Central Africa to 1870

Zambezia, Zaïre and the South Atlantic

Chapters from the Cambridge History of Africa

Central Africa to 1870

Zambezia, Zaïre and the South Atlantic

Chapters from the Cambridge History of Africa

DAVID BIRMINGHAM

CAMBRIDGE
UNIVERSITY PRESS

CAMBRIDGE UNIVERSITY PRESS
Cambridge, New York, Melbourne, Madrid, Cape Town, Singapore, São Paulo

Cambridge University Press
The Edinburgh Building, Cambridge CB2 2RU, UK

Published in the United States of America by Cambridge University Press, New York

www.cambridge.org
Information on this title: www.cambridge.org/9780521241168

This work first published 1981
Reprinted 1994

A catalogue record for this publication is available from the British Library

Library of Congress Catalogue Card Number: 81-9947

ISBN-13 978-0-521-24116-8 hardback
ISBN-10 0-521-24116-2 hardback

ISBN-13 978-0-521-28444-8 paperback
ISBN-10 0-521-28444-9 paperback

Transferred to digital printing 2005

PREFACE

The excitement of history derives from its expanding role in under-standing change in society. The study of history came late to Central Africa but is now developing rapidly. In the pre-colonical period it asks new questions about each facet of population growth, each economic innovation, each interface between the inner world and the outer world, each evolution of religious perception, each new mastery of political skills, each realignment of kinship networks. The three chapters of this book on the greater Zaïre basin and northern Zambezia were first published in the *Cambridge History of Africa* when the new flood of historical questions, historical ideas, and historical informa-tion was in spate. Enthusiastic research continues to add greatly to the debate as the further reading list shows. Archaeologists have studied the lake-side civilizations of Katanga to illustrate the rise of the wealthy fourteenth-century rulers who managed the fishing economy and the copper trade. Oral historians have returned to the Kuba of the forest to rethink the whole relationship between mythical rationalization and historical explanation. The extensive work in the south-eastern savanna has been carried forward in a great stock-taking national history of Zambia. The northern fringe of Central Africa is also beginning to open up at each historical level as archaeologists, linguists, historians and Islamists embark on new research along Africa's remotest academic frontier. In the west a young generation of scholars has embarked on the renewed study of the Atlantic records to enhance the sophistication with which the Afro-European encounter was interpreted. Among the fruits will be fresh analyses of the seventeenth-century Kongo kingdom. These will be followed by new syntheses to carry the work beyond the scope of this present volume. Each new step will encourage yet more Central Africans to explore and re-interpret their rich but veiled past.

Canterbury   *January, 1981*

CHAPTER 1

PRIESTS AND FARMERS IN THE LATER IRON AGE

The history of Central Africa between AD 1000 and 1600 can be broadly divided into three parts on the basis of the historical evidence so far available. In the south-east the territory of Zambia is primarily known in this period through archaeological research. The main theme is the transition from Early Iron Age cultures to Later Iron Age cultures. This transition concerned the spread of more advanced technologies, the evolution of new pottery styles, and the exchange of rare commodities over increasingly long distances. The second region, in the savannas of south-western Zaïre and Angola, saw the emergence in the late medieval period of several important political leaders. Their exploits have been recorded in oral evidence which can be supplemented, in the sixteenth century, by the writings of early European visitors to the region. Finally, the third and largest part of Central Africa covers the equatorial forest and the woodland margin to the north of it. Here historical evidence is extremely sparse, and historical speculation depends largely on ethnographic and linguistic data. The results are so far unsatisfactory, but further work should gradually enable us to understand the two main themes of the history of the north. One is the interaction between forest cultures and savanna cultures both north and south of the equator. The other is the changing relationships between gathering and farming peoples within the forest.

The most important geographical feature of Central Africa during the Later Iron Age and subsequently was its extreme sparsity of population. Nowhere in either the forest or the savanna did population densities approach those of West Africa or the interlacustrine region. Only along the southern forest margin did a slightly greater clustering of villages occur. It was in this belt also that in the later years states began actively to encourage the concentration of population to intensify agricultural production. The sparse Central African populations

1 Central Africa before 1600

belonged to five different categories of peoples. In the north-west peoples
ethnically and linguistically related to the populations of West Africa
spoke languages of the Adamawa-Ubangian group of the Niger-Congo
family. In the north-east the languages spoken were Central Sudanic.
In the forest the Pygmy hunter-gatherers differed from their food-
producing neighbours in culture and economy but spoke the same
languages as the food-producers. The fishing and planting economies
of the forest were practised mainly by Bantu-speaking peoples.
Bantu speakers also occupied most parts of the southern savanna
during the Later Iron Age, together with some communities of non-
agricultural Khoisan-speaking peoples. These five roughly defined
groups constantly interacted with each other, thereby changing the
cultures of individual villages. There were not, however, any major

2

trade arteries or other lines of long-distance communication through Central Africa comparable to the coastal traffic of East Africa or the caravan routes of West Africa. Nothing facilitated the rapid spread of political and economic innovations. The long distances and sparse population also tended to militate against the establishment of domestic markets or the growth of specialized local industries. When foreign contacts between Central Africa and the outside world were established, from the middle of the second millennium, they tended to foster a predatory traffic.

SOUTHERN CENTRAL AFRICA

At the beginning of the second millennium AD the southern savanna of Central Africa was particularly sparsely populated. The changes of the previous thousand years, dramatic though they had been, related to a small number of thinly scattered homesteads, villages and rock-shelters. In many places Late Stone Age peoples survived alongside the Iron Age farmers. Their kits of quartz blades, scrapers, arrowheads and other cutting tools were still being manufactured and retouched with techniques already several thousand years old. By the second millennium, however, these hunter-gatherer communities had become subject to more persistent outside influences than ever before. Some of them managed to obtain clay pots and other Iron Age material possessions by trading with, or possibly by raiding, their new agricultural neighbours. Others probably established a more permanent symbiotic relationship with Iron Age communities. They may have exchanged meat and hides for tools, pots and grain, in a manner still practised between hunters and farmers in the forest regions of equatorial Central Africa. Such a relationship, however, commonly caused the hunters to become absorbed by marriage, by clientship and by assimilation.

Despite the pressure of more advanced Iron Age cultures, many Late Stone Age societies survived in the southern savanna. At Nakapapula rock-shelter in northern Zambia, stone materials have been found on floor levels occupied after the eleventh century AD, and the local Lala people have oral traditions in which they describe the hunting and gathering peoples with whom they associated in the past. At Nachikufu, in the same region, and Kandanda in western Zambia, radiocarbon dating tentatively suggests that lithic technology survived until at least the middle of this millennium. As yet there is unfortunately no evidence to indicate what connection there might be between the Late Stone Age hunter-gatherers of the early second millennium, and the Khoisan hunter-gatherers of the later second millennium. No study of recent hunter-gatherer technology forms an adequate basis for comparison, and linguistic or biological comparisons are even more difficult to make.[1]

Although hunter-gatherer communities survived in Central African rock-shelters until well into the second millennium, they had by then been outnumbered in many areas by the growing communities of iron-working agriculturalists. (This process is described in the *Cambridge History of Africa* II.) The farmers settled especially in the wetter, more fertile, pockets of highland, river valley or forest margin. Where the soil and rainfall permitted, many of them added Asian bananas to their cycle of crops, thus increasing food yields, and stimulating population growth. In Zambia and southern Zaïre, still the only part of the region which is archaeologically known in any detail, the pottery tradition of the Early Iron Age has been classified into several regional styles. The Dambwa and Kalundu groups of southern Zambia did not survive into the present millennium, but were superseded by the 'Middle' Iron Age Kalomo culture which grew out of the Dambwa culture. The Chondwe and Kapwirimbwe groups of the Copperbelt and Lusaka district probably continued to flourish until the early centuries of this millennium, when they were supplanted by Later Iron Age cultures. In eastern Zambia the Kamnama group bore greater similarities to the Early Iron Age cultures in Tanzania, Malawi and Zimbabwe than to other Zambian groups. Finally, two related Iron Age traditions at Kalambo Falls, in northern Zambia, and Sanga, in southern Zaïre, flourished around the turn of the millennium and deserve special attention for the light they shed on the later history of Central Africa.

Early Iron Age peoples settled periodically at Kalambo Falls between about the fourth and the twelfth centuries AD. Related peoples spread over the woodland of northern Zambia, often living in rock-shelters rather than open villages. The land was mostly of poor fertility, and people had frequently to move in search of new sites. Villages were probably smaller than in the fertile southern areas of Zambia. Although the Kalambo villages used iron, there is no sign that they were familiar with copper. This is perhaps an indication of their poverty, since related people at Sanga, in southern Zaïre, had developed the richest of the late-first-millennium Iron Age cultures yet known in Central Africa.[1]

[1] D. W. Phillipson, 'The Early Iron Age in Zambia', *Journal of African History*, 1968, **9** 191–211, and his 'Notes on the later prehistoric radiocarbon chronology of eastern and southern Africa', ibid. 1970, **11**, 1–15, and 'The prehistoric succession in eastern Zambia', *Azania*, 1973, **8**, 3–24. J. E. G. Sutton, 'New radiocarbon dates for eastern and southern Africa', *Journal of African History*, 1972, **13**, 1–24.

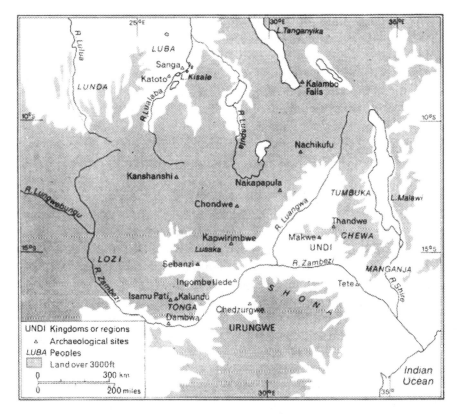

2   Southern Central Africa before 1600

Sanga, by Lake Kisale on the upper Lualaba, is approximately 500
kilometres west of the Kalambo region. Its earliest pottery tradition,
with elaborately bevelled pot rims, and horizontal grooving on
the necks of vessels, is similar to the Kalambo wares. In contrast to
Kalambo, however, Sanga had developed a rich metal-working tradition by the end of the first millennium. The area surrounding the upper
Lualaba valley appears to have been particularly attractive to Iron Age
peoples. Both the river itself and the numerous small lakes were rich in
fish. The vegetation was comparatively light and the woodland good
for hunting game. The rainfall would have been adequate for cereals
such as sorghum and millet, and where the ground retained its moisture
well, bananas could have been grown with little labour. At some stage
oil palms had been successfully introduced into this region and

5

provided an item of agricultural wealth and trade. So far we can only speculate about the degree of agricultural development at Sanga. The archaeological finds do not show farming to have been a prestige activity, like hunting and fishing, which had to be commemorated with grave goods. Yet it need not be doubted that a society enjoying such a variety of material possessions and employing such advanced metal-working techniques practised agriculture. Once their hunting, fishing and agricultural prosperity was established, the Lualaba communities were able to diversify their economy beyond the narrow limits of subsistence. Their iron tools, ornaments, needles and bells show a proficient level of workmanship. The most spectacular manufactures, however, were of copper.

The people of Sanga probably obtained their copper from mines at places such as Tenke along the upper reaches of the Lualaba about 300 kilometres away to the south-east. Although none of these mines has yet been investigated, they may have resembled a mine at Kansanshi, near the source of the Lualaba, which has been exploited since the mid first millennium AD. This mine penetrates a hill roughly thirty metres high, into which hand-dug shafts were sunk. The shafts followed narrow seams of malachite about six to nine metres in depth. The richest ore was probably hand-sorted and then melted in small charcoal furnaces activated by several sets of bellows. The molten copper was cast either into cross-shaped ingots of different sizes, or into long bars. The extent to which the copper was traded at the earliest period is not at all clear. The lake-dwellers of Sanga may have bought their copper from traders by offering dried fish, grain, salt, palm oil or sorghum beer in payment. Alternatively they might have sent expeditions southwards to extract and smelt the copper on their own account. During the dry off-season, when agricultural work was in abeyance, it would have been possible to dispatch teams of labourers and craftsmen. Either way, however, they obtained enough copper to adorn some of their deceased with fitting tributes to their wealth and status. Arms and legs were weighed down with bracelets and anklets of fine copper wire tightly bound round a fibre core. Necklaces were made of copper beads cut from sections of heavy, square wire.

At some period in Sanga history, large numbers of cruciform copper ingots were placed in a few of the graves. The accumulation was so great that one may assume that they had been stockpiled for commercial reasons. The chronology of this development is still obscure. No living floors have yet been found in the Sanga region from which to create a sequence. Although three separate pottery traditions have been found in the graveyard, the stratigraphy of the burials is almost inevitably disturbed. The copper crosses are usually in graves containing Mulongo and 'red slip' pottery styles rather than associated with common Kisalian wares. The initial radiocarbon evidence emphasised the late first millennium origins of the lake-side settlements. The flowering probably came in the following centuries. A wealthy minority, and perhaps immigrant traders, carried the civilization of the Upemba depression far on towards the fifteenth-century dawn of history. Despite the limitations of the evidence, the Sanga necropolis does reveal that an advanced copper-using culture had developed by the late Early Iron Age in south-eastern Zaïre.[1]

While the people of Sanga were perfecting their specialized industries, farming communities were continuing to expand over the more attractive, tsetse-free areas of Central Africa. One of the most attractive of these areas seems to have been the fertile plateau of southern Zambia. By the end of the first millennium the Early Iron Age peoples of southern Zambia had not only assimilated most of the old hunting and gathering population, but had evolved a new culture called Kalomo, which grew out of the Dambwa group and superseded the Kalundu group. This Kalomo culture was marked by advances in both industry and agriculture. Its people lived on village settlement mounds. Each mound gradually increased in height as old buildings were flattened to make way for new ones, and as domestic refuse piled up around the huts. The height of each mound may even have been deliberately increased to raise the site above the floor of the surrounding, marshy plateau. Each mound could have accommodated up to a hundred or so people at a time. The Kalomo mounds, although used over several hundred years, were probably not continuously occupied. After a few years they were probably abandoned, and only reoccupied when the surrounding land had had a chance to recover its fertility. This pattern of spasmodic occupation appears to differ from the continuous occupation of mounds practised further west by the Lozi, though at a much later date. The Lozi mounds were situated on the upper Zambezi plain where annual flooding brought new fertility. The wealth and permanence of Lozi villages may also have been increased by a fishing industry.

[1] J. Nenquin, 'Notes on some early pottery cultures in northern Katanga', *Journal of African History*, 1963, **4**, 19–32; J. Hiernaux, E. de Longrée and J. de Buyst, *Fouilles archéologiques dans la vallée du Haut-Lualaba: I Sanga (1958)* (Tervuren, 1971). The Upemba depresion was further explored in the 1970s by P. de Maret and published in his Bruxells thesis.

The material possessions of the Kalomo people, although more diverse than those of their predecessors, were still limited. Iron was predominantly used for small tools such as arrowheads, spearheads, razors, chisels, knives, needles and bracelets. Some hoes and axes were in use, but it is likely that much agriculture still relied on wooden digging-sticks weighted with bored stones. Occasional ornaments of copper were known, and clay figurines were fashioned to represent human beings and cattle. Relay trade with neighbouring peoples brought a few foreign objects such as conus shells, cowries, and glass beads. More commonly beads were made of local shell of ostrich egg. Ornaments, however, were comparatively scarce, and some people were buried with but a single iron bangle to commemorate their lives.

The development of the Kalomo economy can be traced from material remains. In the early period people were still heavily dependent on wild game for meat. Bones from twenty-odd species of animal were found at the lower levels of Isamu Pati mound. By the end of the Isamu Pati occupation, however, up to eighty per cent of the meat supply may have been derived from domestic animals. Oxen, sheep, goats, dogs and small hens were kept. A similar change in emphasis from gathered vegetable foods to domesticated crops may have occurred. One should, however, be careful not to exaggerate the decline of gathering as an economic pursuit. Even the modern population of the Kalomo region make use of over a hundred wild tubers, green leaves, shoots, fruits, nuts, and even grass seeds, for culinary purposes. The only grain crop surely identified as present in Kalomo mounds is sorghum, though it is likely that eleusine millet was also grown. Grain porridge probably formed a staple part of the diet, and grain beer may have been brewed for feasts, weddings and funerals.[1]

The north-west of Zambia is an area still only sparsely known to archaeology. Because it is an area of Kalahari Sands, clays are rather scarce and pots are not extensively used. This means that it is hard to trace changes in history and culture through ceramic styles. Where pots are used in place of gourds and wooden vessels, they are made by men rather than by women, and commonly have cross-hatched incisions in place of comb-stamped decorations. The style of the north-western pottery, tentatively known as the Lungwebungu tradition, appears to derive directly from local variants of the Early Iron Age pottery tradition. It covers much of the upper Zambezi basin, and spreads into

[1] B. M. Fagan and others, *Iron age cultures in Zambia*, 1 (London, 1967); T. Scudder, *Gathering among African woodland savanna cultivators* (Lusaka, 1971).

Angola and Zaïre as well as across north-western Zambia. This area of apparently unbroken Iron Age cultural evolution contrasts quite markedly with the changes which occurred in the rest of Zambia from the twelfth century AD.

In the north-east and centre of Zambia the Early Iron Age tradition was dramatically replaced in about the eleventh to thirteenth centuries by the Later Iron Age Luangwa tradition, whose style of pottery is still used by the Chewa, Bisa, Bemba, Lala, Eastern Lunda and other peoples. One example of the new culture was found at Twickenham Road in Lusaka. An old hillside village of the Kapwirimbwe Early Iron Age tradition was reoccupied, probably from about the twelfth century. The new occupants built houses of upright poles lashed closely together, and caulked with laterite clay. Their grindstones suggest that they were cereal farmers, and the bones which they threw out belonged to both domestic cattle and hunted game. They had a much more plentiful supply of iron than their predecessors, probably obtained from nearby smelting sites on the Lusaka plateau. This iron was used not only for small razors, needles and bracelets, but for large agricultural and wood-working implements. The people of Twickenham Road used ivory bracelets and copper necklaces. The copper might have come from small ore deposits south of Lusaka, but it might also be evidence of early trade. The possible sources of supply are the copper-mining region of southern Katanga, around 400 kilometres to the north, or, more probably, the somewhat less distant copper-producing region of Urungwe, south of the Zambezi. Similarities between the pottery of Muyove and that of Kapwirimbwe suggest that links between the Lusaka plateau and the Urungwe district of Zimbabwe may have existed even earlier than this. Further evidence that the Later Iron Age occupants of the Lusaka plateau were in trading contact with their neighbours consists of occasional finds of cowrie shells and glass beads. These must have come ultimately from the eastern coast of Africa, however devious the route of transmission may have been. In addition to bangles, bracelets and beads, the occupants of the Twickenham Road village embellished their personal appearance by filing their front upper teeth into points. This custom became common among many peoples of Central and south-eastern Africa in the Later Iron Age.[1]

The sketchy outline of the domestic economy and material culture of the Later Iron Age in the southern savanna will in due course be

[1] D. W. Phillipson, 'Excavations at Twickenham Road, Lusaka', *Azania*, 1970, 5, 77–118.

amplified, or modified, by new archaeological research. So far material comparable to that from Twickenham Road has been found on the Copperbelt, where the Chondwe site was reoccupied in the twelfth century by Later Iron Age settlers. Further north, the long Early Iron Age sequence of Kalambo Falls gave way to a Later Iron Age culture by the fourteenth century. In the east of Zambia, Later Iron Age pottery has been noted at Thandwe and Makwe. Whereas the Early Iron Age pottery of the east was quite distinct from the other Zambian styles of the period, the pottery of the second millennium is clearly of the single Luangwa tradition which stretches from the Lusaka plateau to Mozambique, Malawi, the border of Tanzania, and into Zaïre. It is dated to very early in the second millennium in Zambia and to a few centuries later in sites so far investigated in Malawi. The tradition appears to have spread rather rapidly to all pot-makers in the region. Although it appears to derive from the Early Iron Age styles in the area, and has definite parallels with, for instance, the Chondwe Early Iron Age pottery, no transitional wares have yet been found to illuminate the wholesale change of pot-making over such a wide area. Such rapid and widespread change does suggest that influential communities, sufficiently large to include women specialized in pot-making, must have spread over much of Zambia and Malawi. Immigrant raiders would not have had such a profound cultural influence.[1]

In southern Zambia the Iron Age sequence in the second millennium is a little more complex than in the east. It would, however, appear that the Kalomo culture was gradually replaced by new Iron Age cultures from about the twelfth century – that is, at the same period that the Luangwa Later Iron Age tradition was becoming established in eastern Zambia. The earliest of the Later Iron Age potteries of the south are probably to be found in the Kafue valley or at the lower levels of the Sebanzi Hill site. They do not derive from the preceding Kalomo wares, but from some other Early Iron Age pottery, probably within the Zambian Early Iron Age tradition. From the twelfth century the evolution of Later Iron Age pottery styles is continuous, and leads without a break to the modern potteries of the Ila-Tonga peoples.

One Later Iron Age site in Zambia has attracted considerable attention. This is Ingombe Ilede, on the lower reaches of the middle Zambezi. The riverside hillock on which Ingombe Ilede stands was first occupied for a while just before, or in the early part of, this millennium. The

[1] D. W. Phillipson, 'Iron Age history and archaeology in Zambia', *Journal of African History*, 1974, 15, 1–25.

pottery then used there resembled the Later Iron Age pottery of Sebanzi, in southern Zambia, and had certain resemblances to the styles which evolved into the modern Tonga pottery of the region. This early occupation did not last long, and the site was then abandoned for several centuries. In about the fourteenth century the hill was reoccupied by people of a different cultural group whose pottery was more akin to the northern Luangwa wares. Among these new settlers were traders who established a small town or camp. For a few years around AD 1400 Ingombe Ilede flourished, either as a permanent settlement or as a trading emporium occupied each year during the trading season. The traders who used Ingombe Ilede were wealthy by Central African standards. They were lavishly supplied with glass bead necklaces. They used gold, both for their bangles, and to mount their conus-shell pendants. They wrapped their dead in shrouds of woven cotton or in bark cloth. Their graves were richly furnished.

The basis of Ingombe Ilede's wealth was primarily trade, and the major item was probably copper. This copper was mined in Urungwe, 100 kilometres south of the river Zambezi. The site of Chedzurgwe, at the heart of the copper-mining region, was occupied in the fifteenth and sixteenth centuries by people whose pottery was identical to that of Ingombe Ilede. Their shallow bowls and delicate beakers were far finer than the Tonga or Shona wares of their neighbours. The decoration was a beautiful comb-stamping with skilful graphite burnishing. The copper was cast into H-shaped ingots with a particularly characteristic trapezoidal cross-section. The ingots usually weighed between three and four kilograms. The miners were probably the Mbara people, known to early-sixteenth-century Portuguese visitors as 'the people of Mobara'. Later in the sixteenth century they were apparently conquered by the Mutapa confederacy and the north-western trade-route to the Zambezi dried up.

When Urungwe copper reached Ingombe Ilede, it was probably sold both to the peoples north of the Zambezi and to peoples of the lower valley. One commodity with which peoples of the north may have paid for their copper was ivory, and some evidence of ivory-working is found at Ingombe Ilede. Such ivory could have been sold down river to the coast. The main imports from the coast were probably cloth and beads. The importation of cloth into south-eastern Africa at this time apparently began to stimulate a local weaving industry, and Ingombe Ilede used large numbers of spindle whorls. Although beads were plentiful at Ingombe Ilede, they seem rarely to have reached

Chedzurgwe. One might perhaps surmise that political and economic power rested at Ingombe Ilede and other similar sites, while the sites in the southern hills represented mining outposts under the control of the riverside magnates. Ingombe Ilede did not, however, only represent a flourishing market centre, where copper and ivory were accumulated by wealthy merchants before being sold for exotic luxuries of Asian origin. It was also a manufacturing site. The copper ingots were not merely retailed, but were converted into fashionable jewellery. The tools of the Ingombe Ilede coppersmiths included, in particular, wire-drawing equipment. The wire was either made into fibre-core bangles at once, or wound onto reels for sale. The whole industry was very short-lived on this particular site, however, and by the late fifteenth century Ingombe Ilede had been abandoned.[1]

The archaeological researches undertaken in Zambia have, as yet, provided only rather slight information about the political and social history of the southern savanna. Even the wealthy entrepreneurship at Ingombe Ilede only indicates limited craft specialization and localized class distinction, rather than a growing scale of political organization. No empires emerged comparable to those of south-eastern Africa. The majority of early second millennium peoples continued to live in small isolated villages. Their only institutionalized social contacts were with immediate neighbours. Even the smallest societies, however, required some outside contacts. Marriage, for instance, would be impossible in a small village unit consisting of a single lineage. Procedures for exchanging brides must, therefore, have existed between distinct communities. In some cases warfare may have dominated inter-community relations. Captives became clients or pawns, and young women brought new blood and vigour to the victors. More frequently the transfer, or exchange, of wives was peaceably achieved in long-drawn-out ceremonies, often beginning in childhood. Marriage often required payment by the husband's lineage to the wife's lineage for services lost. This compensation could take the form of livestock or material possessions. The payment of bridewealth was probably the major occasion when exotic or prized possessions were expended. Material wealth was accumulated to acquire enough wealth and status to marry. It is likely that the glass beads and shells which spread from the Zambezi trading camps to the Later Iron Age villages of Central Africa commonly changed hands as bridewealth. Elsewhere copper bracelets,

[1] P. S. Garlake, 'Iron Age sites in the Urungwe district of Rhodesia', *South African Archaeological Bulletin*, 1971, **25**, 25–43.

iron bangles or raffia cloths were probably hoarded for a similar purpose.

Marriage was an important institution not only in the economic and social life of Later Iron Age societies, but also in political life. The lineage, whether patrilineal, matrilineal or unilineal, formed a tightly knit, and exclusive, group. Under some circumstances several lineages were brought together under a political overlord. So far very little is known about the development of chieftainship in Zambia. Many areas were undoubtedly too poor to make centralized control possible or worth while. The Bemba, for instance, only began to expand the scale of their kingship in the eighteenth century, and the Tonga never developed large-scale chiefdoms. Elsewhere, however, a few early clues about political organization have come to light in the form of chiefly insignia. At Ingombe Ilede, and at Katoto in Katanga, iron bells have been found which closely resemble those used in more recent centuries to symbolize military leadership. The Lunda kings, for instance, were accompanied by a royal bell when they went to war. It is likely that the bells used in earlier times may have served similar political functions.

As one advances into the second millennium, the archaeological data connected with political development can be effectively supplemented by oral tradition. This oral data, in which existing societies give a rationalized explanation of their political and religious institutions, may yield clues to actual historical developments. In Zambia oral sources have so far revealed few political traditions earlier than the eighteenth century. Much more oral data has been uncovered in Malawi, Zaïre and Angola. It may be that peoples in the valleys of the southern Zaïre basin created more durable institutions at an earlier period. There are hints in Angola, for instance, that chiefs whose influence transcended lineage boundaries may have begun to develop well before the middle of this millennium. But the earliest layer of oral history so far recovered comes from Malawi.

The traditional political history of modern Malawi began among the Chewa-speaking peoples. In this area the Phiri clan, which attached great symbolic significance to fire, created several kingdoms known by the name Maravi or Malawi. The earliest documentary reference to a Maravi kingdom occurs south-west of Lake Malawi in a Portuguese document of the early seventeenth century.[1] This state, governed by a ruler called the *kalonga*, began to emerge much earlier, perhaps from

[1] Gaspar Bocarro stayed with the great chief Muzura at his town of Maravy in March 1616. Cited in G. M. Theal, ed., *Records of south-eastern Africa* (Cape Town, 1899), III, 416.

the fourteenth or fifteenth century. By the sixteenth century it had spawned a second Maravi kingdom among the Manganja of the Shire river. Another offshoot created the Maravi kingdom ruled by the *undi* in the Tete district of Mozambique. Although the *undi* kingdom was probably founded in the sixteenth century, it was not until much later that it began to derive economic strength from the ivory trade of the Zambezi basin. But although the political and economic power of the Maravi kingdoms belong to a late period in their history, the religious roots of the kingdoms properly belong to an earlier period, during the Later Iron Age.[1]

The earliest forms of organization among the Chewa seem to be connected with shrines. The shrine cults related to areas of land, rather than to lineages and cults of ancestor worship. They somewhat resembled modern territorial cults and were quite distinct from movements of spirit possession concerned with medical and psychological healing. These Maravi cults, like the *malunga* of Angola (see p. 18), were responsible for calling forth the rains, for limiting the floods, for granting success to the huntsman and fertility to the farmer. Each one cared for the well-being of all the inhabitants of its zone of influence, and cut across social boundaries. The cult was managed by an élite of priests and officials. Among the Chewa, as among their Tumbuka and Manganja neighbours, the cults long preceded the development of the Maravi kingdoms of the Phiri clan.

The early Tumbuka of central Malawi claimed that the world was dominated by a high god whose representative on earth was a snake called Chikangombe. This snake lived on hilltops and travelled with the wind. Chikangombe 'married' priestesses whose families guarded his hilltop shrines. These beliefs probably evolved slowly among local Late Stone Age and Early Iron Age ancestors of the Tumbuka, Chewa and Manganja. The early cults were undoubtedly very localized, although they recognized the same type of god. By the Later Iron Age two different trends were emerging. One was a growing regional differentiation. The religion of the southern Tumbuka, for instance, was becoming distinct from that of both the northern Tumbuka and the neighbouring Chewa. A second trend was the development of a hierarchical relationship among some Chewa shrines. 'Mother shrines' became senior to their associates. When this happened, shrine guardians took on political functions, and sometimes became owners of

[1] See B. Pachai, ed., *The early history of Malawi* (London, 1972), chs. 6 by J. M. Schoffeleers and 7 by H. W. Langworthy.

land-holdings. It was onto this basis of incipient political growth that the Maravi concepts of chiefship and kingship were gradually grafted, perhaps from about the fourteenth century. Political power began to pass from the hands of the wives of the 'snake-god' to those of male chiefs. The old shrines faced competition from new shrines around royal graves. Conflict between rival priestly traditions continued for centuries. Only among the southern Manganja, where the old cults had been weak, did the new chiefs of the Phiri clan emerge with unchallenged authority. In this area the Lundu kingdom became a great power on the Shire river. Once its kings were firmly established they had the authority and confidence to reincorporate some of the old cult practices into their new political system.[1]

In addition to absorbing the religious ideas from the old, localized communities of the Chewa, the Maravi kings developed their own royal rituals centred round the chief's perpetual fire. This fire was fed with reed mats, used during puberty ceremonies, in order to symbolize life and fertility. The fire was only quenched when the king died. Royal fire was also designed to assist rain-calling at the end of the dry season.[2] The importance of fire as a royal symbol was also very marked among the southern neighbours of the Maravi, the Shona, on the southern side of the Zambezi valley. There, however, the periodic royal fire ceremonies were perhaps used less to mark a transition of reign or season, and more as a means of uniting diverse people in common loyalty to a king.

WESTERN CENTRAL AFRICA

From the shrines and kingdoms of Malawi, the discussion moves far to the west, to Angola, at the opposite end of the Central African savanna. Our knowledge of the history of Angola has recently been enhanced by fresh work on the oral tradition of the KiMbundu-speaking peoples.[3] The Mbundu[4] groups occupy a large slice of western Central Africa along the lower Kwanza and middle Kwango rivers. They are

[1] T. O. Ranger, 'Territorial cults in the history of Central Africa', *Journal of African History*, 1973, 14, 581–97.

[2] J. M. Schoffeleers, 'The meaning and use of the name Malawi', in Pachai, *Early history of Malawi*, 91–103.

[3] J. C. Miller, *Kings and kinsmen: early Mbundu states in Angola* (Oxford, 1976). I am grateful to Dr Miller both for allowing me to cite his work prior to publication by the Clarendon Press, Oxford, and for commenting on my own interpretations presented here.

[4] It is now conventional to refer to the KiMbundu-speaking peoples as Mbundu, but this can lead to confusion with the neighbouring OviMbundu.

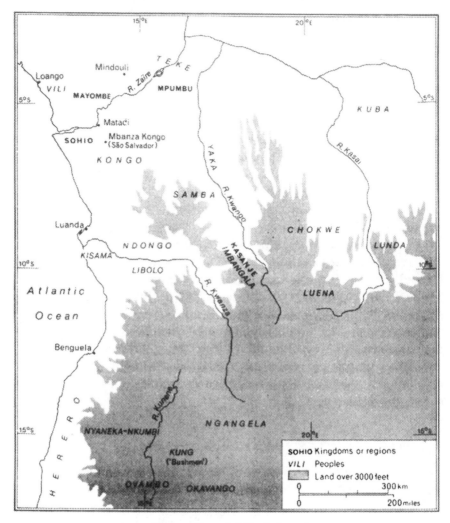

3 Western Central Africa before 1600

bordered in the north by the Kongo, in the south by the Ovimbundu, and in the east by the Chokwe-Lwena peoples of the upper Kasai and upper Zambezi. The history of these Mbundu peoples in the early centuries of this millennium was probably similar to the history of other Later Iron Age peoples of the woodland savanna. In particular it reveals the early importance of religion as a source of wider political influence. Economic ties between the Mbundu peoples appear to occupy a later and more modest place in the growth of political power than do lineages and shrines.

The central Mbundu, known as the Ndongo, may have been settled on the Luanda plateau since Early Iron Age times. This open country was moderately suitable for both agriculture and pastoralism, though it occasionally suffered from inadequate rainfall, and from the depredations of the tsetse fly. The best land was in the north-west, where a pocket of rain-forest separated the plateau from the semi-barren coastal plain. The early Ndongo had few contacts with the coast. Although shoreline villages specialized in salt-drying, in fishing, and in shell-collecting, their trade seems to have been primarily directed northwards towards the Kongo peoples, rather than eastwards to the Mbundu. On the landward side the Ndongo were surrounded by two other Mbundu groups. In the north-east the deep Kasanje depression was occupied by the Pende, who later developed links with the interior of the Zaïre basin. In the south the Kwanza valley was occupied by the Libolo, whose territory stretched towards the Ovimbundu high-lands of southern Angola. At one time or another each of the three groups played a dominant role in the history of the Mbundu, and each created institutions which sought to dominate the autonomous lineages.

The early Mbundu all lived in small villages controlled by the male members of a single kin-group. The village was the home, and spiritual focus, of all members of the lineage, even those who were permanently or temporarily absent. Its theoretical structure consisted of a set of full brothers, together with the older sons of their sisters. Wives belonged to their own kin-groups, but resided with their husbands. Young children stayed with their mothers until they were old enough to join their uncles in their own kin-villages. Rituals destined to ensure good harvests and healthy progeny had to be performed amongst one's own kin. Spiritual well-being was preserved by an elder who had custody of ritual kaolin and red-wood powders. Most of the Mbundu lineages continued to function until the end of the sixteenth century. Over the previous three hundred years, however, many of them had been temporarily subjected by chiefs who sought to make their influence para-mount in central Angola.

The first attempt at political consolidation among the Mbundu was connected with the all-important function of rain-making. The Pende, in particular, came to believe that power to intercede with the weather gods was vested in wooden figurines located in small river-beds. These *malunga* figurines were carefully guarded by their custodians. The *malunga* cults resembled the early 'territorial' cults of Malawi. The shrine custodians used their spiritual authority to exact tribute and loyalty from the Pende. By concentrating both wealth and power into their own hands, some *malunga*-holders came to resemble small kings. A few of the titles of these shrine guardians, together with traditions retelling their great feats, have survived and been incorporated into more recent political institutions. The majority of *malunga* cults were rather narrowly circumscribed by a single valley or stream. They were gradually replaced by a more powerful, and more mobile, form of political authority which spread southwards among the Mbundu.

The second cult to become politically important was associated with new ritual symbols, made this time of iron, called *ngola*. The *ngola* idea was introduced to the Ndongo from the Samba area in the north. The fact that the *ngola* symbols were made of iron may have been related to the increasing economic importance of iron. It is at this time that idealized smith-kings emerged among the Mbundu as guardians of the sacred objects. Until further Iron Age archaeology has been undertaken in Angola, the extent of the technological and economic innovations which may have begun in the fourteenth century cannot be gauged. The emergence of the new *ngola* chiefs is often interpreted in oral tradition in the guise of a conquest by Samba migrants equipped with superior battle-axes and arrowheads. Similar themes of migration and conquest are frequently found in oral tradition to account for the emergence of new policies or institutions. In practice a peaceful diffusion of *ngola* symbols may have occurred. In the ongoing struggle between political centralization and lineage autonomy, the *ngola* were initially mobilized on the side of autonomy. Ndongo lineages found them very effective in resisting alien encroachment, for instance by southern kings from Libolo. Each Ndongo village sought to acquire a protective *ngola*. Its guardian became a Samba by virtue of his function, if not by his ethnic origin, and shrine guardians with Samba titles proliferated. Oral traditions in each village were modified to excise the old records and give legitimacy to the new titles. A newly appointed Ndongo office-holder adopted the genealogy, the history and the prestige of his *ngola*.

Although the *ngolas* were at first local figures, compatible with lineage autonomy, there gradually began to develop among them a hierarchy of authority. As the forces of centralization increased, the holder of the *ngola a kiluanje* title, in particular, began to acquire political and military influence. Although the chronology of this development is still obscure, a recognizable form of *ngola*-kingship may have been emerging several generations before the first sixteenth-century documentary records of it became available. By the mid sixteenth century the kingdom of the *ngola a kiluanje* was rapidly expanding. Spiritual and political authority may have been reinforced by royal control of market-oriented trade. The royal capital was apparently built close to the lower Lukala iron mines and the kingdom also came to control the Kisama salt mines and to receive tribute from them.

In the south the *ngola*-kings came into conflict with another, rather different tradition of Mbundu political centralization. The political methods of the Libolo may have had their roots in an old and shadowy kingdom called Kulembe, where government involved a more fluid and mobile method of control than the fixed shrines used by the northern agriculturalists. The Libolo king appointed regional governors who could visit his subjects and who were personally responsible for their loyalty and support. The Libolo also developed important initiation rites associated with the training of their warriors. For a brief period, probably in the early sixteenth century, the Libolo kingdom succeeded in expanding northwards across the Kwanza. Its governors dominated part of the Luanda plateau. One chief even crossed the plateau to settle on the northern escarpment, where his title is still used by local people. This northern thrust was short-lived, however, and by the mid sixteenth century the *ngola a kiluanje* had succeeded in confining the Libolo to the south side of the river.

In the south the peoples of Libolo were connected rather loosely with the peoples of the southern half of modern Angola. The history of this region in the Later Iron Age is still almost completely unknown. The main Benguela plateau was already occupied by Ovimbundu peoples, but they were not yet organized into the familiar kingdoms of Bihe, Huambo, Bailundu and others. The domestic economy was a mixed one, and it is possible that the Ovimbundu gained their cattle and cattle customs from peoples yet further south. Beyond the central plateau our knowledge is even less adequate. The Herero were probably mainly pastoral, but the Nyaneka-Nkumbi and the Ovambo had mixed planting and herding economies. Along the rivers of south-eastern Angola fishing was an old and important element in the economy of the Okavango and neighbouring peoples. The disunited Ngangela farmers lived in very sparsely populated regions. All of these southern peoples probably had occasional contacts with K'ung (Bush-man) hunter-gatherers, but nothing specific is known about their history until the nineteenth century.

Returning to the northern part of the southern savanna, one finds a rather more thickly peopled region on the borders of the great equatorial forest. This lush belt of forest borderland was occupied by a very large number of distinct ethnic groups. Although the vegetation probably made hunting a little more difficult than it was in the open country, the extra rainfall made agriculture more secure. The ethnic fragmentation among the lower Kasai peoples can be interpreted in different ways. Perhaps an old population was organized into small Early Iron Age societies that were so entrenched that they absorbed all new arrivals. Or perhaps the disruptions associated with the later slave-trade caused small groups of refugees to settle in the forest as independent, embattled villages. Either or both of these explanations are possible. By the end of the sixteenth century some societies living around the forest margin, for instance the Bushong, or Kuba, had begun to experiment with original forms of state-building which later resulted in the emergence of powerful kingdoms. More important experiments in managing growing societies occurred, however, not along the forest border, but in the open savanna. Ultimately the most successful political techniques were devised among the Lunda peoples.

South of the forest fringes the inland savanna was covered by light sandy soils which supported a very sparse population. In the favoured riverside areas where denser populations could be supported, struggles developed between local lineages and centralized chiefs which were entirely comparable to events already described among the Mbundu. In the early centuries of this millennium, the Lunda were probably very like other peoples of the savanna. They farmed, hunted, trapped fish and gathered fruit, drank palm wine and danced at initiation festivals. The old men stayed at home to weave raffia cloth with which to purchase young brides. The young men went to war in order to gain status in the community. The women, young and old, cared for the routine, grew the crops, cooked the food, carved the kitchen utensils and made the great clay pots used for storage and cooking and brewing. The children probably tended goats, collected termites for roasting, scared birds off the sorghum and baboons away from the bananas.

The Lunda were governed by elders known as *tubungu* who commanded respect by their seniority, their experience, and above all their spiritual powers. These elders were known not by their personal names, but by the titles of the offices which they held. Relations between the Lunda title-holders were governed by fictitious geneologies. One title would be deemed to be the brother, son, wife, sister or father of another title, and its holders would treat each accordingly, regardless of their family relationship. Alliances were recorded in oral tradition as marriages, with the senior title described as the husband, the junior title, although held by a male chief, described as the wife. The titles belonged to heads of lineages. The lineages, however, were never of equal strength, and constant rivalry took place between them. Conflict occurred not only over such important lineage questions as matrimony, but also over fundamental economic considerations such as land use and fishing rights. Competition over hunting grounds may have been less important. According to tradition, these early Lunda were not skilled hunters, and did not use bows or possess powerful hunting charms, but relied on simple traps and snares. Personal combat was settled with wooden clubs rather than iron spears, and the scarcity of iron suggests that the Lunda may have belonged at this time to the Early Iron Age tradition of Central Africa.

Among the Lunda lineages, three seem to have played a particularly significant role in the struggle for hegemony. The earliest to achieve a recorded superiority over its rivals was that of the *yala mwaku*. In time, however, it was challenged by the leader of the junior *kinguri* lineage. In the ensuing conflict, which oral traditions remember as a fight between father and son over palm wine, the senior lineage title was suppressed. All lineage headships which had been subservient to it were released from their obligations. There followed a long period of conflict and realignment. A third lineage, called *lueji*, attempted to drive the supporters of the *kinguri* out of Lunda. The rivalry may have lasted a long time, but eventually, perhaps by the fourteenth or fifteenth century, the balance of power was resolved in favour of the *lueji* by the intervention of outside influences.

The new power which emerged in Lunda is orally remembered in the form of exploits by a great hunter called Chibinda Ilunga.[1] This fictional folk-hero represented centralized, chiefly political power, as against the social power of the lineages; he imposed his domination by symbolically 'marrying' the *lueji* lineage. The advent of Chibinda Ilunga provided an outside influence of sufficient prestige and power to arbitrate in the civil wars of the Lunda. This prestige was gained, according

[1] Some accounts of Chibinda Ilunga have been collected by M.-L. Bastin in *Tshibinda Ilunga: héros civilisateur* (Mimeograph, Brussels, 1966, 2 vols.).

to the legends, by his effective use of hunting charms, both to track down his quarry and to protect his master-huntsmen from evil spiritual influences embodied in snakes and predators. His physical power derived from a skilful use of iron, and a much wider range of weapons than had previously been known to the Lunda. The advent of Chibinda Ilunga might be conceived to represent the growth among the Lunda of the technical traditions of the Later Iron Age. It has already been suggested from archaeological evidence that Later Iron Age traditions were spreading in northern Zambia at about this time. A Lunda transition to a more advanced material culture midway through the first half of the present millennium would therefore have nothing surprising about it. The source of these cultural influences is not yet known. In northern Zambia there is a tendency to look across into Zaïre for archaeological antecedents. They may have come from wealthy in-habitants of the Lualaba valley where advanced metallurgical techniques had developed in copper-working by early in the present millennium. Recent versions of Lunda tradition, recorded within the last hundred years, claim that the ideas personified by Chibinda Ilunga were associa-ted with the Luba peoples. This Lunda attribution of their 'civilizing hero' to a particular ethnic group could be an anachronism inserted into the tradition at a later date. Yet the Luba do share several political practices with the Lunda, and later, like them, formed a large and powerful nation. Perhaps the complex and sophisticated political methods which evolved among both the Lunda and the Luba could have common roots in the Later Iron Age societies of southern Zaïre.

Among the Lunda, some political stability was apparently achieved by about the fifteenth century. An alliance was formed between a cen-tralizing foreign chief, independent of the Lunda lineages, and an old lineage title of long-standing respectability. The dissident lineages allied to the holders of the *kinguri*, and to its brother-title the *kinyama*, were defeated and driven out. The *kinyama* title was carried southwards and eventually became the senior title among the Luena chiefs of the upper Zambezi. The *kinguri* title was taken westwards, along with Lunda traditional symbols such as the drum, the double bell and the royal bracelet. The supporters of the *kinguri* also carried charms which had been acquired by contact with the new hunter-king of the Lunda.

From being a small isolated farming and fishing people on the forest margin during the early second millennium, the Lunda spread their ideas and symbols by stages into the southern savanna. The earliest diffusion of Lunda influence, albeit of very indirect influence, was probably carried by short-range relays of refugees, rather than by any purposeful colonizing movement. Small numbers of Lunda migrants were absorbed into surrounding societies. They probably lost their language and many of their customs quite quickly, but they preserved and transmitted a striking political legacy. Their system of perpetual titles spread westwards to become grafted onto the institutions of many different peoples. The new title-holders retained few links with Lunda, although occasional attempts were allegedly made to enlist their support by conflicting factions in the Lunda homeland. The old Lunda lineages took fright at the rapidly increasing power of the new kingship, but were unable to resist. They became absorbed into a centralized Lunda state whose ruler eventually acquired the title of *mwata yamvo*.

Meanwhile the *kinguri* title of the west was gaining increased military power. Its awesomeness was enhanced by ritual acts of great cruelty. At this time, perhaps early in the sixteenth century, the new chiefs of the Lunda-Chokwe political culture came into contact with the easternmost Mbundu peoples of the upper Kwanza valley. In the process an even more tightly organized martial culture emerged which focussed on war camps called *kilombo*. Camp followers were regimented on strict military lines. Recruitment into the *kinguri*'s war camps was exclusively by initiation and not by birth. This effectively destroyed the influence of the old lineages, and enhanced the power of the war-leader. Such a radical break with traditional practice repelled many of the *kinguri*'s followers. They rejected the fierce Spartan life of the camps, and moved away to adopt a sedentary, married life with conventional lineage loyalties. In their search for new recruits to replace those lost, the war camps became even more mobile among new peoples. Even the Chokwe began to reject the *kinguri* and its military dictatorship. In its stead the Chokwe began to adopt Chibinda Ilunga as their folk-hero. The great master-huntsman became the human symbol depicted on beautiful Chokwe wood-carvings. Eventually a revolution occurred which rejected the leadership of the *kinguri*, the most senior Lunda title, and supremacy passed to the *kasanje* title. By the mid sixteenth century, the supporters of the *kasanje* had created a military force known as the Imbangala, with which they rapidly conquered their way right through the southern Mbundu territory as far as the Atlantic.

The Imbangala of the lower Kwanza had lost all their individual ethnic affiliations, and many of their old customs. They had no legitimate offspring and therefore no lineages which might arouse factional loyalty. All Imbangala became so named by initiation. The initiation, and the military training, involved severe forms of anti-social behaviour, including ritual cannibalism, which cut the initiate off from traditional society, and bound him irrevocably to his classmates. Although the Imbangala were united through isolation from their former tribal families, their camps tended to segment frequently, as new war-leaders hived off from the old regiments. One of the camps was described in 1601 by Andrew Battell, a captive English seaman who spent some months with the Imbangala. The camp he lived in was well fortified against attack. Each section was organized as a fighting unit, with its arms always at the ready. At the centre the war-chief was surrounded by a retinue of admiring wives who accompanied him on his cere-monial inspections of the camp, carrying his arrows and his wine cups. The chief decked himself out with elaborate hair styles made of shells, and anointed his many ornamental scars with magical ointments. His followers were particularly fond of palm wine, and their progress was marked by an extravagant felling of palm trees. When the Imbangala reached the Atlantic coast, in the late sixteenth century, they dis-covered an entirely new economic phenomenon: the overseas slave-trade. This discovery soon led them to invade, and virtually to destroy, the populous kingdom of Ndongo.[1]

THE OPENING OF THE ATLANTIC

The history of Central Africa presented so far is mainly one of isolated communities responding to local influences from their neighbours. In the south-east we have some evidence relating to the way in which Early Iron Age societies gradually acquired the technology of the Later Iron Age. In the south-west we have an oral record of the interaction of chiefship and priesthood among neighbouring peoples. All these contacts, however, were predominantly local ones. New ideas seem by and large to have spread without creating lasting, institutionalized links between distant communities. The institutions of Central Africa were in this respect very different from the growing empires and trading systems of western and eastern Africa. In the early second millennium West Africa was becoming linked by regular trade ties to the Mediterranean world. The northern face of Central Africa, between

---

[1] E. G. Ravenstein, ed., *The strange adventures of Andrew Battell* (London, 1901), contains the most vivid primary account of the Imbangala. Their history is to be found in Miller, *Kings and kinsmen*, which seriously modifies this author's own earlier account in *Trade and conflict in Angola* (Oxford, 1966).

the Benue and the Bahr al-Ghazal, had no mineral resources comparable to those of the western Sudan to attract long-distance traders. The copper mines of Darfur may already have been in operation, but nothing brought regular caravans further south, or stimulated the growth of commercially oriented kingdoms. In eastern Africa the early second millennium also saw an expansion of trading horizons. But the wealthy cities of Manda, Kilwa and Sofala derived their profits from the tropical lowlands and from the high interior of south-eastern Africa, not from the remote lands of Central Africa beyond the great lakes. Even in the south, external trade had only a limited effect as a few shells and beads were carried north-westwards across the middle Zambezi. On all fronts therefore Central Africa remained effectively cut off from the growth of world commerce until the second half of the present millennium.

Central Africa's isolation was broken in the late fifteenth century by the opening of the Atlantic Ocean. Until then the Atlantic had remained a closed sea, and Africa's western front, unlike its northern and eastern fronts, had enjoyed no active communication with the outside world. A local sea-borne traffic in textiles or salt may have existed along the coast, as it did in West Africa. Dugout canoes and coastal fishing may have predated the arrival of Portuguese caravels. The odd foreign vessel might have drifted through, after being swept round the Cape and up the Benguela current, with no means of returning to the familiar monsoon lanes of the Indian Ocean. Such occasional, one-way traffic from Asia could have been responsible for introducing innovations of economic importance to western Central Africa. Banana cultivation in the lower Zaïre might have spread from the coast rather than across the continent. Other Asian cultural influences, such as xylophone-playing, certainly reached the area at an early date, though by a route as yet unknown. However plausible occasional visits by storm-driven seamen may seem, the fact remains that no regular ocean-going traffic existed in the South Atlantic until the 1480s.

When maritime trade to the west coast of Central Africa was opened by the Portuguese, its scale initially was small. The primary objective of the Portuguese was to find mineral wealth comparable to the gold of the West African mines. Instead, they had to content themselves with ivory, palm cloth, dyewood and exotic curiosities. Soon, however, they developed a second and more significant interest. This was to supply unskilled labour to the small island-colony which they had created on São Tomé. São Tomé was colonized in the 1490s by sugar-planters sent out from Portugal, partly in order to rid the mother country of convicts and of racial and religious minorities, and partly to foster tropical agriculture. The settlers brought few women with them and not enough men to cut the cane and turn the sugar presses. So they began to buy slave labourers and wives on the mainland. Very soon they were running a surplus of slaves which they could resell, either to the Gold Coast mines, or in Portugal to meet the shortage of agricultural labour. By the 1530s, when Brazil began to be opened up, the slave-trade was becoming good business.

When the Portuguese were seeking trading bases on the Central African mainland, they naturally sought wide estuaries with safe anchorages. These were scarce in the north, along the forest coastline, owing to sand banks and choked deltas, but they found one really good harbour at the mouth of the Congo river, which they called the Zaïre. There they established contact with the important kingdom of the Kongo people. During the next hundred years the Kongo became the best known of all the Central African peoples. Their king even tried to establish his own embassy at the court of Saint Peter in Rome. Numerous reports by Portuguese missionaries, merchants, and chroniclers, and occasional correspondence by western-educated Kongo, shed considerable light on the social culture, the economic development, and the political statecraft of the north-western savanna. It should be remembered, however, that the witnesses who described the scene also represented an intense foreign influence, which brought radical changes to Kongo society.

The origin of the dynasty which ruled the Kongo kingdom probably goes back to the fourteenth century. Oral chroniclers of the seventeenth century indicated that about half a dozen kings had reigned before the first Portuguese merchant adventurers witnessed the scene in 1483. The scope of the early kingdom is but vaguely defined. Essentially, the rulers were kings of Mbanza Kongo, a settlement surrounded by a well-watered plateau of rich soils with numerous villages. There is no sign that Kongo owed its foundation to any spectacular wealth in minerals, or other marketable produce of a specialized kind. It was, above all, a quietly prosperous farming community. The factors governing the kingdom's growth from this central farmland were probably ecological. Mbanza Kongo, apart from enjoying local prosperity, was strategically placed within striking distance of both forest and grassland environments. This access to contrasting, and complementary, sources of wealth probably stimulated the growth of the Mbanza Kongo chiefdom. The central power was apparently based on a modified type of trade conducted through a system of tribute and reward.[1]

The main administrative function of the Kongo king, and of his vassal chiefs, was the collection of taxes at the different levels of society. At the lowest level, the village chief received tribute from his people. Higher up the pyramid, provincial governors received tribute from the chiefs. Finally, at the top, a portion of each governor's receipts was sent to the capital for the king. The system worked, because it was in everyone's interest that it should do so. The flow of goods was not all in one direction. Those who paid could expect return benefits. On the material plane, each tax-collector, chief, or governor would expect to reward those who paid him, with counter-gifts. At the royal court a governor who faithfully paid his taxes in regional produce such as forest palm-cloth, coastal salt or cattle hides might expect to be rewarded with beer or clothing or perhaps dried fish and roast venison. Only a part of the goods paid in tribute were consumed by the court, the remainder being used to reward loyal subjects. This redistribution gave the kings an influential power of material patronage. The increased exchange of goods probably also fostered greater specialization in craft production.

The payment of tribute was undertaken not only for purely material gain. There were also political and spiritual rewards of a kind less visible, but no less real. In homesteads which were poor, isolated and beset by insecurity, it was important to belong to a larger, safer community. The way to belong was to pay tribute to a strong chief in the most public and visible way. Tax-paying was an occasion of great public rejoicing. This visible show of loyalty was rewarded by the chief with feasting and beer-drinking. Even at court the king symbolically handed out edible delicacies to his governors at the annual or biannual tribute presentation. Failure to pay suitable tribute could have drastic consequences. Even the greatest provincial governor could lose his position and become a commoner if he failed to live up to the expectations of his office. The payment of tribute thus fulfilled an important role in determining one's standing in society and in the political hierarchy.

The religious role of tribute-paying is less clearly described than the political or economic ones, but it is nevertheless likely that the payment of tribute, like the payment of church tithes in Europe, was believed to

[1] The following account of the Kongo kingdom is based on the secondary sources discussed in the bibliography. These works themselves are founded on Portuguese writings, modern ethnography, and a very small amount of oral tradition.

ensure against supernatural calamities. The function of a king certainly contained a sacral element. The uncertainties of disease, death and famine could be more effectively countered by divine intervention than by any agency of government. Kings therefore attempted to gain acceptance as the spiritual spokesmen of gods or god-like ancestors. Before the establishment of the kingdom at Mbanza Kongo, the area was controlled by an influential shrine guardian, the *mani kabunga*. The new kings enlisted the support of this shrine, and each king 'married' the lineage of the *mani kabunga*.

The kings and provincial aristocracies which dominated this Kongo system of economic exchange, of political influence, and of religious power, claimed to belong to an intrusive foreign caste which established its overlordship by virtue of conquest. Although some element of foreign influence might have existed in the Kongo kingdom, it is unlikely to have been the sole factor of positive growth. The dynasty's alleged migration from Bungu is probably no more than a symbolic representation of their loyalty to the tribal ancestors. The prestige of the early Kongo rulers undoubtedly owes more to their success in the management of their heritage than to any exotically acquired strain of political genius.

The growth of the Kongo kingdom began as an expansion from the Mbanza Kongo plateau in order to bring it into regular two-way communication with a growing sphere of adjacent communities. By the late fifteenth century, the peoples of the Sohio coast, approximately 160 kilometres away, were linked with Mbanza Kongo. So too were the riverside and island peoples of the lower Zaïre river. Some links were well-regulated tributary ties, but others were more military. The relationship with the estuary peoples appears to have been one of raiding and counter-raiding in which the Kongo king readily welcomed maritime assistance; in 1491 a few Portuguese ships were induced to sail upstream to the Matadi rapids in support of an expedition by the Kongo king.[1] In the north-east of the kingdom the fishing and pot-making villages of the Nkisi river described their links with Mbanza Kongo in the form of real or fictional migrations, each led by a chief carrying the ancestor's basket of religious paraphernalia.[2] The most distant region to establish links with the Kongo kings was the off-shore island of Luanda, located more than 240 kilometres south of the capital. It was there that the king obtained his small, spiralled, *nzimbu*

[1] Francisco Leite de Faria, ed., *Uma relacão de Rui de Pina sobre o Congo escrita em 1492* (Lisbon, 1966).
[2] Van Wing, *Études Bakongo*, 2nd ed. (Brussels, 1959).

shells which served as currency in many parts of the kingdom. These shells formed a significant part of the royal treasure-hoard, and could be issued in carefully controlled numbers to favoured supporters. When Portuguese priests first visited Mbanza Kongo, they received alms in *nzimbu* shells. Once in the hands of Europeans, the shells took on the functions of coinage and were used for the previously unfamiliar purposes of wage-payment and marketing. Their traditional role as a token of measurement, for gifts and exchanges, or as a store of permanent wealth, was now enhanced by the third concept of currency as a specie for purposes of trade.

Little can be said about the chronology of the growth of this complex Kongo kingdom. All that we can be sure of is that in 1600, after a century of overseas contact, it dominated a region more than half the size of England which stretched from the Atlantic to the Kwango. Within that area a relatively high level of craft specialization had developed among potters, weavers, salt-makers, fishermen, blacksmiths and coppersmiths, all of whom traded part of their output, either by the traditional flow of goods through the tribute network, or by the increasing use of regular market-places. In the late sixteenth century, six provincial rulers overshadowed the rest of the king's governors, but their position was not a fixed constitutional one, and other territorial commanders came and went as the balance of power shifted. One force behind the kingdom's development was probably population growth. As villages developed increasingly close together, isolation and independence ceased to be possible. Since favoured parts of Kongo had a rich soil and a good climate, new households did not have to move very far away in search of settlement sites. By remaining close to their neighbours, however, they were faced with the need to create a pattern of government which would regulate inter-village relations. Thus by 1600 Kongo had grown mainly from its own roots on its own soil with its own traditions of loyalty and behaviour. It should not, however, be overlooked that by 1600 Kongo had also been in regular contact for over a century with the Portuguese, who brought a whole new set of ideas and influences. The impact of these influences on Kongo society needs careful assessment.

It has been argued that Kongo was neither a conquest-state, with a ruling élite which belonged to a distinct culture, nor a long-distance trading empire, based on a market network. By the sixteenth century, however, the kingdom was beginning to take on both these aspects. Rulers became increasingly separated from their subjects, and traders became an increasingly powerful middle class. These changes were closely connected with the arrival of the Portuguese.

The Portuguese interest in Kongo, and in the neighbouring territories of Central Africa, was primarily commercial. Strategic and evangelistic considerations played a secondary, though often related role. Before the Portuguese reached Central Africa their early trade in West Africa had been of two kinds. Their skills in cabotage trade had enabled them to carry bulk goods such as cloth, beads, iron, slaves and food efficiently from one part of the coast to another. Their profits were then converted into gold, ivory and pepper for remittance to Lisbon. This cabotage trade, however, could make little contribution to Kongo, which already had a varied economy, and one little able to benefit from coastal navigation. A second form of Portuguese trade therefore became more important. This was the carrying to Africa of Mediterranean manufactures, especially North African textiles. In West Africa this trade enabled the Portuguese to cut into existing markets accustomed to trans-Saharan trade. No such long-distance trade had existed previously in Kongo, but European goods nevertheless gave the Portuguese an effective and original entrée there. By offering expensive and exotic gifts of clothing to the Kongo kings, traders were able to claim counter-gifts from the tribute received at court. They bought raffia cloth, ivory, dyewood and copper, while the court developed a taste for colourful cloaks of wool, cotton and even silk. The redistribution of these textiles, together with iron knives, glass mirrors, Venetian beads and glazed china was carefully controlled and limited by the court. The exotic and ostentatious imports created a new court culture, distinct from the material culture of the common people. Although some foreign trade-goods were probably used to reward provincial governors and even chosen chiefs, the downward percolation of foreign wealth was carefully restricted. Thus men and women of influence began to take on the appearance of a separate, privileged class of rulers. The introduction of a new material prosperity enhanced the prestige of the king and gave new incentives to chiefs to remain loyal to the system. The power of the king in the early sixteenth century appears to have been on the increase. This growth was accompanied by new Portuguese contributions to the ruling group in the form not only of goods but also of services by teachers, artisans, lawyers and priests. The king's spiritual authority was enhanced by new Christian rituals of glittering novelty performed in churches built by expatriate stone-masons. In their search for spiritual security the Kongo kings had found a new source of religious reassurance. They may also have inspired a new kind of awe among their followers.

The first consequence of Kongo's growing connection with world trade was to raise the prestige, authority and wealth of the king and his closest supporters. The second was to involve the new élite in an increasingly frenetic search for resources with which to pay for the goods and services received from outside. The traditional material prosperity of most Central African societies was, as has been seen, rather limited. Even kings had few durable possessions of distinctly greater quality or number than their subjects which could be stored as a permanent form of wealth. Shells, textiles, tools and personal ornaments of copper or ivory were the main symbols of wealth. Central African societies also had very little investment in productive capital. A farmer required only simple tools. A hunter may have invested in a somewhat greater range of equipment, bows, arrows, spears, clubs, game nets, but even his capital resources were limited and probably co-operatively used. The most developed capital investment may have been in fishing communities, where canoes, nets, lines, traps and drying ovens all required an outlay. The traditional capital reserve of early modern Europe was, of course, land, which was gradually being enclosed and brought into private ownership. No such development occurred in the sparsely populated conditions of Central Africa, where common land, of greater or lesser quality, was normally readily available to anyone with the manpower to exploit it. Manpower was indeed the key to all true wealth in these communities. A society with enough able-bodied men and women to clear and plant the land around was a prosperous society by Central African standards.

The kings of Kongo and the merchants of Europe were each aware that the greatest productive resource of the southern savanna was human labour. As a result the sixteenth-century history of the Kongo peoples is tragically bound up with the growth of the Atlantic slave-trade. To the kings, in whom a taste for luxuries had been fostered, slave-trading became an unavoidable solution to their need for foreign exchange. In so far as they also required foreign luxuries to reward their vassals, the trade had also become necessary to their political survival. Yet the longer-term effect of slave-trading was both economically and politically harmful. The loss of labour was not matched by the importation of producer goods. Even the consumer goods acquired became less durable, as the Brazilian trade in tobacco and alcohol partially superseded the more valuable trade in textiles, ceramics and metal wares.

The politics of the slave-trade required very careful management on the African side. A king who succumbed to the inducements to trade could easily split his society and cause uncontrollable rebellions to break out. The initially successful participation of Kongo in the trade raises the important question as to whether the country had an existing class of slaves who could be readily sold without causing severe political stress. The answer is probably that there was no such thing as a 'class' of slaves in Kongo, but that many individuals belonged to a transitory group of servile subjects. These were people of foreign origin, people who had been outlawed for criminal acts, people who had lost the protection of their kinsfolk, or become irredeemably indebted to others. They differed from slaves in European ownership in that under normal conditions they were likely to be reabsorbed into society. Families and clans probably welcomed foreign accessions to their numbers. Women were particularly easy to integrate, but even male strangers probably did not remain the 'slaves' of society for very long.

Since slaves were not readily available inside Kongo, the kings began at an early stage to seek captives from outside. Border raids became a regular feature of the kingdom, and may have led to territorial expansion. In the 1510s and 1520s Mbundu prisoners from the south were on sale at the capital. Portuguese traders also frequented the north, where they bought slaves from the Mpumbu region south of Kinshasa. Traders to Mpumbu, or Pombo, were called *pombeiros*, and this title was subsequently applied to all slavers, both white and later black. The attempt to confine slaving to the periphery of the kingdom was not wholly successful. Local chiefs soon found that neighbourhood feuds were a quick source of captives. The king attempted to institute a system of checks, to ensure that kidnapped Kongo were not sold as slaves, but such controls became difficult to administer as the number of Portuguese traders in the kingdom rose. As a result tensions inside the kingdom increased further.

The king was not alone in finding slave-trading hard to control. The Portuguese also discovered that the traffic was not amenable to discipline. There were two distinct Portuguese policies towards Kongo in the early years of contact. The first policy, devised by kings João II and Manuel I of Portugal, attempted to Christianize and develop Kongo, to make it a prosperous trading partner, and a base for future expansion into Africa. This policy led to the sending of craftsmen, teachers and priests who could westernize the kingdom's institutions. A number of Kongo were also taken to Europe for further education, and one was even elevated to the rank of bishop. In contrast to this policy of modernization, there was a second policy favoured by the governors of São Tomé island. This involved the removal of the wealth of Kongo, largely represented by manpower, and its investment in other spheres of Portuguese activity, notably São Tomé, Mina and later Brazil. When pursued with vigour, such a trade policy rapidly undermined the policy of investment and development inside Kongo. Furthermore, the agents of development, including many of the priests and missionaries, soon became caught up in the slave-trade, and assisted in the exploitation of the kingdom, rather than in its economic growth. The change must be partly attributed not just to corruption and venality among individual colonists, but to a wholesale shift in Portuguese overseas policy. Once India had been discovered, Kongo was no longer so attractive a goal. It accordingly received less capital and human investment from Portugal than it had come to expect in the first flush of enthusiasm. The Lisbon monarchy began to acquiesce in the policy of exploitation.

The government of Kongo during the opening decades of the slave-trade, and during the period of attempted westernization, was in the hands of Afonso I. He reigned from about 1506 to 1543. Although undoubtedly an able and powerful man, he had constant difficulty both in curbing the excesses of the traders, and in persuading Lisbon to maintain the scope and quality of its aid programme. He nevertheless persisted in a policy of co-operation with the Portuguese, and by the time of his death a modified form of Catholic Christianity had become entrenched as part of the court culture. His failure to win more tangible benefits, however, led to the growth of new and severe stresses. The first threat to the kingdom in the latter years of Afonso's reign came from provincial rulers. These were anxious to establish their own direct contacts with foreign merchants. The ones most affected were, of course, those nearest the coast, and the king had constant difficulty in maintaining their loyalty. Other governors challenged his power not by breaking away, but by attempting to capture the king-ship for themselves, with its increasing profits and prestige. The fact that the throne was an elective office may have increased the tensions and disputes over succession; it sometimes ensured also that when a ruler was finally installed he had already proved his political acumen and military ability. The succession to Afonso I, for instance, was in dispute for some time, but when Diogo I finally consolidated his hold on the state he was able to govern successfully for sixteen years. After his reign, in the 1560s, another period of fragmentation and disputed succession occurred. This period of turbulence, however, was over-taken by a second and quite different threat to the kingdom. This was the Jaga disruption.

The Jaga wars, which all but destroyed the Kongo kingdom in 1569, have been the subject of much speculation among historians. Because contemporaries thought of the Jaga as ferocious and entirely alien warriors, who must have come from far away, the speculation has been primarily concerned with their migrant origins. Even serious anthropologists have tended to treat their cannibalism as a fixed cul-tural trait which might be traced to source. More sober comment has suggested that their militancy might have been influenced by the new Imbangala war culture which was evolving at a comparable date in the regions far to the south of Kongo. A more plausible explanation of the Jaga wars ought surely to be sought within the immediate frame-work of Kongo and its near neighbours. For over eighty years the region had been subjected to increasing strains. Any slave-trading society was liable to become oppressive and fractious. There is no reason to suppose that Kongo chiefs were any more considerate of their subjects than others caught up in the slavers' spiral. The Jaga wars might, therefore, be interpreted as a virulent rebellion against authority, wealth and privilege. The main victims were chiefs, traders, Portuguese and the king. The factionalism which had developed be-tween provinces and in ruling clans may have prevented any concerted action from being taken to protect the capital from looting and de-struction. Support for war in Kongo, and even leadership of it, may also have come from border peoples, perhaps in Matamba or among the Teke, who suffered from the king's raiding policy. The evidence, how-ever, is altogether too thin to judge, and the layers of horror-laden myth which began to accumulate immediately after the event are too thick to penetrate.[1]

The consequence of the Jaga disruption for Kongo was funda-mental. It brought a Portuguese military invasion which affected not only the kingdom itself but a wide section of western Central Africa. In the 1560s Portugal was beginning to take a renewed interest in Africa after a period of comparative neglect following the discovery of Asia. This revived interest led to substantial, though ultimately cata-strophic, Portuguese military adventures in both south-eastern and

[1] M. Plancquaert, *Les Yaka: essai d'histoire* (Tervuren, 1971); J. C. Miller, 'Requiem for the Jaga', *Cahiers d'Études Africaines*, 1973, **49**.

north-western Africa. During this phase of militant expansionism the loss of Kongo as a trading base immediately led to a military counter-offensive. Some 600 white troops were sent to restore Alvaro I to his throne at Mbanza Kongo. This restoration brought with it a new class of self-reliant traders, adventurers and rogues, who established them-selves in a kingdom which, in their eyes, now owed them a debt of gratitude. Their presence severely modified the traditional Kongo system of trade through the political hierarchy. From 1571 a commer-cial middle class developed around small nuclei of traders and former soldiers. They built compounds, bought slave retainers, and sired large mulatto families. Their *pombeiro* agents were either sons or trusted slaves, whom they sent on long trading expeditions to the growing slave-markets a hundred and more miles inland. These large trading families maintained close contacts with the king, whom they tried to control and exploit. The king became dependent on the traders for an important part of his revenue of gifts, tolls, tributes and fines. The traders, on the other hand, were dependent on the king for security, freedom of movement, and a supply of war captives and convicts which could supplement the slaves gained by long-distance caravan-ning. In between the rival, but interdependent, groups of the traders and the princes, the priests acted as intermediaries. The court and the merchant community each vied with the other for control of the church, and each sought to have influential priests in its pay. Factions developed on either side and frequent accusations of treason and threats of ex-communication were exchanged between the king's secular canons and the expatriate missionaries.

From the 1570s the kings of Kongo enjoyed a renewed period of stability. Both Alvaro I and Alvaro II reigned for a full generation, successfully manipulating the diverse political and economic interest-groups at work in their kingdom. They kept at bay the forces of the new Portuguese colony of Angola, which had been created on their southern border. They attempted, though unsuccessfully, to diversify their diplomatic connections by entering into direct relationship with the papacy. They claimed sovereignty over a wider stretch of the southern savanna than ever before. This period of stability came to an end with the growth of rival trading groups on the coast. Early in the seventeenth century the Dutch began to frequent the Atlantic sea-board and to offer alternative business openings and competitive prices. The effect was to heighten once again the rivalry between princely factions and so cause renewed political fragmentation in Kongo.

Despite the alternating forces of unity and division, however, the Kongo kingdom remained a major state during the early seventeenth century.

To the south of Kongo, among the people of the Mbundu, the *ngola* kingdom of the Ndongo continued to expand during the sixteenth century. The royal capital, on the plateau some 160 kilometres behind the coast, grew into a small town with fine compounds and royal chambers richly decorated with wall hangings. In 1564 a Jesuit visitor regarded it as comparable in size to the university town of Evora, from whence he came. Distinguished visitors were received at court in regal style and allowed to share palm wine with the king. As a mark of particular esteem kola nuts were handed round. The king, though perhaps not his subjects, kept cattle on his lands. His personal wealth was measured by foreigners in ivory and copper. His association with iron-working continued to be of ritual, if not also of economic, significance.

The king of Ndongo soon emulated his Kongo neighbour in developing commercial relations with the Atlantic trading fraternity. Portuguese prospectors visited the country in search of minerals, and traders camped around the capital with displays of cloth which they brought on credit from ships anchored along the Luanda coast. From the Portuguese point of view, however, trade developed very slowly. It was, moreover, in the hands of private merchants from São Tomé, and not adequately controlled by the royal treasury in Lisbon. In 1571 it was therefore decided to offer Ndongo to a private developer from Lisbon as a proprietary colony of the Brazilian or Virginian type. The 'lord proprietor' was to be Paulo Dias de Novais, grandson of Bartholemeu Dias, who had sailed through Angolan waters eighty years earlier on his great voyage to the Cape.

The creation of Angola as tropical Africa's first conquest colony was not initially a success. It failed disastrously in the terms in which it was conceived, and no other comparable colonizing venture was attempted in Africa until modern times. There were five clearly formulated objectives in the project, but all were abortive. The first was to establish white agricultural settlements on the coast, but the soils proved too poor and the rainfall too precarious. The second aim was to conquer open spaces in the interior as landed estates for European colonists. But the Mbundu were too hostile, and the kings of Ndongo soon showed how limited the effectiveness of muskets was when confronted by massed armies of bowmen with a much faster rate of fire. The Portuguese also found guerrilla warfare beyond them and spent long, cramped months in small earthen redoubts unable to make even short-range sorties until new supplies of powder and lead came from Lisbon. Their third objective was a mythical silver mine, one hundred miles up the Kwanza, but although they spent thirty years opening up the river route and fortifying it with three garrisons, they found no minerals. Their fourth objective was to capture the Ndongo salt-trade, and from it the lord proprietor hoped to recover his costs in the form of tithes. Here again, however, their aim was frustrated, and the salt mines of Kisama, a bare 80 kilometres south of Luanda, permanently eluded the Portuguese grasp. The fifth and final objective of the conquest was the creation of a Christian commonwealth, in which missions would have state support for their proselytizing endeavours. The newly founded Jesuits had been the most ardent lobbyists in favour of the Angolan conquest. They argued that without government support all converts would inevitably return to their own faith and kin. Although the Jesuits remained powerful in Angola, and eventually became large landowners and slave-holders, their missionary achievements were slight.

Although the declared objectives of the colonizing charter of 1571 were not achieved in Angola, the project did meet with success in another direction. The colonizers succeeded in establishing a small state among the western Mbundu. In it tribute was paid not to a traditional chief, but to a Portuguese army officer. This process proved highly effective in accumulating slaves and provided the new state with export revenues. By the end of the sixteenth century the success of the system was so phenomenal that the export of slaves through Luanda was creeping towards 10,000 persons a year. The demographic impact on the Mbundu must have been severe. In addition to slaves exported, many victims died in war or in transit, and whole communities moved away from the slaving frontier towards the north, east and south. In the seventeenth century Capuchins reported that Ndongo, the richly peopled country which had so attracted the Jesuits, had rapidly become a waste land. In less than a hundred years the Luanda hinterland had been raided out and slaves could no longer be recruited by imposing levies on subjected Mbundu chiefs. Long-range raiding campaigns had to be mounted, for which men had to be recruited and supplies bought. The Portuguese crown, now in the hands of the Spanish Habsburgs, intervened in 1591 to rescind the donation charter, and undertake direct conquest, financed by tax-farming. Still the wars proved costly, and in 1603 the alleged silver mountains were reached and the myth of mineral wealth exploded. By the early seventeenth century two new lines of policy were being considered. The first involved the creation of a new colony in Benguela, 300 kilometres down the coast, where mineral prospecting and slaving might prove more profitable. The second involved a gradual return to trade, instead of warfare, as the major means of gaining slaves. This latter policy was stimulated first by the rising prosperity of Brazil, which became increasingly capable of paying for its labour imports, and secondly by the growing competition of the Dutch, who could not be excluded from the slave-trade by the imposition of military monopolies, but had to be met on competitive economic terms. Meanwhile the Ndongo kingdom maintained a policy of retreat and resistance. Unlike Kongo, and some of the West African states, it had difficulty in absorbing, controlling and using to its own benefit a foreign commercial community. It was increasingly forced to resist foreign activity. And when, inch by inch, resistance failed, the Mbundu were absorbed into the semi-colonial, Luso-African community of Angola, with its cultural synthesis of white and black, free and slave, artisan and farmer, trader and soldier. The culture of Portugal often gave way to Mbundu culture in language and custom, and even in religion and medicine, but the links with Portugal were occasionally renewed by the arrival of new governors, judges or tax-collectors, and by the reinforcement of the army with convicts or immigrants from the Atlantic Islands and Brazil.[1]

Although the advent of the Portuguese, and the creation of black Africa's first white colony, was the most important theme in the sixteenth-century history of the western Mbundu, other significant developments were also taking place in the east. New links between the Ndongo and their neighbours probably reached, and crossed, the Kwango river at this time. Salt probably formed an important item in the growing trade of the region. The carefully fashioned blocks of rock-salt were sometimes woven into bamboo cases to make a more durable form of currency. They were fetched by people who came from far away to the east. The long-distance footpaths used by the salt traders probably became avenues for the dissemination of European goods and influences.[2] The material goods obtained at the trade fair were probably not the most important factor of change among the

---

[1] D. Birmingham, *Trade and conflict in Angola* (Oxford, 1966).
[2] D. Birmingham, 'Early African trade in Angola and its hinterland', in J. R. Gray and Birmingham, eds., *Pre-colonial African trade* (London, 1970), 162–73.

peoples of the inland savannas. Far more important were the American food-crops which had been adopted around the trading settlements, and in the vegetable gardens of the Angolan garrisons. At first, from about 1600, maize and cassava spread along the main trading axes to the savanna markets. In later centuries they spread further, to become staple crops among many subsistence farmers. Their diffusion was accompanied by other important plants including tomatoes and tobacco. The latter, however, was never grown on a sufficient scale to meet the demand which had been created for it, and imported Brazilian tobacco remained a key commodity in the slave-trading system. The inland spread of tobacco will one day be plotted through an archaeological study of smoking pipes. The scientific recovery of other imported objects, like glass schnapps bottles, glazed bowls, brass pans, bronze anklets, Asian shells and European beads, will give specific information about the speed with which the new commercial frontier moved into the continent. Traditional evidence from the Kuba region suggests that even the most rapid spread of coastal culture, carried by fast-moving bands of refugees, only reached the middle Kasai after the mid seventeenth century. On the upper Kasai the first influences appear to have been felt at a comparable date. Once new commercial influences did penetrate the area, however, leaders such as the *mwata yamvo* of Lunda used every political device to channel trade to their courts, and to monopolize the benefits to be gained from it. The seventeenth century saw a period of considerable political growth along the new savanna trade-routes.

NORTHERN CENTRAL AFRICA

The history of the southern half of Central Africa, encompassing the woodland savanna of the Atlantic plateaux and those astride the Zaïre–Zambezi watershed, already contains enough pieces to outline some major trends. In the northern half of Central Africa, filled by the great equatorial forest, with its northern woodland fringe, the situation is still much less clear. The tempo of historical change was probably rather slower than in the south. The terrain made communications difficult except by water and hindered the spread of economic and cultural innovations. One effect of this was that the region had a very varied and fragmented ethnic composition. Isolation was further emphasized by an extreme sparseness of population. In the south the different cultural traditions appear to have been drawing together during the present millennium; nearly all the peoples were matrilineal, Bantu-speaking, cereal farmers who possessed some livestock; most of them had progressed from an earlier to a later tradition of Iron Age technology. The north, in contrast, had four major and quite distinct populations which rivalled each other throughout the second millennium AD. Among these four no dated evidence for early iron-working is yet available. Some of them, both in the forest and in the northern savanna, may have remained unfamiliar with metals until late in the present millennium. Agriculture, on the other hand, was probably well established north of the forest at an early date. Hunting and gathering nevertheless remained important economic activities, especially in the forest.

The most important hunter-gatherer groups of northern Central Africa were the Pygmies. Their history can only be surmised from evidence relating to the bands which survived into the nineteenth and twentieth centuries. To the earliest ethnographic observers, Pygmy society seemed conservative and timeless. Each band roamed its ancestral hunting-grounds, camped beside its own streams, and intermarried with familiar neighbours. Despite this appearance of timelessness, important changes had occurred among the forest peoples. Some of the more fertile parts of Pygmy territory had been gradually infiltrated by food-producing peoples. Their economic activities had given the food-gathering peoples a new vision of life. The earliest food-producers may have been ancestral Bantu-speaking cultivators and fishermen, who may have begun to penetrate the forest region from the north as long ago as the first millennium BC. Later, and probably more influential, groups of woodland peoples have penetrated the forest from both north and south in more recent times. These new communities of Negro peoples, who specialized in fishing, intensive vegetable cropping and forest agriculture, may at first have had but slight effect on the Pygmy gathering economies. Nevertheless a kind of symbiotic relationship, or even an interdependence, did develop between some of the Pygmy bands and their food-producing neighbours. Many Pygmies who became aware of the new opportunities presented by a food-producing way of life seem to have defected from their own societies and joined the agricultural communities around them. They became fully absorbed into the new way of life, though physical evidence of the Pygmy heritage is found among many farming societies of the central forest. In some areas identifiable Pygmy groups have disappeared altogether in recent times. Other Pygmy communities retained their cultural identity, but nevertheless maintained regular contacts with their neighbours. These enabled them to exchange hunted game and skins for agricultural produce and artisan wares. Even in the remotest and densest parts of the forest, trading contacts caused Pygmies to acquire cultural features from their neighbours. They acquired some new social customs, such as tribal initiation, and some foreign technological skills, but above all they adopted Bantu and Central Sudanic languages at the expense of their own speech, which has been entirely lost. Thus although by 1600 the Pygmies were the least changed of the Central African peoples, even they had been deeply influenced by agricultural neighbours.

The new forest societies which influenced the Pygmies over the broadest front were those of the Bantu-speaking farmers and fishermen. A few of these Bantu societies have been visited by amateur historians who have collected fragments of oral traditions. Others have had long-established contacts with literate outsiders. Among the latter the best known are the peoples living between the western fringes of the Mayombe forest and the Atlantic coast. Even before the opening of the Atlantic to long-distance shipping, the Vili people had begun to thrive. From a base solidly grounded on subsistence agriculture, they developed an economy increasingly geared to market production. Their foremost achievement was in the field of cloth-weaving. Living on the edge of the forest, the Vili had access to ample supplies of palm raffia. From this they wove cloths which became so refined and so colourful that they could be traded to many neighbouring peoples. By the sixteenth century the Vili showed signs of the advanced mercantile skills which were later to carry them far to the south along the long-distance caravan routes of the savanna. A second important industry among the Vili of Loango was salt-making. Because the Loango coast had a relatively low rainfall and a pronounced dry season, it was possible to collect brine from the coastal lagoons and boil it over wood fires until it had caked into salt blocks. These could be profitably sold to the coastal peoples of Gabon, where high rainfall and coastal swamps made salt-drying difficult. Salt was probably also used to trade with inland forest neighbours. The earliest European traders found that ivory was plentiful in Loango. It is likely that the Vili bought part of the supply from neighbouring Pygmy hunters to whom salt would have been a valuable exchange commodity. The Vili also conducted an early trade in copper which they obtained, either directly or indirectly, from mines on the Teke plateau, north of the lower Zaïre river.

The growth of trade between the forest and the coast had important effects on the Vili systems of government at Loango during the latter part of the sixteenth century. The king of Loango, as seen by the traditions of his people, was primarily a figure of ritual significance. His authority was represented by a royal fire which burnt throughout his reign and was extinguished on his death. Each new king kindled his own sacred fire, in the manner of some other Central African rulers. Envoys from the provinces came to light torches from the new fire and bear them home as a sign of political allegiance. The king also partook in rain-making ceremonies, to give thanks for the cycle of the seasons and the bounty of the harvest, or to plead with the deity for more favourable conditions. Rain-making was usually associated with a priesthood which stemmed from the oldest recognized level of population. The position of priests was powerful but hazardous, as seen in Ndongo, where the rain-makers were executed during one particularly harsh season. The king of Loango also demonstrated his supernatural attributes by carefully disguising his ordinary human needs. Thus, if he was thirsty, he would order his attendant to ring a bell, and all present, even European guests, would fall flat on their faces so as not to behold the king drinking. At mealtimes, he retired alone to a special closed chamber lest any witness of his eating should cause him to die. It was important, also, that the king should be in good health and without physical defect.

The ritual activities of the Vili king were matched by his political functions as chief judge and legislator, as co-ordinator of foreign and military policy, and as ceremonial host to foreign embassies. His councillors and kinsmen received delegated authority as provincial governors, as commanders of the guard, wardens of the wives' compound, watch-dogs against sorcery, administrators of ordeal trials, and king's messengers. A striking feature of Loango government was the existence of a second court, parallel to that of the king. It was ruled by a woman, variously described as the king's sister, his wife, and the mother to his heir. Her key function was a symbolic representation of the women of the kingdom and of their rights.[1] Such women chiefs, or chiefly titles with female attributes, were common among the savanna Bantu, and matrilineal characteristics occurred in many of the diverse and otherwise unrelated political systems of the savanna and southern forest. The northern neighbours of the Vili, as far as the Ogowe, were all matrilineal in their inheritance. In this they contrasted

[1] P. M. Martin, *The external trade of the Loango coast, 1576–1870* (Oxford, 1972), ch. 1.

sharply with the north-western Bantu, and with the nineteenth-century Fang immigrants into the Gabon and Cameroun forests, among whom the male line was the more important.[1]

In the hinterland of Loango, beyond the Mayombe forest, were the dominions of the Teke peoples. The Teke, also known as Tyo and Ansiku, occupied a sandy savanna plateau stretching across the Congo river just where it emerges from the equatorial forest. The river system of the middle Congo has been likened to an hour-glass which widens out into the Ubangi network in the north, and into the Kasai-Lower Zaïre network in the south. It is joined in the middle by the single, broad, island-spattered stretch of navigable river which crosses approximately 800 kilometres of forest. In modern times the link between north and south has become an important channel of regular two-way communication. Bobangi fishing people have been large-scale traders, relaying manufactures, raw materials and staple foods, from village to village up and down the water corridor. In earlier centuries this corridor was probably important as a line along which Iron Age, food-producing populations could span the forest barrier. Fishing communities could flourish along the Zaïre, and, without being composed of long-distance immigrants or traders, could act as agents for the transmission northwards or southwards of new cultural influences. The Teke at the southern end of this corridor may, therefore, sometimes have been the first recipients of new impulses from the north. One of these impulses may have been political, and it is thought that the Teke may have contributed important elements to the western savanna systems of government. Certainly by 1535 the Teke kingdom, or kingdoms, were known to the Portuguese, although their size and influence may have been magnified by sixteenth-century chroniclers in proportion to their remoteness. By the mid sixteenth century the fortunes of the Teke had begun to decline, despite their alleged political prowess. They found themselves caught on the fringe of an expanding Kongo society which was increasingly turning its energies to slave-trading. The greatest slave-markets were found among the Mpumbu peoples of the southern Teke borders. More northerly Teke peoples, under the name Ansiku or Yansi, began to move eastwards into the lower Kasai forest mosaic. They moved either in flight, or in quest of victims of their own, which they sought with increasing intensity as they became caught up in the Atlantic trading complex.

In the southern forest, as elsewhere, contact with the growing

[1] A. Jacobson, *Marriage and money* (Lund, 1967).

long-distance trading economies of the Atlantic zone brought benefits as well as hardship and insecurity. In the sixteenth century the Teke probably controlled or worked the Mindouli copper mines, and benefited from increased sales of copper to the Vili of Loango. Like other savanna peoples, the Teke and their forest neighbours also profited from the introduction along trade-routes of cassava and maize. As these crops supplemented or even superseded millet as the staple crop, levels of agricultural productivity rose. In theory this should have led to rising standards of living and to increased manpower investment in more advanced economic activities. In practice, however, it may have done little more than compensate for the labour loss caused by the slave-trade, and the conversion of human resources into items of conspicuous consumption such as foreign tobacco and alcohol.

The changes associated with Atlantic trade probably only influenced the south-western corner of the forest, and perhaps a few main water-ways, in the period before 1600. Elsewhere the forest farming of the north and east remained untouched by American food-plants. In many areas Pygmy gatherers probably remained relatively more numerous than Bantu farmers, although both were very thinly scattered. In the north-west the patrilineal forest farmers were even more divided and fragmented among themselves than other forest peoples. They formed a large number of small, isolated and divergent Bantu language groups. Only in very recent times has some degree of cultural uni-formity been created by the Fang. One explanation of the great cultural and linguistic diversity may be historical. The north-west forest may contain the oldest Bantu-speaking peoples of Central Africa. Without archaeological evidence we cannot even speculate on the date or cause of the penetration of the forest by food-producers, whether as vege-culturalists, or as neolithic farmers, or as fully-equipped Iron Age agriculturalists. Some of the early people, however, seem to have adapted themselves very successfully to the waterlogged environment of large parts of the northern forest. Their descendants, known generally as *les gens d'eau* – 'the water peoples' – practise highly successful fishing in the perpetual swamps of the Ngiri, the Ubangi, and the middle Zaïre. Even deeper in the forest groups such as the Ngangulu and the Mbochi, sometimes known as *Zwischenvölker*, seem to exhibit cultural characteristics of both the northern and southern forest peoples. A study of their customs and languages might give new clues as to the relative importance of different levels of cultural influence from either north or south among the forest peoples.

The coastal peoples of the north-western Bantu area became cut off from their previous inland neighbours by the Fang conquests of the nineteenth century. Even before this, however, their culture had been somewhat modified by outside contacts. In the sixteenth century they were well-known as fishermen, and had begun to trade spasmodically with the Portuguese slavers. The growth of trading economies in the late sixteenth century led to the shift of small numbers of people from the hinterland to the coast. This shift was large neither in scale nor in distance, but the emphasis changed from riverside settlements a few miles inland to settlements on the river estuaries. North of Cameroun mountain, the Balundu and Bakole began to press in on the old Efik coast-dwellers. In the Cameroun estuary the Duala took up positions where they could trade freely with visiting ships for iron and copper bars. The number of coastal people probably remained small, to be reckoned in hundreds rather than thousands, and their trade was in no way comparable to that of Benin in the west. They nevertheless laid the foundations of a society which grew into the trading states of the nineteenth century. By 1600 an embryonic dynasty of princes had been established among the Duala.[1]

The central part of the equatorial forest presents historical problems which are little better understood than those of the north-west. There does, however, seem to be some slight unity among the numerous Mongo peoples who occupy much of the territory enclosed by the great bend of the Zaïre. The Mongo are patrilineal peoples, like their northern neighbours, and share with them a number of customs associated with marriage, divorce and inheritance. They also show signs of intermarriage with Pygmy stock, suggesting to many observers that this was once a Pygmy territory which has been penetrated by Negro outsiders within comparatively recent times. Some of these influences may have come from the north-western Bantu; others from the Adamawa–Ubangian peoples of the northern savanna. Even the Tetala, at the southern edge of the forest, have traditions which might be attributable to a southward migration, though a detailed judgement will have to await the finds of properly controlled fieldwork. Although the unity of the Mongo group is not very marked, it does seem to require some explanation other than a remote common ancestry, or a series of parallel developments in a uniform environment. The clues may well lie outside the forest, in the central Sudan.

[1] E. Ardener, 'Documentary and linguistic evidence for the rise of trading polities between Rio de Rey and the Cameroons, 1500–1650', in I. M. Lewis, ed., *History and social anthropology* (London, 1968), 81–126.

To the north of the forest, the woodlands which stretch from central Cameroun to the Sudan Republic are occupied by two major groups of peoples. The oldest appear to be the Central Sudanic peoples, whose territory forms a horseshoe round the Uele region of northern Zaïre. Inside the horseshoe, and stretching as far back as the Cameroun Highlands, are the Adamawa–Ubangian peoples, who appear to have intruded eastwards along the forest fringe into Central Sudanic territory. The date of this intrusion by a distinct branch of the Niger–Congo language family is unknown. Both savanna populations are assumed to have an old history of Stone Age agriculture. In recent centuries, at least, this history has also been much affected by the adjacent forest. Although the Central Sudanic peoples generally lost ground to their Adamawa–Ubangian neighbours in the west, and latterly perhaps also to Arabs in the north and Nilotes in the east, some of them appear to have expanded successfully southwards into the forest. Their ability to do so, and to acquire client peoples among Pygmy hunter-gatherers, must have depended on their agricultural skills. The simplest basis of agriculture would have been an indigenous adaptation of food-producing to the many available forest tubers. In a more ingenious theory, Murdock would have liked to believe that Asian cultivars were introduced to the Central Sudanic peoples at a very early date. There is, however, no evidence that banana cultivation spread across Ethiopia and the upper Nile before reaching the forest via the central Sudan. An alternative to the theory of indigenous forest agriculture suggests that Asian food-plants had already reached the north-eastern forest, from the west, south or east, before the Central Sudanic peoples began to colonize it from the north. Whatever the causes of the Central Sudanic expansion, the impact was felt deep into the forest. In the north the Mangbetu and a cluster of related peoples imposed their culture. Further south, the traces of Sudanic influence are less distinct, and Bantu languages are currently spoken, but several peoples of north-eastern Zaïre have traditions referring to northern influences. These include the Bira, the Kumu and the Lengola.

The impact of savanna cultures on forest peoples – and perhaps also of forest cultures on savanna peoples – was not felt only along the eastern forest margin of the Uele area. A similar oscillating interaction took place along the Ubangi on the central border of the forest. Here the savanna cultures and languages were Eastern Nigritic. According to one hypothesis, the Ngbandi were the largest formerly Bantu-speaking group to be overrun, while others, such as the Babwa and

Binza, although retaining their Bantu languages, were nevertheless influenced in other ways which are still remembered. Alternatively, it is possible to argue, in the present state of our ignorance, that the selective change of culture moved in the opposite direction, from south to north. On this showing, the Babwa and Binza would appear to be Adamawa–Ubangian peoples of the Ngbandi group who have been Bantuized to the extent of losing their old speech, as did neighbouring communities of Pygmies.

The major feature of the history of the northern savanna is the continuation into the second millennium of local change among very diverse but interacting farming and hunting peoples. By the sixteenth century, however, there may have been a new factor as the northern savanna came into contact with the long-distance exchange economies of the eastern Sudan and Sahara. In the early sixteenth century, a Spanish Arab, al-Ḥasan b. Muḥammad, later known as Leo Africanus, travelled from Bornu to Egypt via 'Gaoga', a kingdom probably centred on the Wadai–Darfur area, and connected to Egypt by the *Darb al-Arba'īn* route, a journey of forty days. The reigning dynasty of Gaoga appears to have been founded in the fifteenth century, and to have governed a wide, but variable, confederation of ethnic groups. Bornu was a major enemy of Gaoga, but intermittent warfare did not stop trade along the thirteenth parallel, nor the rise in prosperity of the northern oases along the route to Egypt. Egyptian traders sent the king of Gaoga weapons, textiles and horses, for all of which he paid generously in slaves. There is no reason to suppose that the slaves were anything other than local captives. The slaving methods were presumably typical of the Sudanic latitudes, where fast horsemen with modern swords overcame villagers on foot with wooden bows. In time, though perhaps not before 1600, the slave catchment area may have spread southwards towards the Ubangi basin, bringing increasing numbers of the northern woodland peoples into the destructive orbit of the trans-Saharan traffic. The ivory trade was probably based initially on elephant-hunting in the northern woodland, and only later spread southwards. One commodity which may have stimulated real new wealth was the copper of Hofrat en Nahas in southern Darfur, but this was not mentioned by Leo Africanus.[1]

For the time being historical research in both the savanna and forest regions of northern Central Africa will continue to concentrate on the

[1] P. Kalck, 'Pour une localisation du royaume de Gaoga', *Journal of African History*, 1972, 13, 529–48.

question of economic innovation among subsistence communities with a high degree of independent self-reliance. It is unlikely that evidence will reveal the emergence of any large-scale political organization before the seventeenth century. One feature which is of interest, however, is the emergence of trader-fishermen operating over long distances on the great river systems. These seem to have evolved institutionalized friendships, which enabled them to travel safely among remote peoples to whom they were only distantly related. Apart from this instance of external contacts, the focus of all activity seems to have remained the homestead and the village. Outsiders represented a threat to security, rather than an opportunity for wider co-operation and development. This timid isolationism was only reinforced in later centuries, as foreigners began to encroach on the forest margins in search of captive slaves.

The achievements of the later Central African Iron Age can be much more clearly witnessed in the open savanna regions to the south of the forest. There inter-community relations became more important. The diffusion of more advanced technology, the exploitation of scarce mineral resources like salt, iron and copper, the redistribution of raw and worked materials, all took on new importance. Religion became more organized, peoples became more closely united, states became more expansive in attempts to improve the quality of life and resist the threats of famine and war. Success was primarily marked by a growth of population, and an extension of territory to new agricultural lands. Distinctions of wealth and class rarely became important, and few material possessions were of a durable, ostentatious kind. Land never became so scarce as to become a matter of private ownership, with its concomitant centralization of wealth and influence. Within societies, distinctions between freemen and slaves were probably temporary rather than perpetual. Those who lost their kin or clan-fellows became the servants of those who had wider family support around them. Those with the greatest support acquired powers of chieftainship, to which religious functions were commonly attached.

The most important change to occur at the end of this half millennium during the sixteenth century was the gradual opening of Central Africa to outside influences. By 1600 these had only affected the south-western area. During the next 300 years they were to spread, first through the savanna and later deep into the forest, where many of the changes which they caused were of a highly disruptive kind.

CHAPTER 2

KINGS AND MERCHANTS IN THE ATLANTIC ERA 1600–1790

THE NORTHERN SAVANNA AND FOREST

In the seventeenth and eighteenth centuries the northern fringes of Central Africa made up one of the most sparsely populated areas of Africa. Here there were no great population clusters, no expansive cavalry empires, no walled cities and no markets thronged with caravans from the coast or the Maghrib. There were no kingdoms like those of Benin and Dahomey in West Africa and no mines as in Bambuk and Asante. The area had no wealth or minerals sufficient to attract traders across the Sahara. Only in the nineteenth century was its border pierced by Khartoum ivory hunters and Fulani slave raiders. Until that time the occupants of the northern savanna were almost exclusively concerned with subsistence agriculture. Even peoples like the Azande, who expanded the scope of their territory, did not expand the scope of their social institutions. Instead each advance swarm of Azande colonial pioneers cut itself off from its parent society and begun a new, independent, political existence. Not until the nineteenth century did the Bandia clan create the Bangassou 'sultanate' in order to resist the encroachments of slavers.[1]

In the west, North-Central Africa had a small opening on to the maritime world of lower Guinea. This was through the Cameroun port of Duala. The small coastal kingdom of the Duala appears to have been founded by Bantu-speaking peoples from the surrounding forest in the early seventeenth century. They moved to the coast when the first Dutch sailors penetrated the Bight of Biafra seeking trade in exotic African curiosities. The Duala sold them local cloth, beads, and probably ivory, and furnished their ships with grain and goat's meat. The

---

[1] Eric de Dampierre, *Un ancien royaume Bandia du Haut-Oubangui* (Paris, 1967).

49

4   Central Africa in the seventeenth and eighteenth centuries

Dutch were not especially interested in slaves, but in 1614 a ship's surgeon bought four young men as supplementary crew. He paid one pitcher of Spanish wine for them, and they soon learnt fluent Dutch and became effective sailors. The extent to which Duala trade influenced neighbouring peoples of the equatorial hinterland is quite uncertain. In the Cameroun highlands, small kingdoms such as Tikar and Bamum arose during the eighteenth century, but it is not established that their prosperity was influenced by trade with either the Duala coast, or the Hausa market towns of Nigeria. The most fertile and prosperous part of the Cameroun highlands was occupied by the Bamileke. It was not, however, until the nineteenth century, and later, that population growth began to drive these enterprising peoples from their overcrowded farms, to seek commercial employment along the coast.[1]

External relations – whether with the Atlantic or the Sahara – were of much lesser concern to the peoples of the northern savanna in the seventeenth and eighteenth centuries than were their relations with forest neighbours to the south. Both the Central Sudanic-speaking peoples in the east, and the Adamawa–Ubangian-speaking peoples, who, at a very remote date, had apparently overflowed into North-Central Africa from the west, made attempts to colonize the forest borders.[2] Most successful, perhaps, were the Mangbetu in the north-eastern corner of modern Zaïre. Their flourishing banana economy was enhanced by an active relationship with their Pygmy neighbours. The hunters supplied them with more meat than their own herds of goats could provide, and in return received iron wares and vegetable produce. Less successful than the Mangbetu were a related Central Sudanic-speaking people called the Mamvu. When the Mamvu penetrated the forest they came into contact with the Bantu-speaking Babwa. The Babwa had already adapted their agricultural economy very effectively to forest living, and saw no attraction in entering into a symbiotic relationship with the Mamvu, as the Pygmies did with the Mangbetu. Instead many Bantu farmers absorbed Central Sudanic-speaking immigrants into their own societies. In some cases Bantu domination of their neighbours may even have led to temporary Bantu colonization of savanna areas beyond the northern border of the forest.

Along the western sector of the forest boundary, the influence of Adamawa–Ubangian-speaking peoples seems to have been stronger than that of Bantu speakers. Already in the past Adamawa–Ubangian-speaking peoples had expanded at the expense of Central Sudanic ones. Now they expanded into Bantu-speaking areas as well, carrying Ngbandi and other savanna languages to the forest peoples, and adopting in return the South-East Asian complex of forest crops. Some of the influence of Adamawa–Ubangian-speaking peoples may have spread far beyond the forest borderland and brought new cultural attributes to peoples deep in the forest. A more important cultural interaction in these southerly regions of the forest was between Bantu and Pygmy. Many Pygmies

[1] Edwin Ardener, 'Documentary and linguistic evidence for the rise of trading polities between Rio del Rey and Cameroons 1500–1650', in I. M. Lewis (ed.), *History and social anthropology* (London, 1968).

[2] The speculative etho-linguistic distribution and its historical implications for North-Central Africa is adapted from Greenberg and Murdock. The classification is subject to caution, but so far only criticisms of nomenclature rather than alternatives have been offered.

were absorbed into Bantu communities, taking with them their forest crafts and influencing the genetic characteristics of their hosts. Other Pygmies retained a separate identity, but exchange relationships with the Bantu led to slow acculturation. By the nineteenth century Pygmies apparently had no distinct languages but spoke that of their neighbours. A marked case of close interchange of peoples and cultures occurred among the Mongo and their pygmoid clients, at the very heart of the Congo basin. Among these same Mongo, however, there were traits of northern influence which might even be attributable to a southward spread of Adamawa–Ubangian-speaking peoples. Some amateur ethnographers have even thought to discern northern influences among peoples of the southern forest such as the Tetela. In this area, however, more important cultural changes came from the south. In the seventeenth century, and more dramatically in the eighteenth century, the southern forest began to receive immigrants and refugees from the great southern savannas of Central Africa. These immigrants brought with them not only new political forms, such as the kingship which evolved among the Kuba, but a whole new series of American food-crops, which were almost as well suited to tropical forest conditions as they were to the moist southern savanna.[1]

THE KONGO KINGDOM

The first savanna area to receive the new crops, and to be disturbed by events which caused long-distance migration, was the lower Zaïre region. The lower Zaïre was one of the more favoured areas of Central Africa. Several localities, such as Nsundi, south of the river, and Mayombe to the north of it, had fertile soils, reliable water supplies, and prosperous populations of farmers and fishermen. Only in the marginal forests of the north were there peoples who still relied primarily on the gathering of wild plants for their vegetable foods. Elsewhere, even in the eastern forests of the Kwango, agriculture had long since become the primary economic activity. The predominance of agriculture over hunting, fishing and collecting, had further increased in the lower Zaïre during the sixteenth century by the introduction of maize and cassava from tropical America. Although the new crops did not replace the indigenous millets, their obvious success as staple foods in the neighbourhood of Portuguese trading posts led to their wider adoption. In the less populated areas the economic importance of the

[1] Jan Vansina, *Introduction à l'ethnographie du Congo* (Kinshasa, 1966) contains ethnographic data, historical speculation and bibliographical notes for the forest area.

adoption. In the less populated areas the economic importance of the hunter probably continued to match his social prestige. Where population grew, however, and game became scarce, the major source of meat was small domestic stock. Very few parts of the lower Zaïre were suitable for cattle-keeping, and great chiefs who wanted large livestock to enhance their status, had to import cattle from highland country in the south.

The basic economic activities of the lower Zaïre peoples showed a fundamental uniformity, but over and above the subsistence level there was a series of specialized economic pursuits which relied on regional resources. Some areas produced baskets, others dried fish, others pottery. The metal and textile industries were dependent on local materials and local skills. In addition to the local economic differences, there were important political differences between the areas north and south of the Zaïre river. The main kingdom of the north was Loango. The south was wholly dominated by the single kingdom of Kongo. During the sixteenth century, Kongo had been brought into intimate contact with maritime traders from Portugal, and had been effectively compelled to participate in the Atlantic slave trade. Loango, on the other hand, had a more limited experience of early European contacts, and preserved more of its traditional economic and political customs.

In the seventeenth century each responded in its own way to renewed and increased European influence. Although Kongo had been partly successful in absorbing the early alien influences, it now began to falter and crack under the demoralizing impact of intensified slave trading and intervention in its affairs by the Portuguese colonies of São Tomé island, in the north, and Angola, on the mainland to the south. Loango was more successful in retaining its integrity, and in controlling its economic relations with the Atlantic powers. As the political and economic strength of Loango increased, so its influence spread into the northern interior. At the end of the seventeenth century, when Kongo had virtually disappeared as a commercial kingdom, Loango extended its economic control to dominate a new pattern of southern trade routes as well.

In the early seventeenth century, the Kongo kingdom was still remarkably similar to the state first visited by the Portuguese a century before. Its internal structure was still recognizable, with six major provinces and a machinery of government centred on the king. The limits of the kingdom still stretched to the Zaïre river in the north, and to Luanda

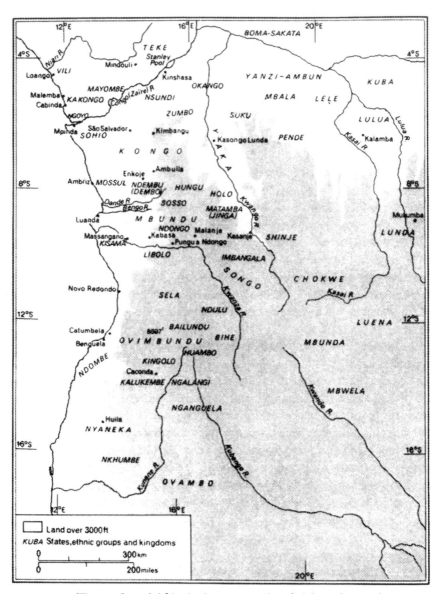

5 Western Central Africa in the seventeenth and eighteenth centuries

in the south. The changes which had occurred in Kongo during the first 100 years of Portuguese contact had not undermined its essential unity. In 1600 the king of the Kongo kingdom was Alvaro II. He was a man of vigour and intelligence who ruled from 1587 to 1614. During this long, uninterrupted reign he became an experienced administrator, and under his guidance the Kongo began to look outward on the world with increasing sophistication.

During the sixteenth century a small foreign community of traders, teachers and priests from Portugal had been built up in Kongo. The descendants and successors of these pioneers formed a Luso-African community whose role in the country was useful, if sometimes ambiguous. Their loyalty, in particular, was distinctly volatile, and they tended to maintain their own economic and social status by playing off the interests of Kongo against those of Portugal. Thus the price which Alvaro had to pay for foreign technical assistance was a diminution of sovereignty. Even more irksome to Alvaro than the potential disloyalty of his semi-European middle-class subjects, was Portuguese control of his foreign relations. So long as he was dependent on Portuguese ships for all external communication, whether commercial or diplomatic, he could not create any counterbalance to their influence. His ancestors had sought to resolve the dilemma by acquiring their own ships, but never with any degree of success. Alvaro sought to open diplomatic relations with non-Portuguese foreigners as a means of breaching his isolation.

Alvaro's first opening was in ecclesiastical diplomacy. To demand better Christian facilities for his people could hardly be construed as disloyalty by the most Catholic king of Portugal. On the other hand, domination of the Kongo church by the bishops of São Tomé had been harmful to Kongo's interests. The Tomistas, including their bishops, were primarily concerned to obtain slaves cheaply and plentifully from Kongo. In order to do so they attempted to subvert the Kongo state monopoly of external trade. For such a committedly mercenary bishop to be the ultimate moral and ecclesiastical authority in Kongo caused fierce resentment at São Salvador, the Kongo capital. Alvaro's father had sought to solve the problem by requesting the creation of a separate Kongo bishopric, and in 1596 his son succeeded in obtaining the concession. Although this move weakened the ecclesiastical power granted to Portugal under the *padroado*, Alvaro's success was less than complete. The first titular bishop of São Salvador was still a Portuguese subject, and Alvaro had to begin a new campaign to persuade the pope that

Portuguese bishops were liable to identify themselves with the interests of Portuguese nationals, notably the new settlers then arriving in Angola. To make his point, Alvaro sent an African ambassador, Antonio Manuel ne Vunda, to Pope Paul V. The ambassador, however, was detained three years in Lisbon, thus highlighting Alvaro's crippling dependence on Portuguese communications. He eventually proceeded to Rome under escort, but died before he could expose the ecclesiastical abuses in Kongo. Alvaro thus failed to break his diplomatic isolation. Even his success in getting a bishop nominated to São Salvador was short-lived. Within a few years the bishops transferred their seat informally to Luanda, where they found more comfortable quarters among their compatriots in the colonial capital of Angola.[1]

Despite this setback, Alvaro continued to seek support for his church. The Christian commitment of Kongo kings was in all probability less a matter of personal belief than one of diplomatic status within the Catholic commonwealth of nations. Kongo kings were anxious to show sufficient Christian enthusiasm to maintain the credibility of their Christian status, yet they did not want to damage the hallowed customs of themselves or their subjects. To maintain world recognition, Alvaro therefore requested the dispatch of new missionaries to Kongo. Three Dominicans eventually arrived and were received by the Duke of Bamba who greeted them with drums and royal bells. They were given hens, goats, food and two million small brown *nzimbu* shells to cover the expenses of their journey by hammock-carrier along the sparsely populated road to the capital. They found São Salvador flourishing and fertile, and estimated that the metropolitan region could raise 25,000 fighting men. The power and prestige of King Alvaro was at this time considerable. His immediate subjects worked hard to support the court and cultivate its surroundings. His provincial governors were still heavily dependent on the royal patronage for their positions. The king controlled the rural clergy, and priests were maintained in each provincial capital, as well as in the important 'kingdom' of Okango, on the caravan route to Kinshasa. Since the king remained so very powerful, the Dominicans soon found that the real positions of influence were among his personal servants and retainers at court. The major rival to the court had become the new cathedral. It had attached to it twelve priests paid out of revenue due to the Portuguese crown. This endeavour to maintain an autonomous Portuguese ecclesiastical in-

[1] Sigbert Axelson, *Culture confrontation in the lower Congo* (Uppsala, 1970), contains full references to the extensive literature on the ecclesiastical history of Kongo.

fluence, and to make foreign priests independent of royal Kongo patronage, had some success. The independence of the cathedral priests was a
flaw in the royal absolutism, and yet the kings were dependent on the
priesthood for the Christian elements of their legitimacy and for the
rituals of their enthronement.

The foreign missionaries were not the only Christian factor in the
Kongo political situation. There had also emerged a limited number of
African and mestizo priests who were able to exercise considerable
power over the partially Christianized peoples of the towns. Their
influence was frequently considered by foreign observers to be pernicious, but no independent Kongo testimonies shed light on their
role. What appeared pernicious and even treasonable to foreigners may
well have appeared to Kongo peoples as highly patriotic. This rivalry
of indigenous and foreign clerics was accentuated when the mestizo
priests in São Salvador, seeing their influence threatened by the better-
educated white Dominicans, persuaded Alvaro II to reverse his policy
and evict them. Despite this episode, however, mission policy still
vacillated in São Salvador, and Alvaro III (1614–22) succeeded in attracting Jesuits into the country in 1619. For a time the power of
the mestizo clergy was eclipsed by an influential Portuguese priest, Bras
Correia, who became confessor to the king. He played a dominant role
in the country's internal politics, and in the succession dispute of 1622
apparently placed his own nominee on the throne. His role, however,
was resented not only in Kongo, but also in Luanda where the Portuguese expected him to defend their interests rather than his own.

Alvaro II's search for external openings was not limited to an
ecclesiastical foreign policy. He also sought tangible technical aid from
the governments of Spain and Portugal. His requests for smiths,
masons and craftsmen were all refused lest he build strategic fortifications against Portuguese military interventions. Alvaro also requested
that a captain of the Portuguese foreign community in Kongo be
appointed who would be independent of São Tomé and Angola. He
would receive a public letter of instruction clearly setting out policy on
matters of extra-territorial rights. The Portuguese government rejected
this request, and expressed concern that Portuguese should be allowed
to reside in Kongo at all, since they were liable to impart military skill and firearm technology to potential enemies of Portugal.
Since a withdrawal of all Portuguese was impractical, however, the
government in Lisbon recommended that a captain should be appointed.
His secret terms of reference would require him to group all the

Portuguese settlers and their women and children in a single, well-enclosed quarter of São Salvador, preferably with a fort for its defence. The captain should be quite free of any grace or favour from the king, and should be replaced in the event of a vacancy by a Portuguese officer from São Tomé or Angola, precisely in the manner Alvaro most resented. This attempt to apply to the traders the West African policy of political disengagement, and military autonomy, did not work. It was clearly inappropriate when the main trading centre was not on the coast but 150 kilometres inland. Traders therefore remained dependent on royal recognition before they could obtain the freedom to travel on business expeditions. Alvaro must have been aware of the traders' dependence when he sought to build up the foreign community to his own advantage. Rather curiously, he requested that he be allowed to expel all Jews from his kingdom, and asked that new immigrants be sent in their place, particularly white women who would marry existing settlers and strengthen the settler community. His policy was of course opposed by Portugal. A growing European community at São Salvador would only strengthen the king's position vis-à-vis his undeclared opponents in the new Portuguese colony of Angola.

Angola became the major subject of concern in Alvaro's external policy. The negotiations outlined above show clearly that, beneath the niceties of diplomatic exchange between equal allies, lay the realities of a rivalry which verged on war. The bitterness of this rivalry was emphasized when Alvaro sent a Portuguese subject, who had attempted to assassinate him, to Luanda for punishment. Instead of receiving punishment, the man was rewarded by the governor and set free. One bone of contention between Kongo and Angola was Luanda island. Although only a stone's throw from the Angolan capital, this island belonged to Kongo and was the source of its currency shells. The Kongo right to the island was commonly recognized by Luanda governors, but João Furtado de Mendonça had none the less granted land on the island to a monastery, and had justified his action by saying that the site would only be used for temporary straw huts in which to baptize slaves. Some claimants to island plots said that Alvaro I had granted the island, or part of it, to Angola in return for the great expense incurred on Kongo's behalf by Portugal during the Jaga wars. A further irritant to the growing conflict between Kongo and Angola was the land along the lower Bengo and Dande rivers. These plains were suitable for cultivation, unlike most of the coastal strip, and Portuguese governors had been granting gardens to settlers.

Alvaro II protested at the infringement of his sovereignty, while the settlers denounced Kongo expansionism. Another confrontation between Kongo and Angola occurred over mining. Alvaro had tried to interest the pope in copper mines during his search for ecclesiastical allies. When that failed, he turned to the Portuguese for skilled mining engineers. At the time, the Portuguese were disillusioned with mines after thirty years of fruitless conquest and mineral prospecting in Angola. The offer did, however, slowly rekindle the old popular belief in Kongo's mineral riches. In the imagination of many, the vision was transformed from copper to gold mines.

In 1622 the various tensions which had been developing between Kongo and Angola finally led to war. The attack was launched by João Correia de Souza, then acting governor of Angola. Correia probably hoped to improve the forward defence of the settlers' farms in the frontier valleys, and perhaps to gain intelligence about Kongo's mineral prospects. He may also have hoped to put a weak king of his own choice on the Kongo throne. A more immediate factor, however, was probably a desire to use his temporary governorship to make a quick profit out of the slave trade. The southern provinces of Kongo were by this time better populated than the war-torn hinterland of Angola, and Correia may have hoped to capture large numbers of war prisoners. In this he was probably spurred on by his auxiliary troops. The role of these black mercenaries, known as 'Jagas', in the war of 1622 left a marked impression on the Kongo folk memory. Plunder was an essential ingredient of the economy of these Portuguese auxiliaries, and their desire to raid the fertile provinces of southern Kongo may have required little encouragement from the Portuguese.

Whatever the motive for the war of 1622, its results were decisive and far-reaching. Although the invaders failed to capture any mining regions, the campaign reinforced a belief in the mines, which became the cause or excuse for a series of wars between Angola and Kongo over the next fifty years. The governor and his captains captured numerous slaves, thus demonstrating the profitability of raiding, despite the protests of the traders whose security they endangered. The war marked the end of the uneasy peace which had persisted between Angola and Kongo during the reigns of Alvaro I and Alvaro II, and the beginning of hostilities which eventually would lead to the destruction of the Kongo monarchy in 1665.

The war of 1622 had another effect which was to prove damaging to the very Portuguese who had initiated it. It undermined the basis of the whole trading system they had evolved in West-Central Africa. The basic essential for a flourishing trade was relatively unhindered access to the main sources of supply, many of which were on the northern and eastern fringes of Kongo. Caravans led by *pombeiros* (trading agents of Portuguese, mestizo or African origin) were dispatched from the business houses of Luanda with trade goods from Europe and India. Within Kongo these agents dealt with resident Portuguese-speaking intermediaries, or went through the kingdom to the frontier fairs. It was estimated that in 1622 there may have been as many as 1,000 'Portuguese' trading agents in Kongo with their own villages, farms and extended African families. When the governor of Angola invaded the southern provinces, xenophobic attacks were launched on many of these establishments. Pedro II, the new Kongo king, intervened to protect many individual Portuguese merchants, while at the same time declaring war on Angola. His success was limited, and many 'Portuguese' were killed or driven out. The king rightly saw this as a weakening of his own authority. The former prestige of Europeans, the influence of the Christian religion, and above all the ability of traders to supply foreign consumer goods, made the Portuguese presence in Kongo a valuable tool of the monarchy. The basis of this Portuguese presence, which had contributed to the long stable reign of Alvaro II, was now being eaten away by the predatory ambitions of the governor of Angola.

The war of 1622 marked the collapse of the diplomatic manoeuvres initiated by Alvaro II and Alvaro III. They had been unable to establish an effective alliance with the papacy, and had failed to persuade the Hapsburg rulers of Portugal to modify the semi-hostile attitude which had developed towards Kongo since the establishment of Angola. It was developments in an entirely different, and unexpected, direction which began to alter the situation in Kongo's favour and postpone her day of reckoning with Angola. By the closing years of the sixteenth century, English, French and Dutch corsairs had begun raiding the Portuguese settlements on the coast of West-Central Africa, and on the islands of Principe and São Tomé. After 1600, expeditions culminated in the development of regular trade to Kongo's western province of Sohio, where the Dutch established factories. Alvaro II welcomed this sudden and unexpected commercial break-through, which gave him an alternative outlet for his own goods and a new source of European imports. Competition led to a rise in export prices, a drop in import prices, and a new appreciation of such commodities as ivory and dyewood. The

Portuguese naturally reacted strongly against their loss of monopoly. They threatened in vain to build a fort at Mpinda, the Sohio port, in order to exclude by force the competition which they were unable to defeat by economic advantage. They warned the Kongo of the moral dangers of associating with heretics, and called on the bishop to threaten Alvaro III if he tolerated Dutch traders in his kingdom.

The success of the Dutch soon presented the Kongo kings with a new problem. Their trade was mostly conducted through the province of Sohio, which had previously been in decline after the main caravan route from São Salvador had been diverted southwards to Luanda. Under Dutch influence, Sohio now revived. Mpinda acquired schools and a priest to run the church. The count of Sohio and his advisers wore fine oriental cloaks, and hats, and gold chains of office in which to receive the Dutch merchants.[1] This new affluence enabled Sohio to become increasingly independent of the Kongo central king. The count began effectively to challenge the principle of monopoly state trading which had theoretically been espoused by both Kongo and Portugal throughout the sixteenth century. The count, more even than the king, was immune to Portuguese threats. He was also relatively immune to threats from his suzerain. The advent of a second trading power thus created a major rift in the kingdom. It was to be followed during the seventeenth century by other divisions.

The war of 1622, and the death of Alvaro III in the same year, marked the end of a long period of relative stability during which the centralized nature of Kongo government remained clearly recognizable. Thereafter centrifugal tendencies became paramount and the centre weakened. Over the next nineteen years, six kings succeeded each other to the throne, and factional struggles became severe. Each faction not only claimed a right to the central throne but simultaneously, though inconsistently, claimed independent rights over individual provinces. Newly introduced European titles of nobility proliferated and new provinces were created. To add strength to the factions, provincial courts were able to welcome and protect some of the 'Portuguese' traders who had fled from the capital. The process whereby trade had strengthened the central monarchy was now transferred to the smaller centres of power. Each state attempted to develop its own monopoly trading, to tax the flow of goods through its lands, and to hinder the business of its rivals.

[1] K. Ratelband (ed.), *Reizen naar West-Afrika van Pieter van der Broecke 1605–1614* (The Hague, 1953).

The next turning point in Kongo history occurred in 1641, when the growing fragmentation was temporarily curbed. By that year, the Dutch had become such large-scale slave consumers that their trade with Sohio was insufficient to meet the demands of their American colonies. They therefore sent an armed fleet from Brazil which captured Luanda in August 1641. In the same year, Garcia II came to the throne of Kongo and began to reconsolidate central power. His reign, from 1641 to 1661, marked the last phase of effective Kongo unity. It also re-emphasized many of the old and deep-rooted problems which contact with European culture had brought to his country. Among the foremost of these was the question of conflicting religious practices. In the traditional structure of Kongo, religion obviously played an important role in the never-ending search for security and for protection against famines, disasters and epidemics. When court circles began to adopt alien religious customs, they were in constant danger of cutting off their traditional grass-roots support by neglecting ancestral religious values and rites. However arbitrary and authoritarian Kongo monarchs may have appeared to European observers, they were nevertheless political figures who had to secure some element of acquiescence from the peoples they ruled. A king closely associated with religious achievements became stronger and more acceptable; if he attempted further to increase his influence by adopting the substance or trapping of European religions, he could still not afford to neglect his traditional religious roots. Garcia II was fully conscious of his religious dilemma.

On the Christian side, Garcia sought to attract the Jesuits back to São Salvador in order to foster European education. He also approached the Italian Capuchins, whom the papacy had long been hoping to send to Kongo, and in 1645, while Portugal was preoccupied in a bitter war with Spain, and when Angola was under Dutch occupation, the first Capuchin mission slipped into the country despite Portuguese protests. Although a Capuchin mission had the advantage, from Garcia's point of view, of being non-Portuguese, it soon showed the marked disadvantage that its members were more numerous, and travelled more widely in the rural areas, than their predecessors had done. They came into regular contact with traditional forms of worship which they condemned with vigour. In 1653 Georges de Geel was killed for interfering with local shrines, and Garcia had to protect the Capuchins. Later in his reign the king had to turn more openly to traditional religious practices for support, and became known as *kimpaku*, the sorcerer. The acceptance of Christian monogamy would, if strictly applied, have precluded his consolidation of royal authority by multiple marriage ties. The church might also have interfered in the royal succession, which the missionaries interpreted through European concepts of family legitimacy, rather than as a Kongo custom of political selection among eligible clan members. Worse still the church tended to favour candidates for sectarian interests, rather than national ones, and so in the latter part of his life Garcia was in constant conflict with the missions.

During the first seven years of Garcia's reign, Kongo had a respite from the pressing problem of its relations with Angola. Under Dutch occupation, Angola showed little of the expansionist ambition of the preceding period. Garcia's most aggressive challenger was his own western province of Sohio, fortified by its special relationship with the Dutch. After a series of wars, battles and skirmishes, Garcia was forced to recognize Sohio independence. Peace did not long survive, for in 1648 the Portuguese returned to Luanda determined to press ahead with the subjugation of the Kongo kingdom which had so treacherously supported their Dutch enemies. Garcia tried to forestall war with diplomacy, and proposed a peace treaty. He wanted the Kongo episcopal see to be restored to São Salvador, and the continuance of the Capuchin mission to be safeguarded. He wanted the integrity of his kingdom to be guaranteed against dismemberment and border raids. He asked that a just price be established for all trade goods coming into his kingdom and that judges be appointed to examine all slaves leaving it to ensure that no freemen were captured. Finally, he wanted a stop put to the importation of foreign shells, which were causing inflation to his *nzimbu* currency.

In Luanda, Salvador de Sá, the conquering governor, rejected Garcia's proposals as impertinent and made counter proposals revealing his own basic interests. Territorially he demanded that Ambuila, the Dande valley, and Luanda island, be transferred to Angola as payment for war damages during the Dutch occupation. Commercially his major concern was the free flow of trade across Kongo. He demanded that Portuguese cloth, salt and slaves be given tax-free transit across the whole kingdom without obligation to ferry dues or other levy. A single and unique duty would be levied on the Angola border. Furthermore the charge for porters must be reduced to its pre-war level and porters must be compelled to carry goods to their destination, and not to some half-way point. This concern with porters' fees and local customs dues was critical for the Luanda traders. Only as an afterthought did they seek control of the copper mines (invariably called gold mines) by offering Garcia the option to retain his *nzimbu* fisheries in return for the transfer of the mines to Portugal. One further clause demanded that all Kongo connections with Europe pass through Luanda, thus permitting the Portuguese to restrict any further activities by the Dutch or the Capuchins.[1]

Garcia initially rejected these Portuguese proposals despite the precarious position in which he had been left by the Dutch withdrawal. As the Portuguese and Brazilians rebuilt their military strength in Angola, Garcia recognized his weakness and signed the Luanda terms. He did not, however, accept the offer to exchange Luanda for the copper mines, and these became a new excuse for Portuguese encroachment during the next decade of simmering dispute. The country's troubles were also increased at this time by the introduction of the plague. In 1661 Garcia died and was succeeded by Antonio I, and four years later full-scale war broke out anew between Kongo and Angola. Antonio called up men from every province and reputedly raised 70,000 supporters reinforced by about 200 white and mestizo musketeers. He met the Angolan army at Ambuila on 29 October 1665. The Angolans, with some 360 'Portuguese' and 7,000 Africans won the day, allegedly killing 400 Kongo noblemen, including Antonio himself. The first effect of the battle was a wave of attacks on European settlements throughout Kongo and a mass exodus of traders. The Portuguese did not, or could not, follow up their victory by seeking and exploiting the copper mines. Neither did they attempt to establish a colonial government based on garrisons of small forts as in conquered Angola. They did try to control the coastal province of Sohio, but after a brief moment of success their invading force was decisively routed in 1672. Instead of imposing control over the kingdom, the Portuguese waited, ready to buy slaves from the warring factions which emerged.

The tensions which caused the breakdown of Kongo after the death of Antonio I had been in evidence for some years. The country had been producing or marketing a large share of the 15,000 or so slaves which were taken out of the lower Zaïre area each year. As exactions grew, villages revolted against their chiefs in protest against slavery, against labour dues, against carrier services and against tribute. The

[1] Garcia's peace proposals were drawn up in São Salvador on 19 February 1649. A copy may be found in the archives of the Vatican's Propaganda Fide, S.R.C.G., vol. 249, fols. 4–4v. and is reproduced in A. Brásio, *Monumenta Missionaria Africana*, x (Lisbon, 1965), 326–8. Salvador de Sá's response was allegedly drafted on 13 April 1649 and is reprinted in Ralph Delgado, *Historia de Angola*, III (Lobito, 1953), 64–9.

chiefs, in their turn, revolted against the impositions of regional governments and the demands of royal factions which pretended to live in royal pomp. At each level, tax had either to be collected by force, thus raising the level of violence and counter-violence, or to be forfeited, thus weakening the power and prestige of authority. The extent to which the government hierarchy had become a chain of greater and lesser oppressors of the people may have been exaggerated by the Capuchin witnesses, but after the death of Garcia II oppression appeared to grow beyond controlled bounds, and after 1665 no central government could effectively limit the powers of increasingly small and fragmented chiefdoms. Three factions claimed the Kongo throne, though none occupied São Salvador. The contenders were not only divided in their territorial hold on different parts of the kingdom, but were split between hostile groups on clan affiliations. The Kimpanzu clan with intermittent Sohio support, attempted to regain power after the long reign of Garcia II and of Antonio I, who belonged to the Kimulaza clan. This western bid to restore the old royal clan was stopped by a series of rival northern kings who established their capital at Lemba, near Matadi. This northern influence was in turn supplanted by an eastern dynasty from Mount Kimbangu. In 1709, after numerous wars, assassinations, and intrigues, the Kimbangu faction regained São Salvador and placed Pedro IV on the throne. His victory, however, was modest, for although the Kongo monarchy retained considerable prestige, the real power of Pedro's successors declined steadily during the eighteenth century. Indeed Pedro himself might never have achieved such wide recognition had it not been for a curious religious revival in the kingdom.[1]

The Italian Capuchin missionaries had been spreading their Christian message through the main provinces of Kongo ever since 1645. Their efforts were greatly impeded by the jealousy of the Portuguese missions, by the catastrophe of Ambuila, where the only Mukongo Capuchin priest was killed, by the civil wars that followed the death of Antonio, and by the burning of São Salvador in 1678. They nevertheless persevered. Much of their teaching was rejected by peoples who could not give up their house-gods, their polygynous families and their traditional safeguards against witchcraft and sorcery. Some of the Catholic rituals and sacred objects found favour among the Kongo, but were incorporated into customary ceremonies and shrines in a way that seemed

[1] François Bontinck (ed.), *Diaire Congolais de Fra Luca da Caltanisetta* (Louvain, 1970) contains information on this confused period of Kongo history.

blasphemous to the provincial Italian Capuchins with no toleration for religious syncretism. Even the movements which tried to give an African form to the spiritual message of Christianity seemed unacceptable to them, but, in spite of mission denunciations, black prophets did occasionally become popular in Kongo.

Few details are known about the early prophets who preached Christianity while rejecting a foreign, white church. In the late seventeenth century, however, when fear and conflict increased in Kongo, and the foreign missions failed to reconcile the political factions, the country was ready to welcome a messianic saviour. This saviour was found around 1700 in the form of a young woman called Beatrix Kimpa Vita. She began to attract attention to herself by claiming to be the voice of Saint Anthony. She travelled the country performing miraculous healings and preaching a religious and national revival. She denounced foreign missionaries and claimed that Christ was a Mukongo born in São Salvador. She attacked traditional fetishes and superstitions, and called on her followers to accept a truly African messianic Christianity. She finally settled in São Salvador and, like Joan of Arc, began to inspire new confidence in the nationalist cause.

The success of the Antonine movement was due to many factors. The extreme fears and uncertainty of the previous thirty years had made people anxious to accept a movement which would offer security and which had an aura of success. The name of Saint Anthony may have revived memories of the last great king, Antonio, destroyed at the battle of Ambuila. Finally, the success of the Capuchins in carrying Christianity to many remote parts of the kingdom may have made people more disposed to accept a movement with Christian manifestations. This successful messianic movement was a threat, however, both to the mission authority and to traditional political authority. Pedro IV and the Capuchins therefore combined to condemn Beatrix as a false saint. In 1706 they had her burnt at the stake. It was shortly after this that Pedro IV was able to move to São Salvador, the capital city which the Antonines had rebuilt.[1]

The recovery of São Salvador did not lead to a large-scale revival of the Kongo monarchy. The country's military power had been permanently broken at Ambuila and was never regained. The peasants suffered from famines and epidemics in the remote areas to which they had been forced to withdraw. The aristocracy no longer possessed the wealth it

[1] Louis Jadin, 'Le Congo et la secte des Antoniens', *Bulletin de l'Institut Historique Belge de Rome*, 1961, **33**, 411–615.

had once derived from agriculture, artisan production, and internal commodity trading. Instead a parasitic class of dukes, earls and princesses lived in a fantasy world where prestige was based on memories, and where kidnapped slaves were the source of wealth. The control of trade, which the central court had once practised, was permanently lost, and the kings no longer enjoyed their monopoly, even in a restricted area. Instead, many separate groups of 'bourgeois' entrepreneurs emerged to take over from the state-controlled system. At the same time, direct Portuguese participation in trade was eliminated. The new class of businessmen did not belong to the old Luso-African community which had mounted the *pombeiro* caravans of the sixteenth and early seventeenth centuries. They were wholly African in their culture and politics. In the west, the most important group were the Mussorongo of Sohio. To some extent they succeeded in maintaining trade relations with the European maritime powers while avoiding their corruptive effects. By the eighteenth century, in order to safeguard their independence, the Mussorongo kept Atlantic shipping out of their own ports and traded through Cabinda and later Boma on the north of the Zaïre estuary. In eastern Kongo, the most influential trading entrepreneurs were the Zombo. They initially controlled some of the trade routes to Kinshasa and the north-eastern Kongo hinterland. From there they gradually took over the management of the trade sector between the Kwango river and the lower Zaïre. In southern Kongo, part of the coast was controlled by the Mossul peoples who attracted English and French traders to their harbour at Ambriz. This port became an important trade outlet for Angola, and a source of supply for all the contraband goods which the Portuguese would not admit through Luanda. The Portuguese tried to limit this traffic on several occasions. They built a fort in the interior of southern Kongo in the hope of blocking the trade paths. When this failed, they tried to capture Cabinda, the French base on the coast north of the Zaïre from which many trade goods came southwards. When all else failed, the Portuguese even attempted an overland excursion into Mossul from Luanda. None of these assaults was effective. Even in 1855, when Portugal succeeded in garrisoning Ambriz from the sea, the pattern of trade had only to be slightly diverted to avoid Portuguese customs duties and administrative interference.

LOANGO

As the trade routes of Kongo passed from the hands of political princes
into the control of trading clans, a new foreign group began to infiltrate
the country and seek economic preferment. These were the Vili from
the Loango coast. Caravans of Vili ('Mubires') penetrated deep into
the old kingdom after the crash of 1665, and by the 1680s they were
even tapping the slave markets of Angola. This growth of the economic
dynamism of Loango needs to be explained by returning to the early
seventeenth century, and examining events in the northern half of the
lower Zaïre region.

The Loango coast, between the Zaïre estuary and the Gabon forest,
had been much less affected by the trading developments of the sixteenth century than the southern areas of the Kongo peoples. It had
preserved its traditional political and economic systems more distinctly.
The area was divided into the three kingdoms of Loango, Kakongo
and Ngoyo, centred on the anchorages of Loango Bay, Malemba and
Cabinda. Loango, the largest of the kingdoms, had an important market
at its inland capital, and the peoples of the coast appear to have been
active traders long before the first Europeans arrived on the scene.
Their economy was already partially geared to surplus production for
marketing and export. The major manufacture was cloth woven in
different qualities and patterns from palm fibres. This cloth was used
for clothing and furnishing, and in some areas it became a ready
standard of currency. As a token of wealth, cloth had an advantage
over agricultural produce, in that it could be more easily stored for
long periods. At all levels of society, cloth became a guarantee against
financial disaster, or a hoard to be spent on great family occasions. In its
role of currency, cloth had the further advantage that it maintained a
fairly stable value, owing to the fixed amount of labour which went
into its production. Although less durable, and more bulky than shell
currencies, it was also less liable to suffer from inflation caused by a
flood of new supplies. Loango cloth therefore became a useful yardstick
by which many lower Zaïre peoples measured relative values in the
seasonally fluctuating market for foodstuffs and consumer goods.

Another important product of Loango was salt, dried from sea
lagoons along the low-rainfall coast. From the seventeenth century
onwards, Loango salt was traded to increasingly remote peoples in the
interior, and may also have been sent up the coast to the high-rainfall
areas of Gabon. A third Loango export was copper from the Mindouli

region 150 kilometres inland. In the seventeenth century the mines were under Teke control, but the trade to the coast was conducted by Vili merchants from Loango. Copper ornaments, together with cloth, were among the major forms of material wealth among the savanna peoples. Copper bracelets and necklace wires were particularly prized as heirlooms or personal property. In addition to the three commodities of cloth, salt and copper, Loango supplied the local and coastal traders with elephant tails, needed for charms and bracelets, and with ivory used for ornamental carvings and musical instruments. The level of locally inspired economic exchanges went far beyond the bounds of a 'subsistence-oriented' trading system. Many of the goods produced required a high degree of entrepreneurial specialization. The cloth weaver produced large quantities of cloth and not merely a small, almost incidental, surplus to the requirements of self-sufficiency. The copper traders, and perhaps also the salt merchants, undertook their commercial activities as more than a sideline to agriculture. The presence of a currency was also a sign of Loango's sophisticated economy and its advanced method of evaluating comparability in the market sector of economy. In exchange for its exports, one of the major imports of Loango was alleged by a late sixteenth-century Portuguese trader to be iron. This essential commodity was needed to make tools, weapons and knives. Since the sandy soils of the Loango hinterland were seriously deficient in quality iron ores, the country was forced to produce exportable goods to pay for its iron imports.

In the hundred years from the late sixteenth to the late seventeenth century, Loango's varied economy was stimulated by the growth of exports to Europe. This development was closely associated with the arrival of the Dutch. Holland had many advantages over Portugal as a commercial power, since its control of the Rhine route into Germany provided her with a large market for colonial imports and a ready supply of manufactured commodities in exchange. Holland began her trade with Loango by purchasing copper in some quantity. At that time the copper mines were probably still controlled by the Teke king, the *makoko*. The rising demand for copper seems, however, to have coincided with a challenge to the Teke by Loango traders who managed the distribution of copper. By the 1660s Loango had a well-organized copper producing enterprise. Each September a large caravan of smiths and unskilled labourers travelled up the Niari valley to Mindouli. While the workers extracted the ore, the craftsmen smelted it until, at the onset of the next dry season, they were able to trek back to the coast.

Payment was made to the local peoples, as well as to those along the route, in the form of royalties, tribute and protection money.

The Loango ivory trade also expanded with Dutch demand. As elephants became scarce near the coast, new supplies of ivory had to be sought farther afield. This advance of the ivory-hunting frontier required the development of new transport enterprises to head-load tusks to the coast. In most of West-Central Africa the rising cost of carriage, the extermination of coastal elephants, and the low prices offered by Portuguese traders licensed under a restrictive royal monopoly, curtailed ivory trading in the seventeenth century. In Loango, where there was no competing trade in slaves from which quicker profits could be gained, a long-distance ivory network emerged which apparently tapped supplies as far afield as the Teke plateau and possibly even as far as the upper Ogowe basin.[1] This growth of ivory trading tended to be a stimulant to other forms of commerce and industry. Traders did not buy their ivory direct from hunters. The exchange process was more complex, and benefited several sectors of the economy. The elephant hunters of 'Bukkameale', who may have been Pygmies, were particularly in need of salt, so that the ivory trade in that quarter stimulated the coastal salt industries. In other areas it is suggested that palm oil was traded for ivory, thus bringing agricultural produce into the market sphere of activity. It is likely that other local products were marketed with increasing intensity in order that capital goods could be accumulated to buy tusks. When the ivory was delivered to European traders, the goods received in exchange began to percolate back through all the channels which the ivory had followed. The trading thus stimulated the whole economy.

The most striking aspect of the international trade of Loango in the first half of the seventeenth century was the virtual absence of any slave trading. Two reasons may be offered. The first was the reluctance of the Loango peoples to trade in slaves. To some extent, they had a choice open to them. Either they could use their labour to manufacture cloth for export, or they could sell their labour and buy cloth from overseas. In the late sixteenth century the price offered for slave labour on the Portuguese-dominated Atlantic market was not sufficiently attractive to entice Loango businessmen. In contrast to this, the Portuguese were offering good prices for palm cloth, which they could readily sell for slaves in Angola. The Angolans, partly because of their comparative economic deprivation, but more especially because of a strong

[1] Phyllis M. Martin, *The external trade of the Loango coast 1576–1870* (Oxford, 1972).

Portuguese military presence on their territory, had no such choice open to them. Angola, unlike Loango, was compelled by economic and political pressures to trade in slaves. In Loango a second reason for the absence of slave trading in the early seventeenth century was the commercial influence of the Dutch. The Dutch arrived at a time when the European demand for African ivory and dyewood was increasing. Already parts of the upper Guinea coast were changing their trade pattern from slaving to commodity trading.[1] The Dutch, who had as yet no tropical colonies, and no need for slaves, responded to this European demand and sought mainly ivory, copper and dyewood in Loango. Only in the 1630s did Holland begin to acquire colonies in Brazil and the West Indies, and to take a more direct interest in the supply of labour to maintain the sugar and tobacco plantations they had captured.

The change in Dutch demand was not sufficient to reverse immediately the Loango refusal to deal in slaves. Several decades of adaptation were necessary. Loango itself had a sparse population, and if the national policy was to switch to slaving, a whole new economic structure would be needed. Only in the 1660s did this new policy become effective and Loango begin to trade in slaves on an expanding scale. The reasons for the change must be sought in the growth of the commercial economy. The country had become accustomed to a high level of international trading activity. To refuse to trade in slaves, when both the supply of other commodities, and the demand for them, was dwindling, would result in an apparent economic decline, and in a dangerous failure to meet immediate expectations. Loango therefore became caught, as Kongo and Angola had been before her. One influential new factor on the demand side was the growing strength of the Portuguese economy in Brazil. From the mid-seventeenth century onwards the Portuguese were better able to pay competitive prices for slaves, and Brazilian rum and tobacco both became very popular in the trade. Loango thus found both the Dutch and the Luso-Brazilians offering more attractive trade terms for slaves.

Once the trade had begun, Loango rapidly became one of the most important slaving areas of the whole Atlantic seaboard. From the late seventeenth to the late eighteenth century, 10,000 and more slaves a year were shipped to the New World. The Portuguese and Dutch were joined in the business by the British, and above all by the French. In

[1] Walter Rodney, *A history of the upper Guinea coast* (Oxford, 1970); K. G. Davies, *The Royal African Company* (London, 1957).

addition to paying for slaves with the traditional imports of cloth, clothing, beads, iron goods, brass, alcohol and tobacco, the European traders began to develop a substantial business in guns and gunpowder. During this period large numbers of guns, perhaps as many as two per slave, were being sold to West-Central Africa via the Loango coast. The effect of such large-scale imports of guns was important. Powerful broker states such as Kasanje (see below, p. 79) developed large armies of musketeers. The potential military and political consequences of these large gun sales were, however, somewhat reduced by the poor quality and inaccuracy of the weapons. On the economic side, the sale of guns had the attractive advantage for the Europeans of creating a permanent demand for gunpowder and for further muskets to replace defective or broken ones, thus encouraging yet further slave sales as payment.

As the Loango trade expanded, so the extent of its trading connections grew, and the sources of its slaves became more diverse and remote. In the north, Loango was linked to the 'Bobangi' peoples of the middle Zaïre, who sent slaves from wide areas of the central Zaïre basin across the north Teke plateau to the coast. The southern Teke had long had important slaving posts which supplied the Portuguese in Kongo and Angola. An even more important dimension was the southern trade which took Vili ('Mubire') caravans across Kongo and into Angola where they posed a severe challenge to the Portuguese at Luanda. The rapid growth of trade to, and beyond, the Teke and Kongo regions meant that during the eighteenth century the slave trade of Loango was probably greater than that of Angola.

The growth and change in the trade of the Loango coast during the seventeenth and eighteenth centuries had important effects on the political and social structures of the coastal societies. In 1600 the *maloango* was a powerful king whose influence extended not only over his own kingdom of Loango, but also along the whole coast from Cape Saint Catherine in the north to the smaller kingdoms of Kakongo and Ngoyo in the south. The advent of foreign traders in the late sixteenth century seems to have stimulated the growth of his power. Internal trade was conducted through the king, whose government collected taxes and used the unconsumed surplus for commercial exchanges. The seventeenth-century *maloango* was surrounded by a class of nobles from whom he chose his royal officers and provincial governors. It was they who levied tribute and exacted export duties in the outlying provinces. It was they who benefited most from the imported luxury goods which enhanced the material culture and prestige of the court and its retainers. Their success was further stimulated by the growth of sharp competition among European buyers. Whereas sixteenth-century Kongo had had to sell to the Portuguese or not at all, seventeenth-century Loango was able to play off rival customers and so improve the terms of trade. Any attempt by one European nation to restrict free competition was severely dealt with by Loango officials.

By the eighteenth century, the position and power of the *maloango* had begun to change. The first cause of this was the rapid rise of the slave trade. Whereas the trade in ivory, timber, elephant tails, cloth and copper had come from within Loango, or from its eastern hinterland, a larger part of the slave trade came from the south, across the Congo estuary. This meant that the southern kingdoms of Ngoyo and Kakongo, with their excellent ports of Cabinda and Malemba, had the advantage over Loango of being 150 kilometres nearer to the main source of supply. They therefore began to assert their independence and to refuse more than token tribute to the *maloango*. They even attempted to close the routes from Kongo to Loango altogether. By the end of the eighteenth century, Loango had shrunk in both territory and trade and was recognized only in name as the premier kingdom of the coast.

A second major change, which came about in Loango during the period of the eighteenth-century slave trade, was a change in the basis of political power. The conduct of the slave trade required many employees with new specializations: brokers, merchants, caravan leaders, interpreters, surfboatmen, water-carriers and house servants. The development of these new forms of employment opened economic opportunities to ordinary Vili who did not necessarily belong to the traditional nobility. Commoners, and even domestic slaves, who showed business skill were able to rise in the ranks of a new 'bourgeoisie'. The most powerful official was the *mafouk*, who collected dues from newly arrived ships. As he, and other trading officials, grew in wealth and authority, they gradually replaced the nobility as the most powerful members of the royal council. They became so influential that by the end of the eighteenth century the *maloango* was almost a captive of his council. When the king died, the council was sometimes reluctant to fill the vacancy and preferred to operate without royal supervision. Whereas in the seventeenth century Loango royal succession was clearly defined, in the eighteenth century there were frequent disputes about succession to the titular leadership of the state.

Between the early seventeenth and late eighteenth century, the internal power structure of Loango, and its economic base, had changed out of all recognition. The kingdom did, nevertheless, remain a whole and recognizable entity. Like some of the coastal states of West Africa, but unlike the Kongo kingdom, it had achieved a stable working relationship with the Atlantic slave traders. Its attempts to gain a monopoly of slave brokerage on the coast north of the Zaïre were a failure, however, and by the late eighteenth century rival ports such as Cabinda had an independent control over a large share of the traffic.

THE MBUNDU AND LUANDA

The highlands of West-Central Africa presented a rather different historical pattern from the coasts of the lower Zaïre. In this region, more notably even than in the Kongo kingdom, the major feature of the seventeenth and eighteenth centuries was the variety of response to Portuguese activity. The Mbundu-speaking peoples of the Luanda plateau were at war with colonial invaders throughout the period. As their resistance was ground down, a small white colony was created in Angola. Only in the upper Kwango was a real degree of Mbundu independence retained. Farther south, the Ovimbundu, on the Benguela plateau, were better able to resist military penetration. By the eighteenth century, however, they became inexorably drawn into the Portuguese commercial system. Thus both the northern and the southern highlands suffered from the steady rise of the Atlantic slave trade, though the Mbundu[1] of the north were the earlier and more direct victims.

The earliest Portuguese attempt to penetrate the highlands occurred along the Kwanza river. In 1571 the colony of Angola[2] was created by royal charter, and three years later an ambitious colonizing expedition set out to conquer and settle the territory of the western Mbundu. Despite repeated reinforcements, the whole venture was a fiasco, and by the early seventeenth century much of the original colonizing and proselytizing zeal had been exhausted. The Portuguese campaigns had,

[1] Properly the Kimbundu-speaking peoples should be known as Ambundu, or Mbundu, with no prefix at all, as cited in David Birmingham, *Trade and conflict in Angola* (Oxford, 1966). This usage can lead to confusion as the neighbouring Ovimbundu have the same root when the prefix is dropped. To avoid confusion the Ovimbundu will always be cited with a prefix.

[2] The name Angola, derived from the Kimbundu title *ngola*, was originally adopted for the Portuguese colony around Luanda, and later applied to the whole Kimbundu-speaking area. In the nineteenth century Angola was joined to the Portuguese colonies of Benguela and Moçâmedes as well as to new territories in Kongo and a large eastern hinterland. The united territories of 'Portuguese West Africa' gradually came to be known by the name Angola.

however, taken on a new momentum of their own. The desire to establish plantations and open mines gave way to a growing thirst for slaves with which to develop Brazil.

The major victim of continued Portuguese aggression was the kingdom of Ndongo. This kingdom had been created in the early sixteenth century by the unification of a series of small Mbundu lineages. The keeper of the *ngola a kiluanje* shrine became king of the new state, and succeeded in synthesizing the political experiences of several neighbouring peoples. While resisting encroachment by Ovimbundu raiders from the south, the *ngola* successfully adopted some of the invaders' political symbols and institutions. In fighting off attacks by mobile warrior units of Imbangala intruders (see below, p. 79), he gained new ideas about the training of youths in military skills.[1] The challenge presented to him from the west by the Portuguese was, however, of a different order. It involved not only a direct military confrontation, but a much more invidious demographic seepage which drained away the basis of the kingdom's vitality.

Ndongo's demographic response to the Portuguese wars and to the accompanying slave trade is hard to analyze with any degree of confidence. In the early seventeenth century both the Portuguese and Dutch talked in terms of 10,000 or more slaves leaving Angola each year. A recent reassessment of the Atlantic slave trade and in particular of the numbers landed in Latin America suggests, however, that it is unlikely that such a level was consistently maintained at this time. An average of 5,000 slaves per year seems more probable.[2] This still represented a major drain on the Mbundu whose total population is unlikely to have exceeded half a million. The loss through forced emigration was therefore extremely high, perhaps proportionally higher than in any other zone of the Atlantic slave trade. This loss was, moreover, accentuated by other factors. First, it was concentrated among the younger element of the population, since slave merchants primarily valued men and women under thirty years of age. Secondly, since Portuguese wars of conquest were a direct source of supply, the major drain was from the central Mbundu region. This was in contrast to normal slave-trade practice in which the capture of slaves occurred on the periphery of strong kingdoms. Thirdly, the Angolan slave trade represented a much more violent and arbitrary exaction of victims

---

[1] Joseph C. Miller, *Kings and kinsmen* (Oxford, 1976), contains details of sixteenth-century Mbundu politics.

[2] D. Birmingham, *Trade and conflict in Angola*; Philip D. Curtin, *The Atlantic slave trade: a census* (Madison, 1969).

than did the trade of some other regions. Where African rulers remained masters of their own house, as in Loango, they could make conscious and moderately rational economic decisions about their participation in trade and about the relative values of slave labour and of European goods. In Angola, on the other hand, the system of Portuguese monopoly trading, and the military enforcement of fixed prices, deprived the Ndongo chiefs of any economic initiative. They received only a restricted economic advantage from trading, and none at all from war losses. It may be also that the intensive Portuguese campaigns of the early seventeenth century were particularly destructive of human life, even if reports of cannibalism by auxiliary troops were exaggerated. Finally, as well as failing to stem the internal haemorrhage of the slave trade, Ndongo increasingly lost its self-governing status as the Portuguese forts and garrisons moved up-country towards the royal capital.

The slave trade was not the only demographic drain on Angola. There was also a growing series of refugee migrations. These may have played as large a part as the slave trade in reducing Angola from the rich and populous country witnessed by the sixteenth-century Jesuits, to the sparse, deserted regions described by seventeenth-century Capuchins. The closest region of refuge for escaping Mbundu was south, across the Kwanza river to Kisama, Libolo and to the Benguela highlands beyond. The north was more thickly wooded and more densely peopled than the south, but the Ndembu peoples of southern Kongo nevertheless absorbed many Mbundu refugees. The third, and most important refuge area during the Angolan wars was in the east, farthest removed from the military depredations. The eastern migrations were initially connected with the fortunes of the Ndongo royal house.

The thirty-year decline of Ndongo's political and military power reached new depths in the critical campaign of 1617, in which Portuguese encroachment penetrated the woody country dividing the coastal plain from the plateau, and a new fort was added to the chain of Portuguese advance. In 1618 Luis Mendes de Vasconcellos made a break-through on to the plateau itself and invaded the heartland of the kingdom. The royal compound was looted and burnt. Large numbers of land-owning chiefs were executed and the king fled to an island sanctuary in the Kwanza river.[1] The campaign was followed by a long drought which intensified the country's distress and caused widespread famine. The destruction of the old kingdom did, however, bring forth

---

[1] Details of these wars are retold in Birmingham, *Trade and conflict*, chapter v and the primary documentation is mostly reproduced in Brasio, *Monumenta Missionária Africana* vol. vi.

a new military leadership which was more capable of resisting the Portuguese advance than had been the declining dynasty of Ndongo. The symbol of this revival was a royal princess called Nzinga, whose personality dominated the Angolan scene for the next half century.

Nzinga took over the leadership of the Ndongo with three policy objectives. She wanted to stop the war which was still devastating the centre of the Luanda plateau. She wanted to obtain from the Portuguese the diplomatic recognition which they had customarily accorded to Kongo. And she wanted to establish a regular and profitable trading relationship with Luanda. These were to remain the cardinal issues of her policy for forty years. If the Portuguese would recognize the independence of Ndongo, and agree to trade with it, the slave trade could be conducted round the fringes of the kingdom leaving the centre unmolested. The traders in Luanda accepted Nzinga's case, arguing that war was of only temporary benefit to the slave trade and was destructive to long term growth in trade routes and markets. The Luanda government also accepted these arguments in the aftermath to its much criticized Kongo war of 1622. In 1623 Nzinga went personally to Luanda to offer peace and trade. She was received with great ceremony, and returned triumphally to Ndongo bearing the baptismal name of Dona Ana de Souza from her newly acquired godfather, the Portuguese governor. Portuguese recognition of Nzinga's pre-eminence on the plateau did not solve all her problems. She continued to be threatened inside Ndongo by bands of Imbangala warriors who plundered her commercial networks and raided her markets. Portuguese help in driving them out proved worse than the raids themselves. The re-entry of Portuguese troops on to the plateau caused such panic among the Mbundu, that Nzinga was forced to join them in fleeing to the east. She finally settled in Matamba, beyond the range of Portuguese intervention. There she created a new kingdom and adopted some of the powerful rituals which had enabled the Imbangala to build strong and cohesive armies. She welded camps of Mbundu refugees into hardened military élites who gained courage and invulnerability by practising such rites as child sacrifice. Her key warriors were adolescent captives who had undergone rigorous military and psychological initiations. Once she was established in Matamba, and had trained her new fighting units, Nzinga was ready to face the Portuguese again and attempt to recover Ndongo.

When Nzinga had been driven out of Ndongo, the Portuguese decided to govern the kingdom by indirect rule. They had conferred the title of *ngola* on a chief called Ari Kiluanji, but their puppet met with considerable resistance. It was not so much his lack of hereditary legitimacy, an essentially Portuguese concept, which bothered Ngola Ari's subjects, as his lack of religious power. A king who had not been installed with full rituals was unlikely to provide effective rain-making or protection from disasters. His Mbundu subjects therefore rebelled as much against his lack of credible authority, as against his Portuguese promoters. Nzinga naturally fostered their rebellion, and from the mid 1620s to the late 1630s war was pursued in Angola as fiercely as ever. The Portuguese military naturally favoured a war policy and ignored the protest of the traders. So busy were they with their annual raids among the Mbundu, that they rather neglected the coastal defence of the colony. Nzinga suddenly acquired a new, powerful and unexpected ally when in 1641 the Dutch landed on the Angolan coast and succeeded in capturing Luanda itself. Nzinga immediately signed a treaty with them and moved her headquarters forward into the western Mbundu region. She hoped, with Dutch support, to be able to destroy the Portuguese in Angola once and for all. Her initial efforts to capture the Portuguese town of Massangano, on the Kwanza, were inadequate, and by the time her forces had been increased it was too late. In 1648 Salvador Correia de Sá was sent from Brazil to drive the Dutch out of Angola. He then forced Nzinga to retreat once again to Matamba. Not until 1656 did she again attempt to negotiate a treaty with the Portuguese.

After 1656, Matamba became an important commercial kingdom. *Pombeiros* arrived with caravans of cloth, rum, tobacco and other luxuries, and went again with coffles of slaves. A Portuguese factor was appointed to control prices and prevent cost-inflating competitions between rival Portuguese agents. A Capuchin mission, headed by Antonio Cavazzi, re-converted the queen and her court to at least the outward forms of the Christian religion.[1] By the time of Nzinga's death in 1663, Matamba had become a major broker in the slave trade. No *pombeiros* travelled beyond Matamba and no inland supplier from Suku, Pende or Yaka was allowed direct access to the Portuguese trading agencies. Nzinga had thus created an effective commercial kingdom. She acted in the ideal manner of the middleman where the distinction was narrow between practising highway robbery and providing an essential economic link in the chain of communication.

[1] G. A. Cavazzi, *Istorica descrizione de tre regni Congo, Matamba et Angola* (Bologna, 1687) is the major source for this period.

While Nzinga was rising to power in Matamba, new political developments took place among the Imbangala settlements in Angola. The role of the Imbangala was seen by contemporary witnesses as entirely predatory.[1] Their only skill was thought to be warfare, either in alliance with the Mbundu or the Portuguese, or else on their own account. The most important title-holder among the Imbangala of the early seventeenth century was the *kasanje*, a chief who in 1617 actively assisted in the Portuguese irruption on to the Luanda plateau and the defeat of Ndongo. After that, the Imbangala began to settle down. They were particularly attracted to the Kwango valley which had good agricultural soils, and a ready supply of salt. The *kasanje* retired there during the 1630s and began to create a trading empire similar to Nzinga's kingdom of Matamba. His followers were both Imbangala and Mbundu. As the Kasanje kingdom extended its trade links towards the south and east, so its capital became a major concourse for Portuguese *pombeiros*. A resident factor was installed to supervise the conduct of trade and check the units of cloth measurement. For nearly two centuries, Kasanje made substantial profits as a commercial gateway from the interior. In 1680 Cadornega described a barter system whereby what were apparently Lunda traders came to the river bank, indicated their arrival with smoke signals and waited for the Imbangala to meet them at the market. They principally bought salt for which they paid with palm cloth and occasionally with ivory. There was also a growing trade in slaves at Kasanje. They were bought by *pombeiros*, who led caravans of Mbundu porters carrying wines and textiles across the fifteen-day waste-land of eastern Ndongo which had been depopulated by the Angolan wars. The main supply of Kasanje slaves seems, during the seventeenth century at least, to have been from the south. Cadornega reported that the kingdom of Kasanje was extremely skilled in warfare and that its raids stretched hundreds of miles into the lands of the Nganguela, the Songo, the Shinje and the Ovimbundu. The king of Kasanje, known proudly to Cadornega as 'Our Jaga', had the bearing of an emperor. He dressed in the finest silks, and was accompanied by a band of xylophones and by the ceremonial double bell of state. He travelled either by horse or in a hammock surrounded by a guard of musketeers. Succession to the office of king or 'Jaga' rotated by election among three founding clans. Cadornega estimated that the kingdom had 300,000 people, of whom 100,000 could bear

[1] Alvaro III of Kongo wrote to Pope Paul V about 'una natione di gente tanto barbara chiamata Giagas et Iagas, che vivono di carne e di corpi humani'. Brásio, *Monumenta Missionaria Africana*, VI, 290, from the Vatican Archives.

arms. Exaggerated though his figures may have been, Kasanje was clearly a major military power.[1]

The relationship between the Portuguese and the Kwango states was not dissimilar to the relationship which other European powers had with coastal kingdoms along the West African stretch of the Atlantic seaboard. It was a relationship of bluff diplomatic threats and hard commercial bargaining. The Kwango states were not accorded the same esteem by the Portuguese as Kongo had been, for although independent, their status was described as 'pagan' and of second rank. Although Kasanje and Matamba were the largest and most powerful brokers, many smaller states also functioned as commercial middlemen. The Holo for instance, who lived a little farther down the Kwango, managed to enter into direct dealings with the Portuguese. The treaty signed with them in 1765 may have been typical of such agreements. In it, the Holo recognized the sovereignty of the Portuguese crown and allowed freedom of worship, and unhindered access to missionaries. The Holo were, moreover, to refrain from war against Matamba, their main enemy and rival, but an important Portuguese trade partner. The Holo were also to ban all Vili traders from their market. This market would come under the care of a Portuguese clerk, the *escrivão*, with privileged extra-territorial rights. In return for all these concessions to Portuguese interests, the Holo received a diplomatic status superior to that of many Mbundu peoples. They were recognized as a self-governing trading community. The culture of this and other broker kingdoms was a curious mixture of African and European tradition. The treaties were drafted in diplomatic Portuguese, but the language of trade was usually Kimbundu, widely spoken by the white community. Although Christianity was formally introduced to the Kwango states, the traditional religion remained far too strong to be ignored, even by Europeans. Kasanje became a particularly important centre of worship and of healing for both black and white. The two-way exchange of culture operated even in Luanda, where white parents were much criticized because their children did not speak Portuguese and because they practised 'pagan' ceremonies.[2]

While Matamba and Kasanje grew as broker-kingdoms on the Kwango, the Portuguese struggled to maintain their colonial state in Angola. Although their original plan to create a settler colony was subverted

[1] António de Oliveira Cadornega, *História geral das guerras Angolanas* (Lisbon edition, 1940–2), vol III, part 3.
[2] Jean-Luc Vellut, 'Relations internationales du Moyen Kwango et de l'Angola', *Études d'histoire africaine*, 1970, I.

by slave-trading interests, a small colony did evolve around the city
of Luanda. This rise of Luanda was comparable, in African terms, to
that of Cape Town, the other European-built city on the Atlantic coast.
The population was of exceedingly mixed social and racial origins.
The élite community never achieved freedom from racial minorities,
and even the earliest settlers probably included Jews, Gypsies and other
persecuted groups from Portugal, Madeira and Brazil. In the later
seventeenth century, there were probably about 100 households in
Luanda whose heads could claim Portuguese citizenship rights. Unlike
the Dutch in Cape Town, however, most of these residents (*moradores*),
like the convicts and soldiers without civic rights, had African wives,
and Cadornega referred to Angola as the country where sons were
brown and grandsons black.[1] This mestizo population of Luanda was
both socially and economically important and many *pombeiros* were
mestizo.

In addition to the city, the Portuguese colony spread out to local
farming communities initially along the Kwanza, near the city of
Massangano, and later in the north, along the Bengo and Dande rivers.
Some of these communities were the country estates of rich city dwellers,
but some were permanent farms and ranches managed by their owners.
Their produce was largely food for local consumption. Suggestions
that sugar and tobacco would thrive, and add diversity to the colony's
economy, were discouraged by Brazilian plantation interests opposed
to African competition. Angolan Portuguese, therefore, limited themselves to selling labour and to growing food to maintain the exported
slaves until they had crossed the Atlantic. The continuing growth of the
Portuguese colony meant that pressure was maintained on the remnant
kingdom of Ndongo. The puppet ruler, Ngola Ari, had frequent
occasion to complain that settlers were kidnapping his subjects on the
pretence that they were run-away slaves from the Bengo estates. An
even more serious burden was Ndongo's role in manning the trade
routes to the interior. The major disadvantage, from the European
point of view, of driving Nzinga and the Imbangala into the backlands
of Angola was the logistic problem which it created in transporting
goods to the inland markets. Elsewhere along the Atlantic coast, the
administration of trade routes was an African matter. Caravans were
mounted either by the coastal brokers, as in the case of the Vili caravans
from Loango, or by inland middlemen such as the Ovimbundu on the
Benguela plateau. In Angola, by contrast, the colony had to create its

[1] Cited in C. R. Boxer, *Race relations in the Portuguese colonial empire* (Oxford, 1963).

own land transport system to reach the Kwango ports of trade. It did so by forcibly recruiting conscript carriers among the subjects of Ngola Ari of Ndongo. The recruitment led to frequent disputes over impressment, over under-payment, over the acceptable scale of carrier fees, and over the abuses of local military administrators who were the official recruiting agents. When Ngola Ari II gained power in Ndongo in 1664, he decided to become a private and independent broker between Portuguese Luanda and the Kwango kingdoms. He seized control of several trade routes, defeated a number of subservient chiefs, and created a fortified camp at Pungu a Ndongo from which to tax or waylay rival caravans. In reply the governor at Luanda resolved to destroy the dynasty which his predecessors had created, and impose direct military rule over the whole of Ndongo. In 1671 he launched one of the most successful of the Portuguese campaigns. The Ndongo royal family was captured and sent to a monastery in Portugal and a fort was built on the site of their last capital.

In the century that followed this final collapse of Ndongo, the economy of Angola hardly changed. The most dynamic sector was still the Atlantic trade, and it was into this that most capital continued to be invested, largely through Brazilian banks. In the 1760s one short attempt was made by the governor, Souza Coutinho, to diversify the modern sector of the economy by investing in iron works, cotton production, a soap factory and in extensive new salt pans, but these activities came to nothing.[1] Both the traders and the soldier-administrators remained wedded to the slave trade. Although the slave trade absorbed most of the capital and enterprise vested in Angola, a small plantation economy survived based on local slaves and servile clients, many of them women. These rather feudal land-holdings were mainly grouped round five Portuguese inland forts. Their security was ensured by militia, auxiliaries, some artillery pieces and an occasional cavalry visit. The captain of each fort had a right to exploit allegedly vacant lands, and to control the operation of the long-distance trade fairs. A few private estates called *arimos* survived and were worked partly by slaves and partly through labour service, but they were not even as economically or socially important as the Mozambique *prazos*. In addition to plantation work, subject peoples in the Angolan domains were expected to perform carrier duties, military service, road and dyke repairs, as well as to pay tithes.

[1] Ralph Delgado, 'O Governo de Souza Coutinho em Angola', *Studia*, 1960–2, nos. 6–10.

During the course of the eighteenth century, the Portuguese slave trade from Luanda normally fluctuated between 5,000 and 10,000 slaves per year. The Portuguese suffered increasingly, however, from the competition of France, Holland and England. Throughout the century they sought to impose barriers to the free movement of trade, and thus compensate for their lack of economic competitiveness. They continued to persuade themselves that they alone had the legal right to trade in Angolan slaves. Their interventions on the coast at Novo Redondo in 1769, at Ambriz in 1790 and at Cabinda in 1787, all failed. So too, as was seen above, did their attempt to control the trade routes in the Kongo–Angola borderland, through which slaves were siphoned from Luanda's natural catchment area both to the English at Ambriz and to the French at Loango. In 1759 a fort was built at Enkoje, but the trade routes were soon diverted to by-pass it. A final factor which weakened Portugal vis-à-vis her European rivals was the growing trade in guns. Portugal, as a semi-colonial power with territorial interests, had always feared the gun trade lest it increase her opponents' military power. Her trade rivals had no such compunction about selling guns, and the French included up to two pieces in every slave lot. In the eighteenth century Portugal could no longer hold out against such competition, but as a non-industrial power she had difficulty in establishing a gun trade of her own. Only the disruption caused to British and French trade by the American war of independence allowed the Portuguese to recover some ground.

THE OVIMBUNDU AND BENGUELA

In the southern part of the Atlantic highlands, Portuguese influence began to be felt in the sixteenth century when preliminary attempts were made to explore the commercial potential of the Benguela plateau. Open boats ran up and down the coast buying small quantities of salt, ivory, dried fish, beef, beans, copper and occasionally slaves. Overland expeditions tried, though with little success, to penetrate the harsh scrubland which separated the Kwanza valley from the southern uplands. In the seventeenth century, these efforts were renewed as awareness of the populous Ovimbundu kingdoms increased. The coastal colony of Benguela was founded as a small off-shoot of Angola in 1617, and in time acquired an outpost in the plateau foothills. It was not, however, until the eighteenth century that a deeper Portuguese penetration caused commercial responses among the plateau peoples which were similar to those seen farther north on the Kwango.

In recent times the population of the Benguela plateau has grown rapidly from one million towards two million. In the seventeenth century the region was already well peopled by crop farmers who held the highlands against the herding, hunting and gathering communities which flourished in the lower regions along the rather arid coast. The Ovimbundu had probably been long subject to political and demographic influences from the north and north-east. Already by the sixteenth century the Ovimbundu had influenced, and been influenced by, the military traditions of the Imbangala. In the seventeenth century they absorbed Mbundu refugees from the war zones of Angola. These refugees probably stimulated population growth and an effective extension of agriculture. The history of these Mbundu refugees will only be convincingly written when the traditions of the Ovimbundu states have been recorded. On tentative evidence, however, it would seem that they introduced novel concepts of state formation to the Ovimbundu. The traditions of Huambo, for instance, refer reverentially to the Ngola Kiluanji, the king of Ndongo. They recorded in particular his conflicts with the 'Jaga', conflicts which presumably took place not in Huambo itself, as the tradition implies, but farther north during the Angolan wars. The old peoples of Huambo belonged, according to tradition, to the Ndombe pastoralists who now occupy the western edge of the highlands. The kingdom probably began to emerge near the middle of the seventeenth century, and, according to some very tentative calculations, may have been the first of the modern Ovimbundu kingdoms.[1] Another link between the Ovimbundu and their northern neighbours may have been forged by the Imbangala. The early roving bands were followed by a more purposeful advance of the Kasanje kingdom conducting slave-trading wars in the eastern highlands. These raids may have led to organized resistance and the emergence of new Ovimbundu kingdoms. Several other late Ovimbundu states, such as Ndulu and Kingolo, have traditions which refer to founders who escaped from the north after the dramatic fall of Pungu a Ndongo in 1671.

Although many Ovimbundu kingdoms may have been founded by, or in response to, Mbundu and Imbangala fugitives or raiders, two states have different traditions. In the far south, Ngalangi has traditions linked to the pre-dynastic history of the plateau and therefore claims a rather dubious historical seniority. In the east, the kingdom of Bihé

[1] G. M. Childs, 'The kingdom of Wambu (Huambo): a tentative chronology', *Journal of African History*, 1964, 5, 367–79.

claims that the ruling dynasty was founded early in the eighteenth century by a Songo princess, who brought to Bihe political influences from the new Lunda state system. Another factor in the late rise of the Bihe may have been the eastward expansion of trade routes from the western side of the plateau.

Once the Ovimbundu kingdoms were created, they slowly came into contact with Portuguese Benguela. The colony had survived precariously on its local trade despite Ndombe enmity, an arid countryside, a frequently rebellious garrison, and a hostile governor in Angola, who resented the diminution of his sovereignty. The most valuable assets were the local salt pans, which were used to supply Luanda, and to buy ivory and skins brought by peoples from the far southern interior. Despite the vicissitudes of its early years, Benguela did eventually become the outlet for plateau trade, and its fortunes rose. The first Portuguese traders to visit the courts of the Ovimbundu kings travelled as private individuals unprotected by the force of Portuguese arms, and dependent for their safety on the goodwill of their customers. The expansion of these *sertanejo* (backwoodsmen) had begun early in the seventeenth century among the mobile coastal pastoralists. By 1680 they were travelling so far that the Portuguese decided to build a fort at the foot of the plateau which could be used as a strong-room for their trade goods. The creation of this fort in the Benguela hinterland marked the beginning of a second phase of the Portuguese activity. The advance was now on two fronts. In the van were the *sertanejo*, who adapted themselves to the culture of their African customers, married into chiefly families, and peacefully created their own compounds near the Ovimbundu capitals. Their situation was comparable to that of the Portuguese trading houses in Kongo before 1665. Behind the *sertanejo* came the military frontier, which advanced in a disruptive manner as it had done in Angola after 1575. This military penetration reached the fringes of the Ovimbundu country in the early eighteenth century when campaigns were fought against Kalukembe in the south-west. As the Portuguese-led armies reached the richer, more populous regions, the slave trade grew rapidly. Benguela began to ship slaves direct to the New World without sending them to Luanda. The volume of Benguela trade rose to match, or even surpass that of Luanda. The two ports became rivals rather than the twin pillars of a mercantilist monopoly.

By about 1770 the growth of trading networks across the Ovimbundu plateau had reached a new peak. The military advance enabled the governor-general of Angola and Benguela to move the fort of Caconda from the lowlands to the plateau, where it became the nucleus of a new Luso-African 'kingdom'. On the advanced frontier of the *sertanejo*, a Portuguese resident was installed at the Bihe court with functions similar to those of the Kasanje resident. Also in the 1770s the Portuguese began to realize that a large part of the Ovimbundu trade was not going north to Luanda or south to Benguela, but along a new route to the coast through the north-western kingdom of Sela. Once on the coast, slaves were being sold both to unauthorized Portuguese ships and to English and French vessels on their way to Loango.[1] In order to cut down 'smuggling', a fort was built at Novo Redondo. The Ovimbundu suppliers reacted violently against this interference with their 'free' route, and the Sela army descended on Novo Redondo and captured its Portuguese garrison. This coup led the Portuguese to attempt the outright conquest of the Ovimbundu kingdoms, a feat comparable to the invasion of Ndongo a century before. By advancing their military front into the central kingdoms of Huambo and Bailundu, they hoped to gain control over all the trade routes. Two columns set out, the first from Angola and the second from Benguela. They were to join forces at a central cross-roads on the plateau. The war was arduous, and spread over the three campaigning seasons of 1774, 1775 and 1776. In such a drawn-out action the Ovimbundu ceased to rely on guerilla tactics, and began to use stone forts like the Portuguese. To counter this new development, the Portuguese hauled in field guns for siege warfare. These engines were finally successful, but some fortifications were so elaborate that they took months to dismantle. During the war the Portuguese defeated Bailundu, the largest kingdom, but the achievement had few lasting consequences, and Caconda remained the most advanced Portuguese military outpost.[2] Traders reverted to their former methods, with Portuguese, mestizo, and African agents all operating under Ovimbundu political protection.

Effective Portuguese domination over the Ovimbundu was not achieved until more than a century after the campaign of 1774–6. Trade, however, continued to grow, and by the end of the eighteenth century Ovimbundu caravaneers, known as 'Mambari', were exploring the upper Zambezi. This southern caravan system matched the central and northern systems of Luanda and Loango. By the nineteenth century,

[1] Birmingham, *Trade and conflict in Angola*, 156.
[2] G. M. Childs, *Umbundu kinship and character* (London, 1949), ch. 12. This is still the only accessible survey of Ovimbundu history, although a wealth of published and unpublished Portuguese data are ready to be tapped.

the network had branches which spread out to cut across some of the older routes. One route reached the Kuba in the heart of Zaïre, and met the Nyamwezi advancing from East Africa. In the south, the Ovimbundu kingdoms used their new-found military skills to conduct large-scale cattle and slave raids on the peoples as far away as Huila, the most southerly plateau of West-Central Africa. Thus the Ovimbundu, who in the seventeenth century had been the victims of Kasanje slave raiding, themselves became the raiders of peoples less fortunate.

THE LOWER KASAI

The middle savanna of Central Africa is divided into two rather sharply contrasted regions. The lower Kasai region is fertile and densely occupied by an extreme variety of ethnic and linguistic groups broken up into small political fragments. The upper Kasai, on the other hand, is dry, sandy, and thinly populated by peoples who mostly bear some kind of ethnic, historic, linguistic or political relationship to the Lunda peoples.

The lower Kasai is currently divided between the Bandundu and Kasai provinces of Zaïre, and the Lunda province of modern Angola. During the seventeenth and eighteenth centuries the whole of the lower Kasai was in growing contact with its western neighbours. Indirect ripples of influence were beginning to be felt from the Atlantic. In the north, along the lower Kasai river itself, the influences came through the Teke, and the people most affected were the Boma-Sakata, the Yanzi-Ambun and the Kuba-Lele. In the south, between the middle Kwango and the middle Kasai, change derived from Kongo, and three more groups were affected, the Yaka-Suku, the Mbala, and the Pende. In addition to the new influences from the west, these peoples were in contact with two other important groups. In the north-east they abutted the great forest cultures of the Mongo. In the south-east they began to be influenced by the even greater savanna cultures of the Lunda of the upper Kasai.

Many of the lower Kasai peoples were closely associated with the rivers in their culture and economy. Fishing was important, both as a local activity and as a large-scale business enterprise involving long-distance expeditions of several months and leading to communication with such far-away peoples as the Bobangi of the middle Congo river. Migrant fishermen also used their canoes to carry such heavy items as pottery, iron and copper, which were difficult to trade far by head porterage. The traditional agriculture of the lower Kasai was founded on sorghum and bananas, but these were gradually being supplemented or replaced by maize, and later by cassava, which became the staple food by the nineteenth century. Other crops, new and old, included groundnuts, beans, sugar cane, colocasia, yams, millet, oil palms, kola nuts and tobacco. This diverse agriculture led parts of the Kasai to become heavily populated by Central African standards. Regional artisan production also led to specialization. At the western and eastern fringes of the region, the Teke and the Lele made up for their sparse agricultural resources by producing fine raffia textiles. The peoples of the lower river, and the Kuba of the Sankuru, were noted for their pottery. The peoples who organized markets usually conducted them on a four-day cycle. The major currency of the region came to be the Kongo *nzimbu* shells, but copper manillas, Indian cowries and various beads also commonly served as currency. Although it is clear that crops, agricultural techniques, currencies and material goods spread from the west into the lower Kasai area, it is not clear by what means these influences spread, or at what periods. There is also much uncertainty about the social, political, linguistic and demographic changes which may be ascribed to the influence of western neighbours.

The traditions of the lower Kasai peoples tend to suggest that they 'came from the west', from the Teke lands or from the region at the confluence of the Kasai and Zaïre rivers.[1] What these traditions mean is debatable. They might imply that the bulk of the population expanded from the west as new agricultural lands were needed by peoples of the rather barren Teke plateau. If so, they might have filled out the area with its present population of farmers. The relative linguistic homogeneity of the region, despite its cultural diversity, might favour such a literal interpretation of the traditions, though over a long time-scale. Alternatively, the traditions might relate to limited prestige groups which spread eastwards. Fishermen, for instance, may have evolved their skill in contacts with the great fishing peoples of the Zaïre river, and then introduced them gradually up the Kasai. On another level, the traditions might relate mainly to the political systems of the lower Kasai. Although the pattern of settlement was almost everywhere one of small villages and hamlets, most peoples were governed by chiefs, or even by hierarchies of chiefs culminating in a king, like the great

[1] Jan Vansina, *Kingdoms of the savanna* (Madison, 1966), ch. 4, especially 110–18, and Jan Vansina, *Ethnographie*, 129–30, cautiously synthesize the amateur ethno-historical observations of early Belgian officials in this area.

makoko of the Teke. Another possible vehicle for the transmission of culture and tradition from the west into the lower Kasai basin was trade. The Teke had early contact with the growing Atlantic trade systems, and by the seventeenth century coastal merchants were familiar with the titles of chiefs in the lower Kasai region. It seems likely that pioneers from the west had begun to penetrate the Kasai and bring slaves to the Teke markets. This penetration may have been responsible for introducing regular markets, American food crops, widely circulating currencies, and chiefs with new traditions of foreign origin. Traditions of the lower Kasai also refer to connections with the lower Kwango. This too could be consistent with trade penetrations, since important land routes from Teke led into the interior by way of the Kwango river crossings.

Hypotheses about the growth of trade and the spread of cultural links still need much research in the lower Kasai region. At the same time attention must be given to the importance of this area as a zone of refuge. It is quite possible that the purposeful and organized penetration of traders was less significant than the hasty retreat of peoples who found themselves in the raiding zone of the Atlantic hinterland. The Kasai might have gained its western cultural features from refugees rather than from traders or conquerors. Only very detailed historical, ethnographic and linguistic researches will be able to shed a more certain light on the assorted components of the Kasai cultures.

Of the peoples of the lower Kasai, three have particularly interesting political histories. The least known are those north of the river who have contacts with their Mongo neighbours. The interaction between the western Mongo and the eastern Teke apparently led to the creation of a new system of kingship with a strong religious core and hereditary court of secular administrators. This pattern of 'socialized kingship' seems to have influenced the Boma-Sakata peoples and led to the evolution of a more complex political hierarchy than existed south of the Kasai.

The second interesting group of lower Kasai peoples are the Ambun (Bambun, Mbuun). They are divided into some twenty-eight clans, each of which has its own history and has brought its own contribution to Ambun tradition and culture. The language of the group is related to that of their north-western neighbours, and the majority of clans claim a north-western origin. There is also, however, an important strand of tradition which refers to a western line of influence from Kongo which affects the dialect and leadership of three clans. A third strand of Ambun tradition claims that one influential stratum of the society came across the Kwango from the south-west. This might have been led by Mbundu migrants who spread far to the east of Matamba to reach the Ambun, and possibly to give them their name. The link with Angola might equally well have been a refugee one or a trading one. The political system which evolved among the Ambun drew not only on the western streams of cultural influence, but also on the growing experience of the Lunda in the east. Lunda emblems of chiefship appear to have been acquired from such Lunda-influenced peoples as the Shinje or the Pende to the south of the Ambun territories. The political culture which evolved among the Ambun does not appear to have resulted in the creation of a centralized kingship. It did, however, influence the Kuba, an important neighbouring people to the east, who went on to create the most interesting and sophisticated political system of the whole Kwango-Kasai area, if not of the whole of Central Africa.

The earliest traditions of the Kuba refer to the drift from the west, be it a drift of peoples or of clan leaders or of ideas and institutions.[1] Reference is made in these traditions to the western Mongo, to the lower Kasai, and even to the region of the Zaïre cataracts. The origins of the drift probably go back into the sixteenth century, and stimulus may have been given to the movement by the turbulence associated with the Jaga wars or rebellions in Kongo (see *Cambridge History of Africa* III, chapter 8). More interesting, however, than these early legends are the changes which occurred among the Kuba and their Lele brethren after about 1600, when their societies began to take recognizable shape on either side of the middle Kasai. Although the Lele and the Kuba are similar in origin and language, they occupy very dissimilar terrain, and have evolved sharply contrasted levels of economic wealth and very different systems of government.

The Lele occupied the poorer, western half of the region, which has inadequate soils, little forest and limited supplies of game. This ecological disadvantage resulted in a low density of population, small villages, greater mobility of population and, it has been argued,[2] less powerful incentives to economic development. This meant that strong political structures did not emerge and the country was constantly

[1] Vansina's main work on Kuba history is his *Geschiedenis van de Kuba* (Tervuren, 1963), but summaries have appeared in his English and French publications, e.g. *Ethnographie*, 130.

[2] Mary Douglas, 'Lele economy compared with the Bushong: a study in "economic backwardness"', in Paul Bohannan and George Dalton (eds.), *Markets in Africa* (Evanston, 1962), ch. 8.

weakened by insecurity and strife. Much of the young men's energy went into defence, thus further hindering economic growth, and causing the economically productive working life of a Lele man to be comparatively short. The improvement of techniques in agriculture, hunting and fishing was discouraged by low yields. This failure of technological evolution affected the design and finish of houses, utensils, ornaments, embroidery, wine tapping and all artisan production except raffia weaving. The lack of variety and specialization in both agricultural and industrial production meant that the Lele developed no markets and no currencies. The most important form of accumulation was not in investment wealth such as canoes, nets and granaries, but in prestige wealth stored in the form of raffia cloths. There existed among the Lele no form of economic incentive whereby an individual could gather riches and wives by inventiveness and initiative. Wealth was reserved for middle-aged and elderly men, who alone were permitted to amass raffia cloths for bride wealth, and thereby achieve a married status. Craftsmanship was limited to the elderly and competition from the young was restricted.

The Kuba, although similar in origin to the Lele, developed along very different lines from the early seventeenth century. Their country was ecologically more rewarding. They were able to build up hunting, fishing and agriculture to a much higher level of skill, efficiency and variety than the Lele. They also grew much faster demographically and created larger villages and communities. The large-scale polygyny which restricted incentive among the Lele was among the Kuba limited to chiefs, while the rest of the population remained virtually monogamous. Technology in house building, food storing, tool manufacture and artisan production soon far outstripped that of the Lele as success bred success. Prestige was gained not just with old age, but by the accumulation of wealth and the production of goods for the important internal market system. Trade in its turn led to increasing specialization among individuals and groups. Exchanges and valuations were carried out in organized markets by means of different currencies, firstly raffia squares, later cowries, and later still beads and copper bars. One of the most important factors, however, which facilitated the growth of the Kuba market economy and which in turn led to its striking development, was the Kuba political structure. This structure was capable of protecting the markets and trade routes and ensuring the smooth redistribution of an increasingly large section of Kuba production which was surplus to the needs of subsistence survival.

The Kuba kingdom or empire was a federation of some eighteen different 'tribes'. The dominant group were the central Bushong, who conquered their related Kuba neighbours and then spread farther afield to incorporate some Mongo and Lulua into the kingdom. The formation of the Kuba kingdom probably began in the late sixteenth century. The Bushong kings appear to have acquired their initial wealth and prestige from their skill as fishermen. Agriculture seems to have been less important in the early period, when populations were more sparse and mobile, but in the reign of the great seventeenth-century innovator, Shyaam, agricultural prosperity was stimulated by the intro-duction of maize, tobacco, cassava and beans. There followed a growth in population. Shyaam also strengthened the kingship by creating a capital and attracting notable traders to it. He established a guard of young men and created new offices of state to reward and strengthen his relatives and supporters. Some prisoners of war were incorporated into the king's army, to further Bushong domination, and others were settled in new villages to strengthen the Kuba economy. The king safeguarded his position by giving preferment to his children, while keeping a severe check on his nephews, from whom his successor would be chosen. In each reign these two factions maintained a balance of power. By the eighteenth century the Kuba empire was at its height and had developed indirect trading relations with distant peoples of the Kwango in the west and the Lualaba in the east. The Kuba are particularly important in Central African history because they show the degree of originality and adaptability which the peoples of the Kasai could demonstrate when creating institutions best suited to the control and exploitation of their own environment. The Bushong kingship permitted the Kuba to develop a thriving empire and drive back or conquer rival peoples who coveted their fertile land. Strong kingship also facilitated the establishment of a rich and varied economy based on a high level of both internal and external commercial exchanges.[1]

South of the lower Kasai, in the region between the Kwango and the middle Kasai similar developments took place to those on the lower Kasai. But whereas the lower Kasai traditions of an eastward cultural drift are mainly connected with the Teke people, the Kwango region is more closely connected with the Kongo. Most peoples in the area, except the recently arrived Lunda and Chokwe in the south-east, speak languages related to Kikongo. Once again it is impossible

[1] Jan Vansina, 'Trade and markets among the Kuba', in Bohannan and Dalton, *Markets in Africa*, ch. 7.

to say how old this affinity is. The fragmentation of ethnic groups is, if anything, even greater than in the north. In recent centuries peoples have moved long distances, either in flight or following more purposeful lines of migration. The Pende, for instance, have two traditions.[1] One relates to a flight from the seventeenth-century break-up of the kingdom of Ndongo, of which they formed part, and whose traditions they accurately remember. The other refers to the emergence of trading relations between the Pende and Angola, and the growth of new prosperity brought by the traders. Each of these traditions may have a level of truth in it. Since the Pende are the easternmost of the Kwango peoples, it is likely that all the others were to a greater or lesser degree influenced by these two strands of influence from the Atlantic zone. The Suku and the Mbala both have traditions which bring peoples or influences from the Kwango valley, and the Yaka claim convincingly that some of their ancestors once lived in Kongo. The traditions concerning the seventeenth century therefore clearly relate to an eastward drift. In the eighteenth century, however, a new spread of ideas, influences and peoples reached the Kwango area, from precisely the opposite direction. This new diffusion was connected with the rise of the Lunda empire.

THE LUNDA EMPIRE

The story of the Lunda empire, and of the many savanna peoples who lived on its periphery in Zaïre, Angola and Zambia, is potentially one of the most interesting, if neglected, themes in the whole history of pre-colonial Central Africa.[2] The basic research data are oral evidence, but although some traditions have been collected over the past hundred years, many are known only to the local sages. A beginning has, however, been made in analysing central Lunda traditions. These speak of the rivalry between clans and clan leaders in the scattered agricultural societies of the upper Kasai. These rivalries often led to armed conflict and one faction or other was forced to flee to new land. In the process several Lunda leadership titles became known among the Luena and Chokwe of the south and west; Lunda epic poems were incorporated into the literary culture of many neighbouring societies; Lunda social and political customs became widely distributed; material symbols of the Lunda were adopted for prestige by peoples as far west as Angola.

[1] G. L. Haveaux, *La tradition historique des Bapende orientaux* (Brussels, 1954).
[2] Jean-Luc Vellut, 'Notes sur le Lunda et la frontière luso-africaine (1700–1900)', in *Études d'histoire africaine*, 1972, 3, 61–166, is the most recent and most competent account.

While this dispersion of refugees, of symbolic artefacts, of legendary hero-worship, and of social customs was going on, fundamental changes began to occur among the Lunda themselves.

During the sixteenth century a new form of centralized leadership began to emerge among the Lunda. A legendary warrior-hero, Chibinda Ilunga, gained domination over the minds of several Lunda clan leaders. His prestige was enhanced by alien rituals and charms connected with the skills of the hunter. Gradually the three strands of religious leadership, of traditional clan leadership, and of practical political leadership began to coalesce round an embryonic royal court. The emergence of a new kingdom out of the old web of kinship ties was extremely slow. Although the process began before 1600, political experimentation and consolidation continued throughout the seventeenth century. As the central government matured it had to accommodate old customs and absorb once-powerful lineage titles. The symbol of political office was the *lukano* bracelet of human (or elephant) sinews. Inheritance among the new political office-holders tended to be through brothers and sons, rather than through maternal nephews of the old matrilineal clans. To compensate for this, many of the supporting titles which ensured lineage loyalty were female titles. They were either deemed to be married to the male royal titles, or were held by female rulers. The offices of *swana mulunda*, mother of the people, and of *lukonkeshia*, mother of the king, were held by women. By the end of the seventeenth century the process of political innovation had culminated in the creation of the kingly title of *mwata yamvo* (or *mwant yav*). A Lunda dynasty was inaugurated which has survived until the present time.[1]

The initial stimulants to the growth of a centralized system of Lunda government have been interpreted as primarily internal factors. During the course of the seventeenth century, however, the Lunda and their neighbours gradually became aware of changes emanating from the commercial economy of the Atlantic. It has already been suggested above that new trading opportunities and new forms of exotic prestige wealth were introduced into the lower Kasai by merchants and refugees in the early years of the seventeenth century. In the dry, and more sparsely peopled regions of the upper Kasai such a process probably occurred more slowly. Communication over land was probably more difficult than the river communication of the north. Even in the eighteenth century, long distance caravans suffered from the unreliability of

---

[1] Miller, *Kings and kinsmen*, contains a new interpretation of early Lunda history.

food supplies and the hazards of river crossing by canoe or pedestrian ford. On the other hand a sparse population offered less resistance to organized parties of foreign travellers than did richly occupied farmland. Although no details are yet available for the opening of the southern trade systems, one can reasonably suppose that by the latter half of the seventeenth century the long distance trade paths were beginning to carry such foreign merchandise as European hardware, Brazilian alcohol and tobacco, and Asian textiles. Many of these paths were not newly created for the purpose of foreign trade but pre-dated the arrival of European and Indian manufactures from Luanda. They had been used to carry indigenous salt bars and raffia strip cloth. They may also have served in the exchange of local metal goods, possibly even copper crosses from the mines of the Lualaba. As this local trade was supplemented and increased, during the late seventeenth century, by the inflow of foreign goods, so the 500 kilometre route-sector between the middle Kwango and the upper Kasai became strategically important. One end of this sector was controlled by the king of Kasanje. The other end was firmly grasped by the new *mwata yamvo* of the Lunda.

The Lunda established their capital in open woodland about 100 kilometres east of the Kasai. The metropolitan region lay between two small rivers, about 15 kilometres apart, and was surrounded by a fortified earth rampart and dry moat of 30 or more kilometres in length. Within this royal zone each new *mwata yamvo* built his official *musumba* compound. The king's personal *musumba* consisted of a large fortified enclosure with a double fence of live trees, or stakes, and numerous inner courtyards, each with well defined practical or ceremonial functions. One part of this large domain was laid aside for royal burials and was watched over by special religious guardians. European visitors who saw several *musumbas* during the nineteenth century were invariably impressed with the straight roads, the open public squares, the cleanliness and the hygiene. By comparison with this 'city', Portuguese Luanda was described by some travellers as small and rather squalid.[1]

During the eighteenth century, eight kings, belonging to the first two generations of the dynasty, governed the Lunda empire. The history of these early kings has been so inextricably telescoped with the early legends of the Lunda, that a detailed account of the period is difficult to reconstruct. Four themes seem, however, to have been

[1] The most observant visitors were Paul Pogge, *Im Reiche des Muata Jamvo* (Berlin, 1880) and Henrique Dias de Carvalho, *Expedição Portugueza ao Muatiânvua* (Lisbon, 1890).

important. The first was the strengthening of the home base of the Lunda domestic economy. The second was the colonial expansion of Lunda and the incorporation into its political system of chiefs from many neighbouring societies. Thirdly the Lunda created an administrative bureaucracy capable of managing the affairs of a growing society. Lastly control of the country's external commerce became a central function of royal authority.

The domestic economy of the Lunda was of course based on agriculture. By the eighteenth century this agriculture was probably undergoing transformation as maize, and more especially cassava, began to supplant millet and bananas as the primary staples. The difficulty which the Lunda faced when trying to expand their prosperity was not that they lacked land – there were still wide open spaces on every side. What they lacked was people. The new state therefore soon developed a military character, and began raiding its neighbours. The objective was not territorial aggrandizement, but the capture of men and women who were brought to the lands round the *musumba* in a large programme of 'internal colonization'. The king, and other members of the Lunda oligarchy, staked out cassava plots where they put their new serfs to work. Population was thereby funnelled from the fringes of Lunda towards the centre, and royal prosperity increased. The status of farm serfs, and household slaves acquired in this way, was distinctly more favourable than that of plantation slaves under European ownership. In this African society, captives rapidly absorbed the culture of their captors and became integrated into their host community.

The expansion of Lunda soon reached beyond the immediate neighbourhood from which captive slaves could be easily brought to the capital. A new policy was devised whereby Lunda kings founded satellite colonies among their more remote neighbours. These satellites were created partly by conquest, partly by settling Lunda colonists, and partly by absorbing local chiefs into the prestigious Lunda political hierarchy. A chief who accepted Lunda overlordship was initiated into the Lunda and became the representative of the *mwata yamvo* among his own tribe. He was granted a cow-hide belt or other symbol of political office and became responsible for dispatching tribute from his own people to the Lunda capital. The obligation to pay periodic tribute was the primary consequence of Lunda domination. Regular tribute caravans provided the essential, if not the only, link between the royal capital and the satellite chiefdoms. Some tribute was in the form of young wives for the Lunda courtiers, or field-hands for their plantations. Other contributions consisted of cassava flour or other farm produce, game, dried fish, household furnishings and agricultural implements. In exchange for their offerings loyal subjects received counter-gifts from the *mwata yamvo*. These rewards might be small luxuries like beads or more practical assets such as livestock.

The growing Lunda empire needed an expanding system of administration. Initially court functions were probably filled by elders called *tubungu* who represented the Lunda ancestors. These elders continued to be influential members of the royal council, maintaining the balance between the old and the new, together with the great lineage office-holders. The most powerful of the old offices was that of the *lukonkeshia*. She ruled over an almost independent court of her own, where she received tribute independently from that sent to the *mwata yamvo*. She had no husband to limit her autonomy, but governed as a great chief. Her counsel was particularly influential in determining succession to the throne, for which reason she was symbolically known as the mother of the king. In addition to traditional leaders, selected according to their quasi-religious status, the new state required administrators appointed by virtue of their political skills. It is possible that new positions at court, and seating arrangements at royal councils, were influenced by the position which officers held in the field during military campaigns. The royal council, like the army, had members designated as 'eyes', as 'wings', and as the 'tail'. Both the *swana mulopwe* and the *kanapumba* combined military rank with political authority.[1] Beside the military captains and courtiers there was a series of great political chiefs called the *kilolo*. In the mid-nineteenth century, thirty-six great chiefs were reputed to pay tribute to the *mwata yamvo*.[2] Imperial stewardship of the outer domains was supervised by numerous royal messengers, called *tukwata*. These, more than any one else, were the personal bureaucratic agents of the monarch and they actually ran the business of state. They travelled up and down the empire, checking on each satellite, and ensuring that adequate tribute was paid at the proper time. When external trade became important to the Lunda, it was the *tukwata* who supervised caravans, escorted foreign travellers, safeguarded royal

---

[1] There is some lack of correspondence between the two most detailed recent descriptions of the Lunda power structure by Léon Duysters, 'Histoire des Aluunda', in *Problèmes de l'Afrique Centrale*, 1958, 12 and Daniel Biebuyck, 'Fondements de l'organisation politique des Lunda du Mwaantayaav en territoire de Kapanga', in *Zaïre*, 1957, 11, 8. See also Vansina, *Kingdoms of the savanna*, ch. 3.

[2] J. R. Graça, 'Viagem feita de Loanda . . .', in *Annaes do Conselho Ultramarino*, 1855; republished as 'Expedição ao Muatayanvua' in *Boletim da Sociedade de Geografia de Lisboa*, 1890.

monopolies, and punished subjects who evaded tolls and tariffs. From the court's point of view they formed an efficient administrative cadre. For the people, their activities were often burdensome and even violent.

The earliest long distance trade of the Lunda was an extension of the tribute system. As Lunda domination spread, new subjects brought in goods such as copper and salt which were scarce in the original Lunda homeland. They also brought an increased range of raffia textiles. Both copper and palm cloth were marketable on the Kwango, and in exchange the Lunda bought tobacco and Angolan salt. It was through this trade that the Lunda first came into contact with the Luso-African economy of the Atlantic seaboard. During the eighteenth century, neither Africans nor Portuguese from the Atlantic regions succeeded in gaining direct access to the Lunda sphere of influence. Their trade, however, spread far and fast, carried either by Lunda subjects or by intermediate middlemen such as the Imbangala of Kasanje. It was suggested above (p. 79) that peoples tentatively identified as the Lunda were selling palm cloth on the Kwango in the late seventeenth century. In the opposite direction, the first Imbangala caravan is alleged to have reached the Lunda *musumba* in the reign of Naweji I, the second *mwata yamvo* title-holder.[1] This was approximately in the second quarter of the eighteenth century. The nineteenth-century data do not suggest that the Lunda themselves were great caravaneers. On the other hand their state-wide administration was extremely competent at supervising the movements of foreign caravans. The *tukwata* led them directly to a specially appointed camp near the royal capital, and there the *mwata yamvo* was given first choice of all their wares.

As the external trade of Lunda grew, a new factor became important. This was the role of the slave trade in the country's foreign policy. There is no evidence as to when the *mwata yamvo* was first seduced by the attractions of this form of commerce. It is likely, however, that slaves were used to buy foreign imports from quite early in the eighteenth century. A substantial proportion of the slaves sold were war victims. Raiding campaigns were launched, notably among the Luba Kalundwe, Luba Kaniok and middle Kasai peoples of the northeast and north. These raids can be distinguished from strategic campaigns aimed at securing control of the great commercial routes to the west. A second source of slaves was internal. Criminal convicts of all kinds found their sentences being commuted to slavery with increasing readiness. When in 1843 Rodrigues Graça told Lunda chiefs of the

[1] Vellut, 'Notes sur le Lunda', 92.

abolition of the Portuguese slave trade, they warned him that this would lead to a most unchristian revival of the death penalty among the Lunda. It seems likely, however, that the internal production of slaves, whether by taxation, by judicial penalties, or by feuds between villages, was only a secondary source of supply. Intensive internal slaving would have had serious weakening effects on the social and political structure of the nation. No such weakening was apparent in Lunda until the second half of the nineteenth century, by which time many of the country's foreign raiding grounds had been lost to rival powers.

It is difficult to understand why the Lunda empire thrived economically on a commerce so disruptive, and so demoralizing, as the slave trade. The first answer may be that the scale of the trade was small, at least when compared to the wholesale extractions practised in Angola. The profits, on the other hand, were high by Lunda standards. The Lunda empire probably governed a million or more subjects, but it is unlikely that the external trade ever rose to 3,000 slaves per annum most of whom were foreign captives. The hardships, fears, and uncertainties of the trade, which had destroyed the Kongo kingdom during the late-seventeenth century, only began to be felt widely in Lunda in the nineteenth century. The profits, on the other hand, amounted to very tangible benefits. Goods obtained in exchange for slaves played an important role in strengthening political authority. Imported cloth and *missanga* currency-beads increased the wealth and prestige of a chief, and enabled him to reward his most faithful supporters. The redistribution of exotic imports was carefully restricted, however, and only the Lunda oligarchy and its retainers acquired the extensive rewards of the trade. The spread of trade-wealth to the Lunda subject states created some conflict between the centre and the periphery of the empire, but at least until the end of the eighteenth century the *mwata yamvo* seems to have remained a fairly effective monopolist. This was possible because the main centres of population from which slaves were captured lay in the north and east, whereas the markets to which they were sold were in the west and south-west. Whether by accident or design, the site of the king's *musumba* was therefore strategically placed to control a slave-exporting economy.

During the course of the eighteenth century, the territorial authority of the Lunda kings expanded in three geographical stages. The first stage was towards the west and north-west. One of the first peoples to be affected were the Pende, some 300 kilometres down the Kasai from the Lunda capital. The Lunda began to impose their form of subtle political domination by intruding into the Pende region and creating a Lundaized ruling group which would pay tribute to the *mwata yamvo*. This intrusion probably occurred quite early in the eighteenth century. Soon afterwards the Lunda created another dynasty, even farther west, among the Yaka on the Kwango. The town of Kasongo Lunda became an important outpost of the empire. The Lunda also gained influence among such other peoples of the Kwango valley as the Suku, Shinje and Holo. Their main concern was presumably to improve access to the western markets of Angola and Kongo. In the 1760s, Lunda attacks on the area caused Hungu refugees to flee westwards and settle under Portuguese protection along the Kongo-Angola border. At the same time a coup d'état occurred in Matamba, and the new king was alleged to have been helped to power by 'Molua' soldiers from Lunda. In 1768 the Portuguese feared that the Lunda might even capture Kasanje town and confiscate its large stocks of trade goods.[1] This fear was not realized, however, and the Lunda later eased their pressure on the upper and middle Kwango. Nothing is known about the history of the lower Kwango at this period, but it is likely that Kasongo provided another gateway to the west. The Zombo traders of northern Kongo seem to have been rising in influence, and may have been the agents of Lunda trade.

The second area of Lunda expansion was in the south and southeast, towards the upper regions of the Lualaba and Zambezi rivers. One of the peoples affected was the Ndembu, whose chief, Kanongesha, was drawn into the Lunda empire. He then became a powerful agent for the spread of Lunda influence among his neighbours and sent slaves north as tribute. Another attraction which drew the Lunda southwards was the copper and salt of the Lualaba. Copper became an important item of trade in the empire, and a new currency of copper-wire bracelets began to circulate among the wealthy. The exploitation of this new mineral wealth caused acrimonious disputes between Lunda factions on the imperial frontier. Disaffected groups began to move away and spread widely and thinly over the featureless woodland of north-western Zambia. For the most part these wanderers remembered their ancestral or acquired allegiance to the *mwata yamvo*, and sent him occasional tributary payments. Towards the end of the eighteenth century the remote backwaters to which they spread suddenly gained a new importance within the empire. Ovimbundu traders from the southwest succeeded in crossing the inhospitable Chokwe forest and reaching

---

[1] Birmingham, *Trade and conflict in Angola*, ch. VII.

the Luena-Lovale peoples of the upper Zambezi. This rapidly led to the opening of a major new high road from the Atlantic to the Lualaba. Copper crosses began to make their appearance at Benguela. In the opposite direction, a whole new branch of the Atlantic slave trade was opened up, and the southern Lunda became dangerously exposed to its demands. Meanwhile, however, the primary attention of the Lunda kings had been diverted from the south to the east.[1]

THE EASTERN PLAINS AND THE UPPER ZAMBEZI

The wide eastern plains of Central Africa stretch across to the Great Lakes and down to the middle Zambezi. They were sparsely inhabited by small clusters of scattered peoples, some farmers or fishermen, others pastoralists or gatherers. The most numerous and influential of them were the Luba, who were spread across the Lualaba and away towards Lake Tanganyika. The history of the Luba has yet to be written, but their traditions reveal an interesting pattern of domination by chiefs of royal blood known as *balopwe*. These chiefs claim to be strangers who invaded the Lualaba and won domination by feat of arms. Their emergence may, in truth, have owed rather more to local political initiatives, for instance among the important Kalundwe group, who seem to have had a seminal influence over other Luba peoples. These royal chiefs acquired a strong religious aura around them. Like many other Central African kings, they were never seen to eat or drink, but were presumed to subsist like gods. When a new chief was invested, he lit a fire from which his subjects were required to kindle their own fires in sign of loyalty. The snake and the rainbow were adopted as royal symbols. More personal chiefly paraphernalia included a *lukano* bracelet, and a basket of dried bones from former kings. Luba chiefs, like the king of the Lunda, received material tribute from their subjects. Goods flowed towards the centre of the chiefdom and power flowed out from it. The Luba systems, like the Lunda ones, were operated by a hierarchy of officials. The *kilolo* were village and district chiefs, the *mwine ntanda* were land chiefs, and the *mfumu* were court councillors.[2] Although the Luba had a very clear concept of royalty, there was no single Luba state. By the seventeenth century, four kingdoms had

[1] New research on southern Lunda history is being carried out by Robert Schecter of the University of Zambia.

[2] The most recent collation of the ethnographic data on the Luba was undertaken in the mid-1960s by Stephen A. Lucas and presented together with his own field work in 'Baluba et Aruund: étude comparative des structures socio-politiques', unpublished doctoral dissertation (Paris, 1968).

gained a degree of unitary strength, but many Luba chiefs remained independent of them. At this time, in fact, many Luba were migrating out of their traditional homelands and colonizing the more fertile country of the Lulua and eastern Kasai. They took with them their language and their clans, and some features of their culture, but they did not create kingdoms such as those which developed south-east of them in the eighteenth century.

Some oral tradition suggests that the growth of Luba kingship preceded the growth of Lunda kingship. It may well be true that the concept of a royal authority transmitted through the male line was known earlier among the Luba than among the Lunda. The application of that principle to imperial expansion seems, however, to have taken root rather more quickly among the Lunda. The development of the small Luba kingdoms of Kikonja, Kaniok, Kalundwe and Kasongo may have paralleled the Lunda genesis, but the emergence of a dominant Luba empire probably only occurred rather later. Before the late eighteenth century, the Luba had only limited commercial relations with their neighbours. Kaniok and Kalundwe were heavily preoccupied with western defence against Lunda raids. The Kikonja had a prosperous internal economy based on lake fish and oil palms. The major copper mines were exploited by Sanga and Lamba chiefs, whose culture was similar to that of the Luba, but who remained independent of them. The wider economic opportunities of the eastern savanna were not, therefore, grasped by the Luba at all, but by Lunda immigrants from the west.

The Lunda expansion into the eastern part of Central Africa came only very shortly after its western drive towards the Atlantic. The first Lunda action on the eastern front took the form of raiding wars against the Luba. Although these wars yielded captives, the Luba frontier states succeeded in mounting such resistance that no permanent Lunda penetration or conquest of the lands of the Lomami and middle Lualaba occurred. Instead the Lunda turned southwards to the upper Lualaba, where people were more thinly scattered and less well organized. Long-distance Lunda expeditions not only reached the Lualaba copper mines, more than 300 kilometres from home, but pressed on eastwards into the plains, to reach the Luapula. The *kazembe*, the chief who led these advance excursions, sent back salt and copper and slaves to his sovereign. Gradually, however, he discovered a new and potentially greater source of wealth. This was the East African ivory trade.

The ivory trade of East Africa was about 2,000 years old, but only in the seventeenth century had an increasing demand made itself felt beyond the lands of the lower Zambezi. The agents who carried the search for ivory from the river ports out into the plains of Central Africa were probably the Bisa, whose territory lay mid-way between the Luapula and the Zambezi. They hunted ivory over a wide area and carried it to the Portuguese markets at Tete, and perhaps Zumbo, farther up the Zambezi. Another outlet for Bisa ivory was by a more easterly route across, or around, Lake Malawi. Here the Bisa sold their tusks to Yao traders who became the great ivory caravaneers of the eighteenth century.

The Lunda role in this growing commerce was a largely political one. As in the west, the Lunda were not themselves great mercantile entrepreneurs. They were, however, adept at the administration of trade, and so built an eastern wing to their empire through which to concentrate the collection of ivory. A convenient central point was found at the Luapula crossing. The Lunda explorer of the region became a colonial king and took the title *mwata kazembe*. He created a court similar to the *musumba*, though he remained a fairly loyal vassal of the *mwata yamvo*. The initial growth of the *mwata kazembe* state was based on less prestigious, though perhaps more fundamental, economic bases than the external trade in ivory. The Luapula valley had a stable and flourishing economy of its own. The indigenous people had both an important fishing industry and a successful agriculture. The latter was enhanced by the Lunda introduction of cassava, which rapidly replaced older crops as a more reliable staple food. On to the local social system, the *mwata kazembe* grafted the prestige of belonging to the Lunda. Chiefs who supported the new court were given a seal of approval and became Lunda by virtue of their function. Many, if not most, of the chiefs and courtiers were Lunda by appointment, rather than migrants who had settled on the Luapula. Once the Lunda system was established, it began to collect tribute from newly subjected peoples. At first this came from domestic subsistence activities, but soon the court was able to profit from regional trade. Lualaba copper was channelled through the *mwata kazembe* to the peoples of northern Zambia, and later Tanzania. The salt trade provided royal revenue. When longer range trade became important, it was managed through the traditional tribute system. Bisa traders came to the *mwata kazembe* and offered him gifts of Asian textiles, which they had brought from the *va-shambadzi* agents of Portuguese trading houses (see *Cambridge*

History of Africa IV, chapter 6), or from Yao caravan leaders in Malawi. In return Kazembe gave them gifts of tusks which had been brought to him by his tributaries. During the eighteenth century, the Bisa changed their role of ivory hunters for that of trading intermediaries between Lunda and the eastern markets. The Lunda, at the same time, found a major new source of foreign earnings which they succeeded in guarding as closely, and jealously, as they did their western monopoly in slaves. Only towards the end of the eighteenth century did Kazembe's control of the ivory trade become weakened. Elephants became so scarce, and ivory so dear, that the Bisa sought means to by-pass the Luapula and move farther north. They carried their trade to the Lomami river, where the Luba Kasongo state was able to build the same kind of ivory-based power that the *mwata kazembe* had gained a generation earlier. From this base Luba Kasongo defeated Luba Kalendwe and began a rapid wave of expansion to the north and east. This created the unified Luba empire which became familiar to the first foreign travellers who visited eastern Zaïre in the nineteenth century.[1]

Kazembe was the only major kingdom of the eastern plains in the eighteenth century. Its territorial expansion was, however, limited by the Bemba, a strong warrior people who occupied the plateau due east of the Luapula. From their inhospitable retreat, the Bemba conducted raids on more fortunate farming and cattle-rearing peoples. By the end of the eighteenth century, these raids were beginning to take on a systematic quality which led to the creation of Bemba chiefs among conquered peoples. Later in the nineteenth century, these chiefs formed the foundation of a strong military kingdom which attempted to disrupt the orderly pattern of trade which the Lunda had fostered. Meanwhile, however, the *mwata kazembe* had enjoyed his undisputed hegemony over the area for nearly a century before the rise of the Luba Kasongo and Bemba empires to the west and east.

The southern half of Zambia was beyond the range of the Bisa trade routes, or even of Lunda raiding activity. Of the many peoples in the area, two are particularly worthy of mention. These were the Lozi, in the Zambezi valley, and the Tonga on the neighbouring plateau. The Lozi, although a small and isolated people, present an interesting example of political evolution in South-Central Africa. The upper Zambezi flood plain provided environmental opportunities of a kind which did not exist along other stretches of the great rivers. This flood

[1] This interpretation of the chronology of Luba history follows Anne Wilson, 'Long-distance trade and the Luba Lomami empire', *Journal of African History*, 1972, **13**, 575–89.

plain provided a long, narrow oasis in the southern woodland. The recurrent fertility of the soil and natural pattern of irrigation may long have been recognized, and may well have attracted gatherers or farmers from as far afield as Zaïre or eastern Angola. By the seventeenth century, intensive occupation appears to have begun, and large settlement mounds were built above the flood level to permit year-round occupation. Cattle were skilfully moved from the mainland to the mounds in large canoes. By about the late seventeenth century, a political system began to emerge in the north of the valley. Later a secondary centre was created in the south, and by the nineteenth century the Lozi state had succeeded in dominating the whole area, though tension still arose between north and south. One role of its government was to co-ordinate the labour force necessary to build mounds and dams and drainage canals. A system of labour regiments was created on a kinship model. The Lozi kings, like the Kongo kings, maintained an economic balance between the various parts of their empire. The woodland peoples surrounding the valley supplied game, hides, iron, woodwork, cloth and honey as their tribute. The valley people supplied fish, grain, baskets, and pastoral produce. The court, after consuming many of these goods, acted as the centre of exchange for the remainder. This economic role of the king was further enhanced by the distribution among his followers of captured cattle and slaves. The cattle were held on trust from him. The slaves were attached to the land as serfs and were rarely, if ever, sold outside.[1]

The Tonga have sometimes been presented as the epitome of the stateless, self-sufficient, subsistence peasant, living in total isolation from his neighbours and caring only for his crops and his cattle. His situation contrasts quite sharply with a powerful Lunda chief commanding a wide range of African or foreign luxury goods, and selling his ivory and slaves on the world market, albeit through the hands of rapacious middlemen. The contrast, however, is not quite complete. The Lunda chief still had his feet firmly planted in the soil, and even at the *musumba* the rotation of the seasons and the bounty of the harvest were important. Furthermore the Tonga peasant was not altogether devoid of material aspirations. He traded with his neighbours to obtain essential materials like hut poles and iron ore and arrow shafts, or to gratify a luxury taste for honey, shea butter and dried fish. Some of his possessions, such as beads and wire bangles, were relayed by many peoples before they reached him. Even when a Tonga had a narrow

[1] Mutumba Mainga, *Bulozi under the Luyana kings* (London, 1973).

range of material wealth, his cattle provided him with a form of prosperity which was never available to the Lunda or other peoples of the Zaïre woodland.

During the seventeenth and eighteenth centuries, three innovations had affected the predominantly small-scale farming societies of Central Africa. The first, and perhaps most pervasive, was the agricultural change brought about by the introduction of American maize and cassava from the west. A change of staple crop must have been seen as beneficial by local peasants since the new crops had spread rapidly, if selectively, to reach such far-off regions as the Kuba kingdom in the north and the Luapula valley in the east by the eighteenth century. Higher yields, greater drought resistance, better storage qualities and reduced labour requirements made the American foods popular. In good years there may have been some decline in the quality of diet as people moved a step farther from the mixed and varied eating habits of the hunter-gatherer to increased dependence on low-grade starch crops, but in bad years famine was more readily staved off.

The second change to be seen during this period was commercial. The local societies had never been totally isolated and self-reliant. Exchanges of material goods always occurred at two levels. One concerned the production and supply of essential raw materials and tools. The large majority of Central African peoples were now dependent on iron. Even when hoes were made of wood, iron adzes and chisels were needed to fashion them. Game may have been caught in nets and pits, but iron knives were used to clean the skins and share the meat. Other important items of early trade were various kinds of cooking salt and domestic pottery. A second important kind of exchange was based on luxury objects, often connected with the circulation of bride-wealth. Here items were governed as much by cultural preference and tastes in fashion as by basic necessity. Raffia textiles, copper beads, ostrich shell pendants, livestock and grain beer were forms of wealth which could be consumed or exchanged during marriage negotiations. It was into this group of prized possessions that external trade made important new contributions. Glass beads and sea shells were bought, metal objects of iron and brass were introduced, new stimulants like rum, brandy, and tobacco came into use, and cotton textiles or European-cut clothing acquired prestige value. This new range of material wants gradually drew more and more peoples of the lower Zaïre, the western plateaux, and the woodland middle-belt into the sphere of influence of the Atlantic slave trade. Only a small minority succeeded in gaining the new riches. Others lost everything and were carried away as destitute slaves. To the majority, the growth of trading meant a rise in the daily level of fear, insecurity and violence, while only rare samples of the new material wealth filtered down to the villages.

The third set of changes to affect Central Africa in this period was political. The old kingdoms were profoundly modified, like Loango, or even dismembered, like Kongo, and new states emerged in positions of growing strategic importance. The first of the new states was the intrusive Portuguese colony of Angola which established the pattern for small, aggressive, trader-states equipped with firearms. The African rivals of the colonial state drew on older customary political skills in the political management of small societies, as their growth was stimulated by new commercial opportunity. Even the greatest of the broker kingdoms, Kasanje, did not, however, rely on commercial acumen alone for its acquisition of wealth, but built up a raiding empire in which slaves replaced cattle as the pre-eminent prize, and soldiers could be alternately used to loot enemies or to protect trade routes and markets. State-formation, however, had only a minimal effect on most Central African peoples, who continued to live in small isolated villages, rather than in kingdoms. Their isolation may even have increased rather than diminished when elders were forced to lead their people into hidden and remote woodland areas. Yet the Central African kingdoms, even though only affecting a minority, do enable interesting parallels to be drawn with the more familiar field of West African history. Loango, Kasanje, Bihe and Lunda bear some resemblance to the merchant kingdoms of West Africa in seeking to defend their autonomy while at the same time acting as the indirect agents of the Atlantic trade. This similarity between the broker kingdoms of Central Africa and those of Guinea did not outlive the eighteenth century. In this ill-fated southern region the nineteenth century was possibly even more destructive than the eighteenth. It left a legacy of violence, cruelty and despair which has been the burden of the area until the present day. Neither colonial tutelage nor nationalist idealism has succeeded in restoring the freedom from fear which was so rudely shattered two centuries ago.

CHAPTER 3

IVORY AND GUNS IN
THE NINETEENTH CENTURY

In the nineteenth century Central Africa remained as it is today one of the most thinly populated of the habitable areas of Africa. Currently averaging about six people to the square kilometre, or about one sixth of the density found in the wooded areas of West Africa, Central Africa has no great concentrations of rural population, such as are found in the Niger delta to the west, or in the interlacustrine highlands to the east, and the only urban growth has been in recent commercial, administrative and mining centres such as Duala, Bangui, Kinshasa, Luanda and Ndola.

Late in the nineteenth century Central Africa was divided into four political zones which are reflected in the subsequent history of the area. The central and north-eastern zone consists of the republic of Zaïre, an area of about 1 million square miles and twenty million people, who were ruled during the first half of the twentieth century by Belgium. The south-west consists of Portuguese-speaking Angola, an area of half a million square miles and five million people. In the quarters adjacent to these two huge territories there developed the spheres of British influence in the south-east, and of French influence in the north-west. The Cameroun section of the French sphere was under German rule from 1884 to 1914, and a small pocket of the northern Gabon forest is Spanish-speaking. Three of the four main colonial influences had their roots in the pre-1875 period. The Portuguese and French had traded extensively along the coasts north and south of the Zaïre river, from the fifteenth and seventeenth centuries respectively, and the Portuguese had created settlements in Angola and Benguela. The northward expansion of Dutch and English-speaking settlers in southern Africa was creating reverberations across the Zambezi into southern Central Africa by the mid-nineteenth century. In the fourth quarter, that of

Zaïre, the roots of external influence also lay in the pre-1875 era, but in this case a dramatic change of leadership occurred. The economic system pioneered from the east coast by Swahili and Arab initiative, was captured and transformed into a European colony by Belgian-led initiative from the Atlantic coast.

The study of nineteenth-century Central Africa involves much more than seeking the roots of twentieth-century colonialism. With adequate research it will one day be possible to reconstruct a detailed account of the pre-colonial societies of the area. The oral traditions are fresher than for earlier periods, the eye-witness accounts more plentiful, the institutions more closely related to the present, and the ethnic rivalries and partnerships more alive. From this wealth of evidence the complex structure of government institutions and trading systems could be recreated. This pattern of sometimes very localized societies, rather than the four quadrants of the modern map, should form the primary focus for the nineteenth-century historian. From there, he must seek to understand the tensions and alliances, the loyalties and fears, the unity and conflict which were central to the lives of people in many hundreds of societies and communities. The peoples of these communities spoke 200 or more different languages, Bantu languages in the forest and the south, Central Sudanic and eastern Niger-Congo languages in the north. They occupied a wide range of different ecological environments, the most favoured being the medium rainfall belts immediately north and south of the forest. Their everyday economic activities ranged from forest gathering, through grain and tuber cultivation, to nomadic pastoralism, with a significant minority graduating out of primary food production to become handicraft specialists, caravan traders or political and religious leaders. So far, however, research is in its infancy, and a survey based on the work undertaken in the 1960s is liable to dwell on economic factors, and more particularly on factors of trade, to the detriment of politics and religion, demography and nutrition, law and social organization.

THE LUNDA EMPIRE

The history of the savanna half of Central Africa, although but dimly illuminated by the standards of West African historiography, is already considerably better known than the history of the northern forest and beyond. By the end of the eighteenth century it had evolved several large-scale political institutions and far-reaching economic systems. The most important of these was the Lunda empire. This empire had

6. Central Afric

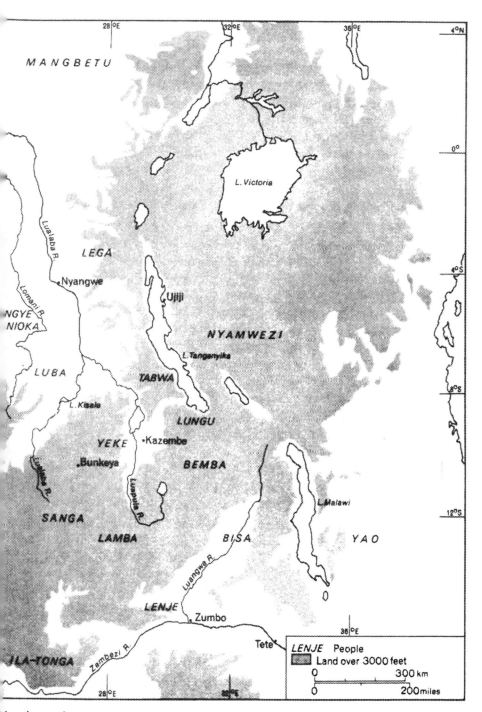

MANGBETU

L. Victoria

LEGA

Nyangwe

Ujiji

NYAMWEZI

L. Tanganyika

TABWA

NGYE
NIOKA

LUBA

LUNGU

L. Kisale

YEKE

•Kazembe

BEMBA

•Bunkeya

SANGA

Luapula R.

LAMBA

BISA

L. Malawi

YAO

LENJE

Luangwa R.

ILA-TONGA

Zambezi R.

•Zumbo

Tete•

LENJE People
Land over 3000 feet

0 ———— 300 km
0 ———— 200 miles

its roots in the eighteenth century. From about 1700, or a little before, the fusing of new commercial opportunities with old political skills enabled a Lunda dynasty to emerge which rapidly came to dominate the upper Kasai basin. As the empire developed, Lunda peoples colonized the central provinces, while their agents spread Lunda political influence among numerous surrounding peoples. During the first three-quarters of the nineteenth century the central part of this Lunda domain continued to thrive and prosper. The hub of the empire was a royal capital or compound called the *musumba* which was rebuilt anew by each successive king. A successful and long-lived ruler attracted courtiers and retainers who built satellite compounds at the *musumba*, until it came to resemble a town, with well-fenced courtyards, broad streets, and a great piazza for public functions. The *mwata yamvo* (or *mwant yav*) ruled this metropolitan complex with two sets of supporters. The traditional elders, descendants of early Lunda clan leaders, were custodians of continuity, rooted in the soil. Some held hereditary posts associated with leading figures of the Lunda 'creation'. One such figure was the influential *lukonkeshia*, 'mother of the nation', who governed an independent sub-court where she entertained state visitors and received tributary taxes of her own. The second set of supporters were bureaucratic office-holders, appointed by the king, and responsible to him for the day-to-day administration of the over-kingdom. These functionaries operated both as senior court dignitaries and as travelling government agents. Until at least the middle of the nineteenth century the forces of unity remained effective in Lunda. Village chiefs paid their tribute even when they lived as much as two months' journey away from the capital. Official *tukuata* travelled the length and breadth of the empire checking caravans, escorting foreign travellers, and warning chiefs whose tribute was late, or inadequate. This continued political well-being was reflected in great stability at court. During the period between 1790 and 1873 the empire appears to have been ruled by three great rulers, Yavo ya Mbanyi (early nineteenth century), Naweji ya Ditende (c. 1821–c. 1853) and Muteba ya Chikombe (c. 1857–1873). Even allowing for disputed successions and short intermediate reigns, this continuity was remarkable in so large and diverse a country, especially at a time when fundamental changes were occurring all around in eastern, western and southern Central Africa.

One factor governing the success of the Lunda empire was the old and strong tradition of unity which related both to the early Lunda migrations, and to the eighteenth-century political expansion. In addition to these quasi-nationalist sentiments of unity, the country was held together by its government. The administrative structure, evolved over many generations, stabilized by many checks and balances, tested by many succession crises, had acquired a certain political permanence. An equally important factor of stability was the economic basis of Lunda power. This basis began with agriculture. The capital was situated in open country with perennial streams and good rainfall. Even at the height of his power, a *mwata yamvo* continued to take personal care of his plantations and regularly visited his large cassava fields manned by serf labour. A safe agricultural base was necessary to sustain the small towns which developed around the court. A second source of Lunda wealth was derived from the copper mines in the south-eastern part of the empire. Copper crosses called *muambo*, weighing two or three kilograms each, were widely disseminated across the savanna. Lunda craftsmen were skilled at converting these copper ingots into an alloy which made fine trade wire. This wire was wrapped round elephant hairs to form bangles, both for personal ornamentation and as a ready form of currency. Both the province of the Lualaba and the eastern, Kazembe province of the Luapula included copper in the tribute payments which they remitted to the *mwata yamvo*. Another important item of trade, and of tribute, was salt, which was scarce and valuable in all the Lunda territories, and had to be imported from both the eastern and the western marches of the empire.

In addition to its internal prosperity, Lunda enjoyed a considerable level of wealth derived from its external trade. One feature of this was the slave trade. In the early nineteenth century, as in the two preceding centuries, the Atlantic slave trade remained the most pervasive factor of foreign influence in Central Africa, even in the savanna heartland 1,000 kilometres from the coast. As yet no detailed, quantitative analysis of the nineteenth-century slave trade from Central Africa has been attempted, but in about 1850 Magyar estimated that one-third of all the slaves leaving Luanda and Benguela in the previous hundred years had come from the Lunda territories. This would suggest that at least two or three thousand slaves a year were being sent out from the Lunda sphere of influence. Even if the true figure were to be considerably less, it raises serious questions as to why Lunda should have become involved in the trade and how the victims acquired their slave status.

Some of the slaves exported from Lunda were undoubtedly prisoners of war. The empire had constant difficulty in defending its northern border, which never lay very far from the *mwata yamvo*'s capital. The king himself frequently led wars against Kete and Luba border groups who threatened his capital. A second share of the export slaves appears to have been collected within the empire as part of the tax system. In 1847 Rodrigues Graça made an estimate of the tribute revenue which the *mwata yamvo* received at approximately annual intervals. The estimate listed thirty-six chiefs who contributed slaves and ivory to the royal exchequer, as well as locally produced iron, copper, hoes, bows, spears, food, palm oil, skins, raffia, cloth and earthenware. Small chiefs paid as little as 600 milreis (£130), but more important chiefs such as Kasongo and Kanioka, when not in revolt, paid the equivalent of 12,000 and even 16,000 milreis. The total revenue, according to Graça, came to about 260,000 milreis (£60,000), substantially more than the colonial revenue of Angola for the same year.[1] The manner in which the *mwata yamvo* prevailed upon his subject chiefs to pay tribute was apparently threefold. Some military force was used, and chiefs reported that government officials 'seized' their children and ivory, if tribute had not been adequately paid. Secondly the veneration in which the *mwata yamvo* was held must have been a powerful deterrent to those contemplating tax evasion. Thirdly, the tribute system was a two-way exchange, and loyal chiefs were rewarded with foreign cloth, ornaments, beads and rum in which the *mwata yamvo* virtually held a trade monopoly. The integrity of the empire was thus maintained by armed strength, by religious sanctions, and by the judicious use of material rewards.

The internal slave trade, on which the wealth of both chiefly and royal courts was partly based, still needs much clarification. One important factor was probably judicial action in sentencing criminals, or alleged criminals, to slavery. When Rodrigues Graça explained to provincial Lunda chiefs that Portugal had outlawed the slave trade, they protested. Portugal, they said, continued to transport convicts to Angola, and so why should not the Lunda be allowed to transport convicts to Portugal? A second means whereby people fell into slavery was in numerous small-scale feuds, either between chiefs, or over disputed succession within a state. Explanations of enslavement in Lunda are closely tied to the relationship between ruler and ruled, and the concept of 'slavery' may often have been not very different from that of 'subject'. Thus a chief, under extreme pressure, might have been able to use considerable discretion in selecting 'slaves' among his entourage of serfs.

[1] Joaquim Rodrigues Graça, 'Viagem', in *Annães do Conselho Ultramarino* (Lisbon, 1855), 145–6.

A controlled trade in slaves was capable of assisting in the growth of political authority. Chiefs were intimately involved in the administration of justice and in the conduct of both local and national wars, the two important means of obtaining slaves. They also controlled the redistribution of foreign goods, thus gaining further power. One factor in the trade which, surprisingly, does not seem to have been significant, was the sale of guns and powder. As late as 1875, Pogge reported that guns were worth very little in Lunda compared to the high prices offered by peoples nearer the coast. Some guns were in use, but were exceedingly ineffective in Lunda hands, even at a range of twenty paces. In 1874, when a chief who controlled the western route to the Lunda capital planned to take over the government by a military coup, he recruited Chokwe musketeers as mercenaries to assist him. In 1876, when Pogge gave the new *mwata yamvo* a single breech-loader, this was an event sufficiently important to be recorded in Lunda tradition as having increased the power of the ruler. In general it would seem, therefore, that although foreign trade played an important role in the power-structure of the empire, this role did not involve the significant supply of firearms.[1]

Although the century before 1875 was marked by conspicuous stability in the heart of Central Africa, and by long uninterrupted reigns at the courts of the Lunda kings, changes of great importance were taking place in all the peripheral areas of southern and western Central Africa. In the west these changes involved the opening of southern Angola to long distance trade and to foreign settlement, the expansion of the Ovimbundu trade network into the upper Zambezi basin, the undermining of the Mbundu–Kasanje trading axis of Angola by Chokwe expansion into western Lunda, and the development of the proto-colonial Luso-African society of the Luanda hinterland. In the east the main developments were the growth of trade from the lower Zambezi into eastern Central Africa, and the establishment of Nyamwezi, Swahili and Arab trade routes between eastern Zaïre and the Indian Ocean. Each of these developments had effects which, as will be seen, undermined the old political and commercial systems, so that in the 1870s Lunda suddenly disintegrated, and the central rump of the empire was overrun by invaders and torn by factionalism.

[1] Paul Pogge, *Im Reiche des Muata Jamvo* (Berlin, 1880); A. Petermann, 'Ladislaus Magyar's Erforschung von Inner Afrika', in *Petermanns Geographische Mitteilungen* (Gotha, 1880); Joaquim Rodrigues Graça, in *Annães do Conselho Ultramarino.*

SOUTH-WESTERN ANGOLA

The late eighteenth century marks the beginning of several important changes in the western part of Central Africa. For over a century the region had been dominated by the Atlantic slave-trading system. In the second half of the seventeenth century the forces of Portuguese conquest had spent themselves, and the trading system had become dependent on a working relationship between Portuguese traders and a series of frontier states such as Matamba, Kasanje and later Bihe. Portuguese enterprise was restricted to two spheres of influence, in the hinterland of Luanda and Benguela; beyond that the effects of overseas trade were transmitted by African enterprise. From the 1780s the Portuguese began to make fresh attempts to gain information about the remoter parts of Central Africa and to establish new areas of activity and more direct trading links with the interior. The Luso-African sphere acquired a new dynamism and began to push its frontier outwards.[1] In the south this process began when several expeditions were sent from Luanda to explore the lands in the far south-west of Angola.

South-western Angola had not been greatly influenced by external events in the first three-quarters of the eighteenth century. Along the coastlands a few small groups of Herero-speaking pastoralists, such as the Kuvale and Ndombe, remained largely isolated and self-sufficient. What external contacts they had were either with client groups of Kwisi hunter-gatherers, or with the larger Bantu nations of the highlands who occasionally raided cattle below the Chela escarpment. On top of the south-western plateau the Mwila peoples were organized into kingdoms such as Huila and later Njau. It was these kingdoms which first established regular trading contacts with the Atlantic markets. In the late eighteenth century ivory began to flow northwards through Quilengues to Benguela, and a few Portuguese tried to settle in and around Huila, but their settlements did not survive. Slavery was still the staple of the Benguela trade, and southern slaves were unpopular, as well as being hard to obtain in such a sparsely peopled area. Neither the Huila market, nor a coastal expedition organized in 1785 by the Baron of Moçâmedes, was of any immediate consequence. Farther east, indirect trading influences were beginning to percolate inwards at about the same time. The Nkumbe sold ivory to Ovimbundu intermediaries

[1] For a clear analysis of the Luso-African sphere of influence in the eighteenth century see two articles by Jean-Luc Vellut: 'Relations internationales du Moyen-Kwango et de l'Angola dans la deuxième moitié du XVIIIe s.', in *Études d'histoire africaine*, I, 75–135; 'Notes sur le Lunda et la frontière Luso-Africaine (1700–1900)', in *ibid.* III, 61–161.

at Caconda, but rigorously excluded the Portuguese and their agents clad in European dress. The Ovambo made their first outside contacts with ivory merchants in Damaraland in the south. Not until the mid-nineteenth century did these indirect trading links give way to more direct foreign contact between the peoples of the south-west and the traders.

In 1840 merchants from Luanda founded the trading port of Moçâmedes on the south coast and began to seek direct access to the highland ivory markets. Within a few years they had opened the route as far as the Nkumbe, and even the Ovambo, and trade increased to include cattle, slaves, gum, orchilla and wax. A major new trading axis had thus been created to parallel the older systems of Luanda and Benguela. In 1849 the new colony was strengthened by the admission of Portuguese refugees from Brazil who introduced sugar and cotton planting in watered pockets of the coastal desert. The cane was used for rum to increase the inland trade, and the cotton became reasonably profitable when prices rose during the American civil war. The Moçâmedes colony was further strengthened in the 1860s by the arrival of Portuguese fishermen who successfully established a coastal fishing industry. The fishing port also developed market gardens from which to supply foreign whaling fleets. All of these new industries were in part based on the local absorption of slave labour which could no longer be legally exported. But they also represented a real attempt at white colonization, as opposed to white trading, in Central Africa. As such the Moçâmedes colony formed an important stage in the Portuguese transition from an exclusively mercantile economy to one including agricultural settlers.

Attempts to use the toe-hold gained in Moçâmedes to extend the new southern colony into the highlands met initially with sharp resistance. The coast was sparsely occupied and defended, but the plateau was organized into militant kingdoms. In the late 1850s Portuguese military expeditions reached Humbe, despite Ngambwe resistance and long-range Ovimbundu and Kwanyama opposition, but they were soon forced to withdraw to Huila. Meanwhile long distance Ovimbundu raids for cattle and slaves became increasingly severe in the south. On one occasion the raiders even descended into the desert and threatened Moçâmedes. They were bought off with European goods as protection money. Military opposition was not the only barrier to the extension of the southern colony. Settlers who had reached the foot-hills found the plateau unsuitable for tropical agriculture. Various colonizing ventures failed before Boer trekkers from South Africa arrived in the early 1880s, and effectively began to clear the highlands of both trees and people in order to facilitate white settlement. The early trading communities had in the meantime become increasingly Africanized and subject to Nkumbe political control.

Two sets of commercial rivals challenged the growth of southern Portuguese trade. From south-west Africa traders penetrated the Ovambo and Okavango regions to capture much of the ivory market and develop a trade in ostrich feathers. The southern traders were accompanied by influential Christian missions. The Ovimbundu traders from the north found that the best way to buy southern ivory was with cattle. They obtained their cattle with European trade-goods in the far east of Angola, in the Zambezi region. By the 1870s the extensive networks of inter-regional trading were causing a decline in the supply of ivory, and all three major buyers were competing for the Ovambo trade by the 1880s.[1]

SOUTH-CENTRAL ANGOLA

The commercial network of south-central Angola also began to expand towards the east in the late eighteenth century. The Portuguese and the Ovimbundu had long been anxious to gain access to the upper Zambezi basin, both in order to open up new spheres of trade and to seek a possible land route to Mozambique. Two major barriers lay in their way. In the north the Chokwe were hostile to foreign penetration and had developed very little trade which might afford an opening. In the south the Mbunda chiefs prevented the passage of caravans in order to protect their own slave and ivory trade. When a route to the east was finally pioneered from Bihe, it crossed a stretch of uninhabited land between these two blocks and reached the Luena–Lovale lands along the Luena and upper Zambezi rivers. This route to Lovale was first described by a trader who had reached the Zambezi from the west in 1794. The new opening probably had considerable effects on the trade of the southern Zaïre region. Lunda copper went to Lovale, for instance, and the Lovale had become skilled in the making of copper wire. Eventually copper crosses from Katanga were being traded right through to Benguela. By 1800 the governor of Angola was speculating that the upper Zambezi might be an extension of the Lualaba which,

[1] Carlos Estermann, *Ethnografia do Sudoest de Angola*, 3 vols. (Lisbon, 1956, 1960, 1961). Alfredo de Albuquerque Felner, *Angola: apontamentos sôbre a colonizaão dos planaltos e litoral do sul de Angola*, 3 vols. (Lisbon, 1940). J. J. Monteiro, *Angola and the River Congo*, 2 vols. (London, 1875). This section owes much to the advice of W. G. Clarence-Smith, who has since written a history of south-western Angola, 'Mossamedes and its hinterland 1875–1915', Ph.D. thesis (London University, 1975).

amazingly but correctly, he thought might be the upper Zaïre. He was also aware that the upper Lualaba was one source of Lunda copper. Thus by opening a route to Lovale, a new communication had been established with Katanga which bypassed both Kasanje and the metropolitan areas of the Lunda empire in the north. Chiefs along this new high-road into the interior soon began to benefit from their position. Angarussa, who controlled the upper Kwanza crossing, charged up to 200 fathoms of cloth for each caravan that passed eastward, and a further two or three slaves on the return journey. He also accepted commissions from traders to waylay their rivals. In view of the profitability of the new opening to the east, other nations began to offer alternative routes, so that they too might draw profit from trade tolls. The Mbunda, in particular, opened up access to the remote Mbwela lands of the south, where slaves were particularly cheap.

THE LOZI

The western traders who reached the Zambezi hoped to go on to the rich lands of the Lozi along the river between Lovale territory and the southern bend of the Zambezi. They were not welcomed by the Lozi, who showed little enthusiasm for trade. Only much later did the Lozi become linked to the trans-African trade routes. The Lozi were essentially a pastoral people, who kept fine cattle both on the banks of the river and on islands in the flood plain. They used large canoes to ferry their cattle to the richest or safest pastures. The Lozi probably had an organized political and economic system, even in the early nineteenth century. The rulers operated a system of tributary exchanges whereby production of many goods was stimulated: the king received canoes, weapons, iron tools, meat, fish, fruit, salt, honey and a range of agricultural foods including maize and cassava. In return he lent to his subjects cattle, all of which belonged to him. Silva Porto, visiting Lozi in 1853, listed twenty-eight 'tribes' who came under the jurisdiction of the king and supplied the central authority with their specialized products.

From about 1840 to 1864 Bulozi (or Barotseland) was ruled by Sotho conquerors from the south called the Kololo. They arrived on the Zambezi after several years of marauding in Botswana, with occasional forays as far afield as Namibia and Zimbabwe. Their main base was in the southern part of Bulozi, between the Chobe and Zambezi rivers. Their economy continued to depend to a significant extent on cattle raiding, but two new sources of wealth became important when they reached the Zambezi. One was the old Lozi flood-plain economy, which the Kololo effectively took over. They became as skilled as the Lozi in the management of canoes, and in the collecting of tributary payments from the many sectors of the plain. The second new dimension was external trade. Before the Kololo invasion the Lozi had rebuffed the traders who came from the west via the court of the Lovale king, Kinyama. The reason, in all probability, was that this rich agricultural area was not a potential source of labour exports. On the contrary it imported labour, and Mulambwa, the Lozi king in the 1830s, had nothing to offer to slavers. The advent of long distance trade occurred at a later date along the more southerly Mbunda–Mbwela route. About 1850, 'Mambari' traders from Angola began to frequent the southern Kololo area, below the flood-plain, where they found people more willing to sell slaves. These slaves, obtained as a byproduct of cattle raiding, were of no immediate economic benefit to the pastoral, pre-dominantly non-agricultural Kololo society. Soon after its opening, this southern route was enhanced by the development of ivory trade. A combination of rising prices, soaring demand and the abolition of the Portuguese royal monopoly on the Angola coast made it profitable to carry ivory 1,400 kilometres to the Atlantic. This trade proved attractive to the people of the flood-plain, as well as to the southern Kololo, and in 1854 Livingstone pioneered a northern trade route to Angola, which was later used by at least one Kololo-led caravan. This northern trade may have intensified conflict between the northern and southern poles of the Kololo kingdom. The traders may have become independent of both Lozi and Kololo traditionalists, and so helped to cause the breakdown of political stability. This breakdown occurred in the 1860s, after the death of Sekeletu, the second Kololo king. When a strong king re-emerged in the 1870s, it was no longer a Kololo leader, but Lewanika, king of the Lozi. Although the rise of the western ivory trade may have facilitated the Lozi 'restoration', ivory also helped to cause its downfall. After a few years of independence, Lewanika came under the influence of ivory hunters from southern Africa who eventually brought colonial conquest in their wake.[1]

[1] Eric Flint, 'Trade and Politics in Barotseland during the Kololo period', *Journal of African History*, 1970, 11, 1. António Francisco da Silva Pôrto, *A travessia do continente africano* (Lisbon, 1936) and *Viagens e apontamentos de um Portuense em Africa* (Lisbon, 1942). David Livingstone, *Missionary travels and researches in South Africa* (London, 1857).

THE OVIMBUNDU KINGDOMS

One of the most important developments in the south-west of Central Africa between the late eighteenth and late nineteenth centuries was the growth in power and prosperity of the Ovimbundu kingdoms. This growth was linked to both southern and eastern trade developments. The Ovimbundu states may have been founded by seventeenth-century immigrant groups. By the eighteenth century they had crystallized into half a dozen major kingdoms with several lesser satellites on the periphery. Their early history was noted for the long distance raids organized to obtain cattle for themselves and slaves for Benguela. Gradually some states developed into regular trading centres to find a surer and more permanent means of prosperity than plundering. Other states profited from the routes which crossed their territory by charging tolls or supplying services and food.

The most important of the trading kingdoms was Bihe. It was the easternmost of the Ovimbundu states and therefore had the most ready access to the interior. It seems that Bihe also had an established prosperity, which may have formed the basis for its entry into long distance commerce. Bihe had a particularly good supply of iron, and so became a centre of iron working, supplying hoes and other implements to neighbouring peoples. Immediately east of Bihe was a pottery industry, which supplied a wide area where sandy soils made good-quality potting clay scarce. The profits from local trades, together with the experience in communications, may have stimulated the growth of Bihe entrepreneurship in organizing slave, ivory, wax and, later, rubber caravans. Initially, in the first half of the nineteenth century, the main route out of Bihe ran north-west towards the Kwanza. An important fair flourished at Dondo, the main crossing point into Portuguese Angola. Two other Ovimbundu states also lay along the north-western routes, at Ndulu and Bailundu. They became important as trading kingdoms, either in their own right or as agents of the transit traffic. The more direct exit for Bihe trade was to the Benguela coast, but this involved crossing the whole Ovimbundu territory and paying protection money or other dues to several intermediate states. A variety of routes was used, passing either through Bailundu or through Huambo depending on political conditions. The growth of this direct trade to the coast led to the founding of a new Portuguese trading settlement at Catumbela. This was more accessible from the plateau than Benguela, which had been geared to the southern trade through Caconda. The number of traders grew steadily; in 1879 Silva Porto travelled from Catumbela to Bihe in a month and met about forty caravans. The growth of entrepreneurship gradually affected all the Ovimbundu states, as increasing numbers of long distance caravans were sponsored. The development of these wealthy, experienced, commercial kingdoms gradually came to be felt as far afield as Luba and Kuba.

THE CHOKWE

A fourth topic in the history of south-western Central Africa was the creation of an entirely new trading 'empire' by the Chokwe. These pioneers struck northwards from the uplands of eastern Angola to capture part of the trading system of the Zaïre basin. The Chokwe had played a very slight role in Central African trade in the eighteenth century. Their country was remote and underpopulated, and they took little part in the supply of slaves. Their main exports were ivory and wax, but in the heyday of the slave trade, they were difficult to transport and less profitable than slaves. The Chokwe did, however, manage to sell some of their commodities, and in return specialized in the purchase of flintlock muskets. In the 1840s a great change occurred among the Chokwe. The trade in wax from Benguela and Luanda rose some thirty-fold, as trading houses tried to remain solvent despite the decline of the slave trade. Chokwe wax went both to Kasanje and nearby markets on the route to Luanda, and to Bihe, for transmission to the Benguela coast. Chokwe wax was highly esteemed and was collected from carefully prepared log hives. Production occurred throughout the upper Kasai woodland and even beyond into Luchaze territory, though transport costs reduced the profits farther east to a marginal figure.

Another important change occurred among the Chokwe, when a rapid rise in the ivory trade came to overshadow wax production. The Chokwe played a large part in the revival of ivory which followed the abolition of the Portuguese royal monopoly in 1834 and the consequent rise in prices. The Chokwe had the advantage of being skilled hunters. They were also expert gunsmiths and had been able, through their wax trade, to build up and maintain a substantial armoury of guns. Thirdly, the Chokwe woodland was the nearest region to the coast in which elephants were still plentiful by the late 1840s. Under these conditions, the Chokwe were able to take up intensive ivory hunting. The volume of the exploitation, however, soon depleted the elephants. New hunting grounds had to be sought and the Chokwe sent out hunting parties to the north and east. They offered their skills to the Lunda, in whose territory elephants were still available. One half of the ivory shot in Lunda was kept by the Chokwe hunter and the other half went to the Lunda chief. Both the chief and the hunter usually sold their ivory to Kasanje and Bihe traders, who had travelled in the hunters' wake, and switched part of their interest from slaves to ivory. By this adaptation to new circumstances the traditional large-scale trader continued to prosper for a few years longer. At the same time the Chokwe emerged as a new entrepreneurial group in the Kasai basin.

The increase of Chokwe prosperity had the primary effect of increasing Chokwe population. The ivory which they hunted was primarily converted into women. These women were bought from Kasanje and Bihe caravans at increasingly favourable rates as the demand for slaves, and especially women slaves, slackened on the coast. In Chokwe society, investment in women was the soundest means of economic development. Agriculture prospered, families increased and by the 1850s the upper Kasai was beginning to experience a shortage of cultivable farmland. As a result a slow process of migratory expansion began towards the north. Chokwe villages moved a few miles at a time beyond the national frontier, occupying forested river banks and other familiar terrain. The migrants avoided conflict with the Lunda by occupying the more wooded areas and by contributing, through trade and hunting, to the economic well-being of their neighbours.

Having successfully exploited first wax and then ivory until each was exhausted, the Chokwe economy underwent a third change in the late 1860s and began to embark on the production of rubber, tapped from forest vines. In the Chokwe home territory this activity was very short-lived, because of the wasteful methods used for tapping latex. The rubber collectors had to move north, thus swelling Chokwe migrations, and spreading the rubber trade along the forest galleries of the Kasai basin.

The exhaustion of ivory and rubber along the upper Kasai caused important changes in the Chokwe economy. From being mainly producers, who sold to the established caravaneers from Kasanje and Bihe, the Chokwe became traders who fetched their ivory from the middle Kasai and eventually from among the Luba. To do this they established their own long distance caravan system, with their own routes, carriers and leaders. Once they had launched into the business of carrying, the Chokwe began to rival the old entrepreneurs. Furthermore, when they reached the Lulua and Luba areas, they found themselves among people who hunted their own ivory and tapped their own rubber, so

that the traditional skills of the Chokwe as producers became super-
fluous. They gradually adapted to the single role of trading intermediaries.

In the short space of fifty years the Chokwe had risen from being a
small, remote, forest people to being one of the most dynamic economic
forces in Central Africa. They had also become one of the most powerful military forces, and their early, inconspicuous migrations were increasingly replaced by violent raiding. By the 1870s they were a match
for any rival including the large, organized empire of their Lunda
neighbours, which they succeeded in subverting and almost destroying.[1]

NORTHERN ANGOLA AND LUANDA

The history of northern Angola in the nineteenth century involved
changes of a rather different kind from those at work in southern
Angola during the same period. In the south new trading axes were
being pioneered to tap a wide variety of new resources and commodities and to stimulate new economic growth and diversification. In the
north the nineteenth century was associated with decline and retrench-
ment. It was, however a decline in slave trading which should have
released new forces of positive growth. For a long time this growth was
not greatly in evidence, and Luanda stagnated. When the history of this
period comes to be written, one will of course have to treat with caution
the perennial traders' cry that business had been ruined. It is, nevertheless, true that such trade as there was on the old slave route through
north-central Angola continued to decline after its hinterland had been
partially captured during the eighteenth century by Loango in the
north and Benguela in the south. Despite the decline of this route, the
western coast of Central Africa remained the most lucrative slaving
area on the Atlantic during the nineteenth century. A British Foreign
Office estimate of the total slave exports from 1817 till 1843 gave the
figures shown opposite.[2]

The striking thing about this table is that only 4,400 slaves were listed
as shipped from Luanda, barely 7 per cent of the total listed from
Benguela and less than 3 per cent of the Cabinda figure. Although some
of the unclassified 'Angolan' slaves may also have come from Luanda,
one can nevertheless assume a serious decline in the city's trade.

---

[1] Joseph Miller, 'Cokwe expansion 1850–1900' (mimeographed, Madison, 1969), and
'Cokwe Trade and conquest', in Richard Gray and David Birmingham, *Pre-colonial African
trade* (London, 1970); Gladwyn M. Childs, *Umbundu kinship and character* (London, 1949).
[2] Philip Curtin, *The Atlantic slave trade* (Madison, 1969), 261.

Loango	1,100
Malembo	26,800
Cabinda	102,500
Congo river	16,400
'Angola'	144,100
Ambriz	30,600
Luanda	4,400
Benguela	58,400
Total	384,300
Annual average	14,800

The decline was also felt at other points along the route into the interior. In 1790, before the Napoleonic wars had reduced the overall quantity of shipping available to slaving interests, Kasanje was still the focal point of the Luanda trading system. For over a hundred years it had effectively controlled a large share of the trade between the Lunda empire and the west coast. The Portuguese, however, driven by falling profits, were no longer satisfied with the old broker kingdoms and sought direct contact with their suppliers. In 1806 Anastacio and Baptista, two Luso-African *pombeiros*, reached the Lunda capital of the *mwata yamvo*, and were able to reveal to the Lunda details of the European trading system so long concealed by Kasanje middlemen. Two years later an embassy from the *mwata yamvo*, and another from his mother, the *lukonkeshia*, arrived in Luanda to present royal letters to the Portuguese governor. This breach of the Kasanje barrier by diplomatic envoys led to the creation of new commercial routes which by-passed the Imbangala territory altogether. The resulting decline of Kasanje led to increasing disputes between the Portuguese and the Kasanje kings. These disputes finally led to a major war in 1850 in which the kingdom was disrupted and the Portuguese *feira*, or staple market, was moved back to Malanje in Portuguese-held territory. Although Kasanje was subsequently re-established, and although in 1852 David Livingstone was able to receive copies of *The Times* there, it no longer flourished. Malanje became the departure point for caravans to the interior, and its trading houses became fully capable of equipping long distance traders. By the 1870s all that remained of the long association between the Kasanje plain and Angola were a few Portuguese cattle ranchers and sugar planters. Most caravans used other routes, leaving Kasanje independent, but largely deprived of its life-blood.

A second major change in the Luanda system came in mid-century with the penetration of Ovimbundu and later Chokwe enterprise into the Kwango–Kasai region. The effect of this was to cut across the old east–west trade routes and replace them with new north–south routes. This was not done without a struggle, and battles between Kasanje and Ovimbundu caravans occurred even before the Chokwe captured a share of the trade. In the south, as seen, this growing north–south trade triggered off a major northward expansion of Chokwe peoples. In the north, as will be shown later, it began to affect peoples on the forest fringe who had little previous contact with market-oriented trade. On the central routes, however, the effect was to depress trade yet further and cause the Portuguese to think once again about developing the local economic potential of their coastal provinces in Angola.

There had been attempts in the eighteenth century to diversify the economy of Angola by investing in the salt and hide industries, and by introducing Iberian technology into the iron-working industry. These endeavours had come to nothing, however, and in the early nineteenth century the colony was as dependent as ever on the slave trade. Even food and building timbers were brought in from Brazil. A large proportion of the 2,000 white inhabitants of Luanda city were deported criminals, and much of the military garrison consisted of local African convicts. The rest of the population consisted of a few hundred mulattoes and free Africans, and some 3,000 slaves, many of them charwomen and laundresses. The 'colony' was divided into about a dozen districts ruled by ill-paid and ill-trained government agents. Their main function, and incidentally their main source of income, was the forced recruitment of conscript carriers to be hired to passing traders. This conscription led to severe forms of extortion, and the contract was between the agent and the trader only, not between the carrier and the trader. As the slave trade declined, efforts were made to seek new trade goods and a new hinterland. As early as 1790 the Portuguese had tried to expand northward along the coast. They had been severely defeated by the ruler of Mossul, who continued to dominate the coast north of Luanda for many years. In 1855 the Portuguese tried to overcome this barrier by establishing a garrison at the English settlement of Ambriz. They had little success in attracting more trade, however, and their high tariffs drove the traders to the neighbouring bay of Kinsembo. Despite the difficulties, some agricultural produce began to flow into Luanda by the 1860s. Cotton, coffee, beeswax, and palm oil were all produced by small-scale African farmers and collectors in the Kwanza, Bengo and Dande valleys. Farther inland, cattle-keeping revived in importance, and when a steamer service was introduced on the lower Kwanza, attempts were made to establish sugar plantations there. In Cazengo and Golungo Alto a few Portuguese traders branched into coffee planting, but the colonial economy remained weak even in the last quarter of the nineteenth century.[1]

SOUTHERN CENTRAL AFRICA

When one moves eastward, beyond the immediate sphere of Luso-African influence in western Central Africa, one eventually enters a region in which the earliest international trade came across eastern and south-eastern Africa from the Indian Ocean. This commercial penetration of southern Central Africa, like the Atlantic penetration of western Central Africa, was marked by several distinct phases, each pioneered by separate groups interested in exploiting different resources. In the north of the southern savanna the two spheres of economic influence were linked by the growing political and commercial empire of the Lunda. In the south an economic watershed divided west from east, and parts of southern Zambia remained a no-man's land unvisited by foreign caravans until the nineteenth century. The fact that this region was untapped by direct long distance trade did not mean that its population was inactive. On the contrary, many interesting developments were taking place, particularly on the fertile Tonga plateau. The Tonga were mixed farmers and pastoralists who remained isolated from the outside world until colonial times, although after the 1830s they experienced periodic cattle raids from the Kololo and Ndebele. They did not, however, constitute exclusively self-sufficient subsistence communities. Within a middle Zambezi framework they operated a system of exchanges and specialisms which supplemented their subsistence activities. The Tonga had valuable supplies of salt with which they could purchase goods of external origin. On the other hand they lacked good quality iron ores, and so had to rely on imported hoes and other metalwares. Other items of exchange, such as shells, beads and cloth, filtered through from farther afield and reached the Tonga after multiple exchanges had taken place among neighbours who were trading in fish, grain, game, ochre, building materials and specialized items of food. These exchanges enabled Tonga communities to build up a small quantity of material wealth which could be converted either into

[1] J. Lopes de Lima, 'Ensaio sôbre a statistica d'Angola e Benguella', in *Ensaios sôbre a statistica das possessões portugezas*, III (Lisbon, 1846). J. J. Monteiro, *Angola and the River Congo*, 2 vols. (London, 1875). E. Alexandre da Silva Corrêa, *História de Angola*, 2 vols. (Lisbon, 1937).

personal ornaments or exchanged for food in times of famine and hard-ship. They did not become specialists in trading, or in any form of market-oriented production, as did the Chokwe or the Lozi, but they nonetheless took steps to increase their economic well-being, and to cushion themselves against economic disaster.[1]

Eastward from this central region where the penetration of nine-teenth-century trade was only slightly felt, were the lands of the Luangwa and Luapula basins, where direct and strong contacts with the outside world developed during the nineteenth century. The earliest of these contacts was with the lower Zambezi. Already in the eighteenth century the people of the middle Zambezi bend, especially the Lenje, had been conducting some trade with the Portuguese at Zumbo. A more important trading state in the area, however, was the eastern Lunda kingdom of Kazembe.[2] This important state had been established in the mid-eighteenth century by groups of Lunda explorers, colonizers and fortune hunters. In an otherwise sparsely inhabited region, they found that the Luapula valley contained a flourishing community centred on the fishing industry. The diversity of the Luapula economy somewhat resembled that of the upper Zambezi. The migrants from Lunda were able to contribute in several ways to its growth. They were probably able to introduce cassava as a new and hardy staple crop, with a higher yield than the traditional grain crops. The Lunda immigrants were also able to establish a pattern of administration which en-couraged economic co-operation. The early rulers built a state structure, and imposed a produce tribute on the various peoples of the region. The Lunda tribute system of two-way exchanges between the king and his chiefs was probably used to redistribute the surplus. The Lunda colonization of the Luapula also increased external trade. In particular salt was sent west to the court of the *mwata yamvo*. It is likely, though not yet adequately proven, that the eastern Lunda of Kazembe also supplied slaves to central Lunda, both for internal re-absorption, in agriculture, and for relaying to the Atlantic. In the early years Kazembe received its exotic imports from the Atlantic. Metal wares, ornaments, shells, and even crockery, were carried from the west coast over enormously long lines of communication. Much shorter, however, and potentially more important, was the trading axis between Kazembe and the lower Zambezi.

[1] Marvin Miracle, 'Plateau Tonga entrepreneurs in historical inter-regional trade', *Rhodes-Livingstone Journal*, 1959, **26**.

[2] Kazembe was the hereditary title of the ruler of this Lunda state. Kazembe is here used to denote the state ruled by the *kazembe*.

By the 1790s Kazembe and the Zambezi Portuguese were each anxious to establish direct trading links. Indirect trade between them had been in the hands of the Bisa, who conveyed slaves, ivory, and copper to the Portuguese and carried cloth back to Kazembe. At first Bisa trade was only a small branch of Portuguese business, along with ranching, gold panning and local slave trading in the Zambezi valley. Gradually, however, they became aware of Kazembe's potential value as a gateway to the interior. In 1798 an expedition led by Francisco de Lacerda e Almeida was instructed to sign a treaty with the third *kazembe* and open a road to the west. The *kazembe*, although anxious enough to attract traders, naturally had no intention of allowing foreigners to open his much cherished route *à contra costa*. The Lunda knew all about the economic advantages of the strategic middleman. Lacerda e Almeida's great expedition therefore failed in its economic aims, if not in its scientific ones.

The second Portuguese attempt to establish links with Kazembe started from the west. The two Portuguese-speaking *pombeiros*, agents of a European trader at Kasanje, who visited the *mwata yamvo*, also had instructions to travel to Tete on the Zambezi. They reached Kazembe safely in 1806 and, after being delayed for four years, were eventually allowed to complete their journey. On their return they were again waylaid in Kazembe and relieved of the presents they carried. These presents had been sent by the Portuguese to induce chiefs of the interior to direct their trade to the Zambezi rather than the Atlantic. This journey of the *pombeiros* was undoubtedly one of the most dramatic and famous episodes in the annals of African exploration, but it did little to increase the eastern trade of Kazembe or to further Portuguese trading ambitions in Central Africa. By 1831, when the Portuguese made their third attempt to open trade with Kazembe, the situation had altered and the king had established contact with the expanding trade systems of East Africa. Monteiro and Gamitto found him disdainful of their goods. He was unwilling to accept plain cloth at any price, and he would not pay ivory or copper for even the better quality coloured and woollen materials, but only rather inferior slaves. The Portuguese penetration from the south-east was thus halted, and the way opened for a new enterprise to move onto the Central African scene from the Zanzibar coast.[1]

[1] Ian Cunnison, 'Kazembe and the Portuguese', *Journal of African History*, 1961, 2. A. Verbeken and M. Walraet, *La première traversée du Katanga en 1806* (Brussels, 1953). Nicola Sutherland-Harris, 'Zambian trade with Zumbo in the Eighteenth Century', in

Swahili-Arab penetration of north-eastern Zambia and south-eastern Zaïre was more like the Chokwe penetration of western Lunda than the Portuguese activity which it superseded. The Swahili-Arabs probably began to arrive in the early nineteenth century, although it has been suggested that by the time of Lacerda's visit to Kazembe a few traders had already reached the Luapula.[1] They came as peaceful traders, and settled in small compounds near established local chiefs while they built up their trade in slaves and ivory. Caravans were periodically sent back to the coast, and returned not only with new trade-goods but also with more guns and powder. As the Swahili-Arab trading-posts increased their military establishment, the factories became stockades or even forts. Eventually the traders became sufficiently well-established to overthrow the local chiefs and gain independent political power for themselves. Thus they slowly undermined the communities on the eastern fringe of the Lunda empire, just as the Chokwe were undermining those on the west. In both cases ivory was the fundamental stimulus to advance; but in both cases a trade in slaves, including women slaves, was an important secondary activity.

The development of Swahili-Arab ruled communities in Kazembe's sphere of influence was especially significant in the 1850s and 1860s. Kazembe itself was not initially subject to outright challenge, but many of the eastern chiefs, who had previously been under its influence, were now more directly under Swahili-Arab influence. Kazembe seems to have retained considerable control over the supply of ivory from beyond the Luapula, but in the 1860s this supply was either becoming exhausted or being tapped by rival west-coast traders. The kingdom was probably also losing its grip on the important copper trade. As a result Kazembe's power and prestige was definitely on the wane by the time Livingstone visited the capital in the 1860s. By 1872, the influence of the traders had become so strong that they became involved in serious political disturbances in which the seventh *kazembe* was replaced first by the eighth *kazembe* and soon after by the ninth *kazembe*. This disruption was part of a pattern which was to become familiar in other

Gray and Birmingham, *Pre-colonial African trade*. F. J. de Lacerda e Almeida, *Travessia da Africa* (Lisbon, 1936). A. C. P. Gamitto, *King Kazembe*, tr. Ian Cunnison, 2 vols. (Lisbon, 1960). Andrew Roberts, 'Pre-Colonial trade in Zambia', *African Social Research*, 10, 1970. Andrew Roberts, 'Tippu Tip, Livingstone, and the chronology of Kazembe', *Azania*, 2, 1967.

[1] The term 'Arab' has often been applied to coastal Muslims more properly called Swahili. Tippu Tip, the greatest 'Arab' trader of all, was probably more African than Arab by culture, race, and language, and would be described today as a Swahili. The term Swahili-Arab is used throughout in referring to East Coast traders since the contemporary nomenclature is so unclear.

parts of Central Africa. Failure to satisfy rising expectations created by the opening, or increase, of external trade, led to situations of internal conflict which could easily be exploited by outside agents. The situation was made more volatile by the rapid increase in the supply of guns. In the first half of the nineteenth century guns were rare in southern Central Africa. A few were brought in by traders, but they were inefficient and short-lived weapons, which few people learnt to use with any skill. They became a symbol of power, a badge of office, but not a real military asset. The development of the ivory trade in the period after 1850 brought in new entrepreneurs, such as the Chokwe and the Swahili-Arabs, who had a much larger supply of guns and, above all, were much more skilled in their use than the population which they met in the remote interior. The new traders rapidly gained considerable power and prestige, and were often only too willing to accept invitations to support one faction or another in the internal disputes of states such as Kazembe, thus weakening the old order and increasing their own power.

The third major people to penetrate Central Africa from the east, along with the Portuguese and the Swahili-Arabs, were the Nyamwezi. The Nyamwezi acquired their commercial skills, and accumulated their capital, in the internal trade of western Tanzania. They became important traders of iron, salt, hoes, cloth, food and other local staples or specialties. At about the same time that the Swahili-Arabs were beginning to seek access to the interior of East Africa to buy ivory, the Nyamwezi were beginning to seek access to the coast to buy foreign cloths, beads and copper. By the 1850s the Nyamwezi, like the Swahili-Arabs, had become large-scale caravan operators in East Africa. Their major trading partner was Kazembe, from which they bought ivory and Katanga copper. In the 1850s the Nyamwezi began to circumvent Kazembe, in order to trade more directly with the copper-producing areas. In this the Sumbwa Nyamwezi were particularly successful, and became known in Katanga as the Yeke.

The Yeke penetration of Kazembe's western domains, and of the frontier-lands of *mwata yamvo*'s Lunda, began, like the Chokwe penetration in the west and the Swahili-Arab penetration in the east, as an essentially peaceful commercial operation. The Yeke were welcomed because they brought foreign goods, increased the scope for local exchanges, and put a new value on commodities which were previously hard to export because of transport difficulties. In particular, the Yeke traded with chief Katanga of the Lamba. They bought large copper ingots, moulded in the traditional cross form, but weighing as much as a man could carry.

Although the Yeke had penetrated the Lamba country in the capacity of traders, they soon began to aspire to political power under the leadership of Msiri, the son of an early Sumbwa trader. Msiri made use of his superiority in firearms to dominate his neighbours and spread fearsome rumours of his military prowess. His first conquests were made on behalf of local chiefs who welcomed his help in suppressing insubordination. In return they gave him captives, whom he could use as porters to carry ivory and copper to Unyamwezi. Msiri rapidly followed up this success by challenging the power of chiefs Katanga and Mpande, whom he overthrew, to make himself master of the Lamba and Sanga peoples. He then directed new campaigns against the Luba, in the north, until by about 1870 he had sufficiently gained in power to challenge the overlordship of Kazembe. Thus at the same time that the Swahili-Arabs were weakening the power of Kazembe in the east, the Yeke were breaking his authority in the west, to declare themselves an independent nation. Yeke independence not only reduced the size and power of Kazembe, but also threatened its route to the *mwata yamvo*'s capital.

The success of Msiri led many peoples from all parts of Katanga to join him. He called his new heterogeneous kingdom Garenganze, and by the 1880s his capital, at Bunkeya, had grown to over forty villages of followers who had migrated to safety under his suzerainty. By intervening in the disputes of his neighbours, Msiri was able to spread his influence to cover most of the area between the upper Lualaba and the Luapula, a vast territory carved out of the two main branches of the Lunda empire. Garenganze became one of the most important and most successful conquest states of nineteenth-century Central Africa. Its initial success may have been associated with the advent of plentiful and effective guns, but in his administration Msiri adopted traditional and well-tried methods of government. A Lunda-type system of provincial governors administered his more remote subjects, and levied the ivory tax which lay at the base of Msiri's wealth. A hierarchy of war chiefs organized expeditions against Msiri's Luba and Lunda enemies. The Yeke military élite, numbering perhaps some 2,000 men, was armed with guns, while the bulk of the state's armed force consisted of locally recruited soldiers with lances, bows, and other traditional weapons.

Although Msiri's empire was apparently a more aggressive, military kingdom than the old Lunda states, it remained, like them, dependent on trade for prosperity and long-term success. Ivory remained Msiri's foremost source of state revenue, and he held a monopoly of tusks from elephants killed on his land. Garenganze was so remote from the major trade arteries that elephants were still plentiful after the 1870s, and could provide an important revenue to the state, when most regions nearer to the coasts had been almost hunted out. In a second revenue-earning field, the copper industry, Msiri began by imposing a percentage levy on production, but soon moved towards a state monopoly, recruiting Yeke smiths to smelt copper and produce wire, bracelets and ingots for the surrounding markets. The supply of slaves to Garenganze was mainly satisfied by warfare, but Msiri also instituted orders of merit with treasured emblems of office which could be purchased by donating slaves to the royal court. Slaves were also a current means of paying fines for judicial infringements. Finally, Msiri gained control of the salt springs of Mwashya, and the marsh salt supplies of the Lualaba, which gave him an important stake in the internal trade of Katanga.

The original outlet for the Yeke trade was eastward via Kazembe, or other Luapula crossings, to Unyamwezi and Zanzibar. With the decline of Kazembe, Msiri began to seek new caravan routes. He established direct links with the Lovale by about 1870, and thereby became linked to the expanding Ovimbundu trade system of southern Angola. Caravans from Bunkeya began to travel fifteen hundred kilometres right through Bihe to Benguela on the Atlantic. From the west Silva Porto, an established Portuguese trader, began sending caravans from Angola to Bunkeya. Msiri was able, by means of this new link, not only to export additional quantities of ivory and slaves, but also a certain amount of rubber and wax. In 1875 Vernon Cameron followed much of this route in his journey across Africa from east to west, and met a 'Nyamwezi' caravan in Angola. In the next decade Frederic Arnot came up the route from the Atlantic to establish the first Christian mission in Katanga.[1]

Although the Lunda state of Kazembe was perhaps the major kingdom to attract Swahili-Arab and Nyamwezi traders into the southeastern quarter of Central Africa, two other kingdoms of rather different character were also important. These were Bemba and Luba.

The Bemba state developed during the nineteenth century to cover much of the plateau country east of Kazembe, between the Luapula and Luangwa valleys. The origins of the kingdom probably reached back into the seventeenth century, and may have been vaguely related to early Luba or Lunda states, but the emergence of an important terri-

[1] Auguste Verbeken, *Msiri: roi du Garenganze* (Brussels, 1956).

torial claim by the *chitimukulu*, or king, only took place from the late eighteenth century. The reasons for the rise and expansion of the Bemba state are not at all clear. It has been suggested by Roberts[1] that the initial stages of Bemba expansion were related to raiding. The Bemba homeland was poor in many respects, and the Bemba took to raiding their neighbours for cattle, for salt and probably for many other regional products which they themselves did not produce. By the end of the eighteenth century the *chitimukulu* began to found Bemba chiefdoms in the raided lands and to appoint to them relatives who would tie the new lands to a central dynasty. Among the earliest 'colonies' was the western chiefdom of Ituna, the ruler of which was given the title *mwamba*. This expansion was rather different in character from the expansion of Lozi or Kazembe, which started with a comparatively wealthy nucleus, based on rich fishing, cattle-keeping, or farming, and gradually expanded to bring neighbours into an increasingly diversified sphere of economic exchanges. The Bemba, in contrast, started out as a poor group of military raiders and expanded into the better endowed country around them.

The Bemba kingdom received a new stimulus to expansion when, about 1850, it began to establish contact with the Swahili-Arab traders moving into the territories around the south of Lake Tanganyika. The Bemba country still had supplies of prime-quality ivory which it could offer to such traders. Furthermore, the Bemba pattern of raiding was eminently suited to the capture of slaves. Since Bembaland was too poor for large-scale, slave-using agriculture, as in Lozi or even Chokwe regions, a slave surplus was available for export. In about 1860 Chileshye, the *chitimukulu* who had pioneered the first phase of Bemba expansion, died and was succeeded, after an interval, by Chitapankwa. He began to make use of the country's new-found trading potential to acquire guns which had not been used in the establishment of the kingdom, but may have become a major factor in its later expansion. Guns increased the scope of slave raiding and elephant hunting in the west, and from about 1870 relations with the East Coast traders, including Tippu Tip, could have supplied them in the east. But there is little evidence for their importance even in repelling the Ngoni.

Although the Bemba state can be described as a 'brigand' kingdom, like those of the Yeke and Chokwe, the Bemba showed considerable skill in creating political cohesion within their domains. The first link

[1] A. D. Roberts, *A history of the Bemba: political growth and change in north-eastern Zambia before 1900* (London, 1973), 125-7.

was in family ties between the central rulers and the appointed governors of the conquest territories. To enhance the loyalty of these governors, appointments were not made for life, but were subject to promotion and advancement. The second unifying factor in Bemba was a ritual one. Local chiefs came to pay their tribute to royal chiefs in order to obtain religious sanction for their office. It may be that, as in Kazembe, material exchanges were also a part of the tribute system, thus making loyalty profitable as well as spiritually comforting.

By the 1870s the Bemba economy had successfully integrated the needs of local commerce with the opportunities of external trade. Trade did not consist simply in the exchange of imports for slaves, but in the circulation of a wide range of commodities. Spears and hoes could be exchanged for cloth, either bark cloth for immediate use, or imported cloth, which was commonly preserved as a current means of exchange. Cloth in turn could be sold to buy salt, and salt was a recognized means of buying slaves. Thus a wide range of forms of production and of trading prosperity was fostered before the final sale of slaves for goods. To conclude, as Roberts has demonstrated, the power of Bemba chiefs was due to their ability both to sustain local interchange of goods and labour, and to attract long distance trade.[1]

THE LUBA EMPIRE

The history of the Luba is one of the most interesting and important stories in Central Africa. The traditions refer to 'empires' as far back as the fifteenth century, and archaeological excavations have shown that as early as the eighth century some areas which were, or later became, Luba, had achieved a high degree of technical ability in the field of metallurgy and may even have been part of an early trading system. Until the end of the eighteenth century, however, the Luba apparently remained divided into small or medium sized states; Kikonja controlled the Lualaba lakes, and their dried fish industry, while other states specialized in salt production or oil palm cultivation. Among the Songye to the north, raffia cloth was produced both as a commodity and as a currency, which circulated widely among the Luba. Related peoples in the south worked copper which they sold to the Luba principalities.

Among the Luba, trade, or more precisely the exchange of produce,

[1] A. D. Roberts, *History of the Bemba*, 182-214. See also Marcia Wright and Peter Lary's useful and well-documented article on the history of this region, 'Swahili settlements in northern Zambia and Malawi', *African Historical Studies*, 1971, 4, 3, 547-73.

was mainly conducted through the system of tribute and reward. It was a vertical exchange, with producers paying a part of their produce in kind to the chief and receiving in return material rewards derived from the tributes of others. Such a system did not encourage horizontal trade directly between producers, and did not lead to the emergence of full-time professional traders, or even part-time, dry-season, traders. The incentives which enabled a 'class' of traders to emerge among the decentralized Nyamwezi and Bisa did not operate among the centralized Luba kingdoms. On the other hand, when outside traders established links with Luba leaders, these rulers were immediately in a position to go into business as monopolist entrepreneurs, and thus greatly to strengthen their economic and political standing.

The growth of Luba under the impact of long distance trade came last in a series of political developments which spread across the southern savanna from both east and west. Maravi in the east and Kasanje in the west had been seventeenth-century trading empires. In the eighteenth century the twin empires of Lunda and Kazembe had grown to dominate the western and eastern trades. Finally in the late eighteenth and early nineteenth century the effects of long distance trade began to be felt among the Luba. The state which most rapidly and successfully responded to these new opportunities was Luba Lomami. It was probably the largest and most centralized Luba state, with an effective mechanism for collecting tribute from producers in a rich and varied economy.

The first traders to reach Luba Lomami were Bisa ivory traders. They had been trading in the Kazembe region since about the 1760s, but by the 1800s ivory was becoming scarce, so they began to push northwards. The market for ivory which they created had a stimulating effect on many aspects of the internal trade of Luba. Durable goods such as cloth, mats, bracelets, rings, hoes, axes and hides were exchanged and hoarded until sufficient capital had been accumulated to buy tusks. The tusks could then be sold, subject to royal or chiefly supervision and taxation, to the Bisa. The main items acquired in return were cotton cloth, beads, and in some areas cattle. The Bisa used no guns in their penetration of Luba, either as trade-goods, or as a means of hunting elephants. They did not even have guns for their own protection, and relied instead on their stable relationship with the Luba rulers. Any attack on them would have been damaging to the new centralized commercial economy from which the Luba aristocracy was so greatly benefiting, and would therefore have been internally suppressed without use of Bisa arms. The advance of the Bisa trading front through the Lualaba–Lomami basin was preceded by the advance of a Luba political front. Pioneering chiefs moved into the virgin lands and arranged the purchase of ivory which they then transferred to central depots. They simultaneously created a more or less permanent Luba political superstructure. The Bisa followed behind, selling their cloth and beads in the new outposts of Luba frontier society.

The expansion of Luba was concentrated in the reigns of three great rulers. Ilunga Sunga (c. 1780–c. 1810) began the process with an unsuccessful attack on the Kalundwe in the west. Meeting strong resistance in that direction, he turned eastward and rapidly spread Luba influence over the region between the Lualaba and Lake Tanganyika. One of his sons, Kumwimba (c. 1810–c. 1840), carried Luba expansion still farther. He first of all conquered the Lualaba lakes and took over the rich fishing and palm oil industries. He then moved southwards to control the copper workings of the Samba. At the same time, in response to the continuing ivory trade, he consolidated Luba domination over the conquered eastern territories and created a new, north-eastern province in Manyema. By the time the Luba empire was at its height, under Ilunga Kalala (c. 1840–c. 1870), it was at the centre of a wide-ranging and varied international trade. In the east, oil and salt were brought across Lake Tanganyika from Ujiji in return for arrow poisons, drums and slaves. In the south-east the empire was linked to its main long distance customers via the Bisa. In the south-west a new link was developing with the Bihe–Lovale route, along which the Ovimbundu were carrying copper and slaves to the Atlantic. In the west Luba was in contact with Lunda through the Luba Kaniok kingdom. In the northwest an important trade including palm cloth, baskets, iron, zebra skins, and fish was carried on with the Songye and, through them, with peoples as far away as the Kuba.

About 1870 the economic and political growth of Luba began to weaken. In his study of the savanna kingdoms, Vansina attributed this decline of Luba to institutional instability, especially in the succession system. An open succession system, far from being a safeguard against the advent of incompetent rulers, appeared to be a major cause of weakness, leading to constant feuding between royal factions, and laying the country wide open to foreign interference through ready-made fifth columns. He saw a further weakness in the overwhelming importance of the king. The fortunes of empire appeared to fluctuate with the personality of the ruler, and no government seemed capable of compensating for the personal inadequacies of the king. This interpretation of Luba history in structural and personal terms may have been largely inspired by the nature of the historical evidence. Even in the nineteenth century this consists, for the most part, of oral chronicles, which inevitably lay emphasis on the exploits of great men, and blame national calamities on the deficiencies of weak ones. Such emphasis, however, may obscure some of the less visible changes, particularly in the economic sphere. During the period 1800 to 1870, there had, in fact, been only one great ruler in each generation and, although disputes and short reigns had intervened between these three great reigns, the overall pattern was one of growth and stability. What caused this pattern to change radically after 1870 was a fundamental change in the country's external relations. This had the effect of increasing internal dissension, but the structural defects which then became apparent were the consequences, and not the causes, of Luba decline.

A crucial factor in the decline of Luba was probably the exhaustion of its ivory supplies. So long as ivory was available, Luba maintained a stable working relationship with the foreign trading groups. By 1870 the most important of these were the Yeke-Nyamwezi in the south and the Swahili-Arabs from Ujiji in the north. When ivory became scarce, the Yeke-Nyamwezi concentrated increasingly on copper, and in the 1860s began to conquer the copper producing areas of chiefs Mpande and Katanga. Their success was increased by the first large-scale use of guns in the region. The creation of Msiri's state based on military power and direct exploitation, rather than trade, presented one major threat to Luba. A second and even more serious threat arose on the northern frontier among the Swahili-Arabs. These Swahili-Arabs had overtaken the Luba frontier of expansion, and were driving north into the forest in search of ivory by more direct means than state trading. Luba was then cut out from both the northern and the southern trading circuits. This situation of declining opportunity occurred just when Luba most urgently needed outside trade contacts to buy guns. These new weapons had suddenly become crucial for military survival. In the absence of any ivory to sell, the Luba attempted to buy guns with slaves. The traders, however, accepted slaves only at very low prices, and when nothing more profitable was available. Thus to get guns in the 1870s, Luba had rapidly to expand its slave trade, thereby causing a new set of problems. The empire was now enclosed, north and south, by strong, gun-using, trader-states, which prevented slave-seeking expansionist wars by the Luba. In fact, the roles were reversed, and Luba was in danger of becoming the raiding ground of others. In order to obtain slaves for sale, Luba rulers had to find them internally, thus causing new conflicts and tensions, and further damaging their declining authority. The result, during the 1870s and 1880s, was that Luba began to break up into warring factions, each faction trying to capture the kingship and re-establish authority where a previous ruler had failed. The more the country declined, however, the more it became prey to Yeke-Nyamwezi and Swahili-Arab slave raids. Eventually the Yeke kingdom of Garenganze in the south, and the Swahili-Arab kingdom of Nyangwe in the north, imposed foreign 'pacification' over the area they had so effectively disrupted. This domination by the new trader-states did not last long, however, and within a decade they were challenged, in their turn, by yet stronger and more determined traders, who took over their political and economic systems, and harnessed them to Leopold's Congo Independent State.[1]

The demise of the Luba-Lomami empire was closely matched by the decline and fall of the older and more influential empire of the *mwata yamvo* of Lunda. Until the 1870s Lunda had survived in strength and stability. But the forces of change crept closer during the century, and eventually removed both the western and the eastern spheres of influence. It was the Yeke who reduced the power of the *kazembe* in the east. The Chokwe did the same to the *mwata yamvo* in the west. With the final decline of the overseas slave trade, the kings of Lunda had sought alternative items of state trade such as wax, ivory and rubber, but each had proved a very temporary solution to the fundamental decline of export revenues. For a time the flow of slaves was reversed, as Lunda sold slaves eastward to the Luba in return for ivory, but this too was a short-lived phenomenon. The Chokwe continued to expand and increase their power at the great western market of Mona Kimbundu. As the *mwata yamvo* became unable to meet the expectations of even his closest supporters, factions arose to replace him and stem the catastrophic decline of the empire. One of these factions called in Chokwe mercenaries to support its cause. The result was but a temporary restoration of central power. Soon the Chokwe began to settle in central Lunda in increasing numbers. They overran the kingdom which, having lost its provinces to new gun-using trader-armies from east and west, now lost its capital as well.[2]

---

[1] Jan Vansina, *Kingdoms of the savanna* (Madison, 1966), 227–44; Anne Wilson, 'Long distance trade and the Luba Lomami empire', *Journal of African History*, 1972, **13**, 575–89.
[2] L. Duysters, 'Histoire des Aluunda', *Problèmes d'Afrique centrale*, 1958, **12**.

NORTHERN CENTRAL AFRICA

The history of the equatorial north is rather different from the history of the Central African savanna. Changes from the outside were slower to penetrate into the forest. By the nineteenth century, however, an increased tempo of change was being felt among all the peripheral peoples of the forest. In the west the forested segment of the Atlantic coast belatedly became a maritime trading sphere. In the south a whole complex of agricultural, commercial, and political changes began to percolate northward from the societies of the savanna. In the east an almost revolutionary set of explosions occurred, as Swahili-Arab traders broke into the forest in a desperate last effort to maintain their ivory trade. And finally in the north the centuries-old interaction between forest and woodland peoples was deeply affected by the military expansion of several savanna states.

In the huge central forests, where people were often scattered as thinly as three or four to five square kilometres, change remained slow. A shifting balance was maintained between three groups, the farmers, the fishermen and the nomadic hunters. There was, of course, some overlap in their activities, as farmers often hunted and fishermen sometimes farmed. There was also some interdependence, as when hunters bought grain or farmers bought fish. These occasional contacts, or even a more permanent, symbiotic, relationship between agriculturalists, and client hunters, did not, however, lead to the development of markets, trade routes, kingdoms, and to the regular, institutionalized communications which became so important to some peoples of the more favoured savanna. This lack of large states and absence of contacts with the outside world did not imply, as has sometimes been supposed, a complete stagnation or a lack of historical evolution. It did, however, mean that the galaxy of minute polities showed considerable diversity, as each village or group of villages evolved its own method of meeting the challenge of its environment. The rich variety of cultures was expressed not only in improved material possessions, but also in the sophisticated social structures developed to meet the needs of small-scale communities.

The most specialized of the forest peoples were the various Twa or Pygmy groups. In the nineteenth century they were probably declining as a proportion of the population, if not in absolute numbers, by gradual absorption into neighbouring societies. The first facet of their distinctive culture to be lost was apparently language, and by the twentieth century at least all surviving Pygmy groups spoke the Bantu or Central Sudanic languages of their agricultural neighbours. Evidence for a more wholesale shift from hunting and gathering to iron-age farming is difficult to obtain, but the process undoubtedly went on, and many forest farmers owed part of their cultural and demographic heritage to the Pygmies.

The second distinctive group to occupy part of the forest were the river-line fishermen. Small, stretched-out communities of fishing folk developed their specialized way of life along the Lualaba, the Ubangi, the Kasai and many other waterways of the Zaïre basin. Many of these communities remained inward-looking, but a few developed outward contacts on a growing scale. The Bobangi, in particular, mounted long distance expeditions by canoe. During these ventures they came into contact with other river peoples and acted as long distance commercial carriers. By this means contact was established between the Teke, and other savanna peoples of the lower Zaïre and Kasai, and the riverain peoples of the forest. By the late nineteenth century some waterways were carrying a heavy traffic in food and ivory.

By the nineteenth century the farmers probably outnumbered the hunters and fishermen in all but the densest forest, like that of the Ituri, or the most waterlogged river basins such as the Ngiri. Even at the heart of the forest region, the farmers were receptive to changes in crops and technology, as well as to new ideas about the management of small societies. The large and diverse Mongo nation, which occupied much of the low central land of the Zaïre basin, has clear folk memories of immigrants joining the society from the north over many generations. The Mongo pattern of succession and inheritance, which distinguishes them from their neighbours, may be a social trait introduced by immigrants. Although the peoples of this remotest forest heartland welcomed change, their remoteness militated against them. In addition their sparsity of population was probably not conducive to fostering such agricultural change as occurred, for instance, in the more populous Kasai region of the southern forest.

The best documented of the changes which influenced the periphery of nineteenth-century equatorial Africa occurred in the west. The forested segment of the Atlantic coast had had an altogether different history from that of West Africa or Angola during the slave trade era. In the far north, along the southern shore of the Bight of Biafra, lay an area which had been little favoured by seventeenth- and eighteenth-century traders. Dutch, English, and French vessels made occasional

visits to the coast, but no trading posts or ports were regularly established. As a result of this neglect by foreign traders, Cameroun was one
of the few parts of Africa with plentiful supplies of good quality ivory
near the coast. About 1800 ivory was fetching £240 a thousand kilograms in this area, the value being made up of fifteen thousand kilograms of salt, seventeen kegs of powder, fifty 'Tower' proof guns, ten
pieces of Indian 'baft', ten pieces of Indian 'romal', forty cheap
Manchester prints, twenty good-quality prints, two kegs of brandy,
thirty copper pots-and-pans, and a residual sum in beads, ironmongery,
crockery and cutlery. The superior quality of the ivory attracted increasing numbers of traders, but they found negotiating a delicate
business. The tastes and demands of the Duala merchants, and of their
inland suppliers, fluctuated disconcertingly with changing fashions. To
transact any business, gifts had to be given to the local trade prince, and
goods of the right variety and quality had to be offered for sale. Exces-
sive importations of any particular kind of cloth rapidly depressed its
price. Spirits formed a major part of the trade, but their sale involved
acrimonious bargaining, because of the common European practice of
adulterating the liquor.

The development of the ivory trade in Cameroun also brought
traders to the coast who were willing to deal in slaves. Although
Cameroun slaves had a reputation for being weak and sickly, the numbers exported in the early nineteenth century were rising, and the area
became important in the last stages of the trans-Atlantic traffic. Business
was further enhanced by the sale of palm oil, beeswax, ebony and red-
wood, so that as many as twenty-five ships at a time were sometimes
reported in the Cameroun estuary. The growth of trade had a markedly
divisive effect on the political structure of the Duala peoples who controlled it. The practice of paying 'comey' to the chief off whose shore a
ship anchored created strong incentives for each village, or even each
section of a village, to claim independence and the right to levy
'comey'. One major division occurred in Duala society in 1814, when
chief Mbele, known to the traders as King Bell, lost his dominant position and was faced with the rival kingdom of King Akwa. The two
kings dominated the estuary for a time, but the process of political
fission continued, and by 1861 there were at least three trade kings on
the estuary. It may be that 'secret' societies, such as Mikuka and
Bangolo, had become more important than the trade princes in controlling the Duala communities.

The survival and growth of the Cameroun slave trade had the effect of attracting official British interest to the Bight of Biafra from the 1820s, when efforts were being made to suppress the traffic. In 1827 a British naval base was established on the island of Fernando Po. A small settlement of freed slaves, similar to that of Freetown in Sierra Leone, grew up at Port Clarence, and in 1843 the Baptist Missionary Society arrived to care for the spiritual life of the recaptives. The mission also began to establish settlements on the Cameroun mainland and, under the guidance of Alfred Saker, Jackson Fuller and George Grenfell, the Baptists became the most important mission in the area until the German colonial occupation of 1884. While missionary influence grew, the British government also began appointing consuls for the Bight of Biafra to encourage mainland chiefs to outlaw the slave trade, and to promote a more 'honest' conduct of the 'legitimate' trade. The suppression efforts of Beecroft, Hutchinson and Burton were arduous, but slow-yielding. As late as 1861 a ship from Montevideo was caught buying 400 slaves in exchange for rum. Gradually, however, the export of palm oil rose to become the major commodity of Cameroun trade.

The trade of Cameroun used two forms of money as well as credit transactions. In transactions with inland suppliers and producers, the Duala calculated their prices with the copper manilla, a heavy open anklet. About twenty manillas were called a bar, a money of account worth about one quarter of a pound sterling. In transactions with Europeans, a different unit of account was used called the 'crew'. This consisted of a variable assortment of trade-goods, some of them large items, such as guns and powder kegs, and some measurable goods such as alcohol, cloth and metal. Although the crew was apparently linked to the price of a measure of palm oil, it could be used in any financial transaction; pilot dues, for instance, were measured in crews at the rate of one crew per metre of draught.

In addition to calculating 'prices', and to bargaining over quantities in an assortment of goods, traders also faced the difficult matter of negotiating credit. Credit was supplied by the ships, not by the Duala. Goods were unloaded, valued, and then despatched to the inland markets, while captains awaited their payment. If they were lucky, and got quick and full payment, they could hope for profits of 100 per cent and more. For those less lucky, the risks of this 'trust' system were high, and many ships suffered long hold-ups, or even lost the entrusted cargo altogether. The oil traders welcomed the appointment of British consuls, and the establishment of courts of equity, not only because they would reduce the competing slave trade, but also in the hope that they would assist in the recuperation of bad debts.[1]

Southward from Cameroun lay another area with a similar history. The coast of Gabon had been comparatively unimportant in the early centuries of European trade. It was of fairly difficult sailing access, and had only attracted the occasional vessel seeking ivory, wood or slaves. The Gabon hinterland was even more densely forested and thinly populated than that of Cameroun. Here too, however, the growing demand for ivory brought increased trade. The main trading people were the Mpongwe, living on the Gabon estuary. They were merchants, middlemen and commercial entrepreneurs, similar in many ways to the Duala. Each chief tried to control a slice of the trade. Here, too, the slave trade increased in the early nineteenth century, with the rise in general trading activity, and traders dealing with the Spanish-speaking Americans were especially prominent. One difference between Cameroun and Gabon was that in Gabon the French, rather than the English, took the official initiative in trying to suppress the slave trade and to increase the production of 'legitimate' commodities with which the Gabon peoples could earn their foreign exchange requirements. Despite the official contacts initiated by France, and the establishment in 1848 of Libreville, the French Freetown, trade was very much dominated by British interests before 1875; French industrial manufacturers were unable to compete with the cheap and plentiful cottons and metalwares brought in by the British, and also by the Americans. The growth of trade in ivory and wood was very slow in causing a decline in the slave trade. From the 1840s the slave trade shifted from the relatively well-patrolled Gabon estuary to the many creeks farther south, where vessels could hide and be supplied by small canoes carrying slaves through numerous waterways. Not until the 1860s did the real end of the slave trade set in.

In the early part of the century, the Gabon trade was conducted by a complex system of credit. This credit seems to have operated in two directions at once, thus giving maximum profit to the middlemen. The European traders landed their goods at the settlements of the Mpongwe trade princes such as King Denis and King Glass and then waited, sometimes a year or even eighteen months, while the goods were relayed by a system of multiple exchanges to sources of production in the interior. When the supply of ivory began to decline, the firms tried to stimulate it by increasing credit, but this tended to aggravate the delays. At the

[1] J. Bouchand, *La côte du Cameroun* (Paris, 1952).

same time that Europeans were supplying credit from the coast, ivory producers in the interior were apparently sending tusks to the coast also on credit. They too had to wait a long time for their profits and lost a percentage every time their tusk changed hands. This multiple exchange through a wide range of middlemen seems to have been temporarily reduced as the Mpongwe gained a monopolist grip on the trade routes. When they did so, however, their position as middlemen was rapidly challenged from both ends. From the interior it was challenged by the Fang expansion, and from the coast by the European penetration.

One of the most dramatic features in the nineteenth-century history of Cameroun and Gabon was the enormous and rapid expansion of the Fang peoples. In the eighteenth century the Fang, Bulu and Beti had lived in the Sanaga region of eastern Cameroun near the northern border of Bantu speech. They seem to have come under pressure from raiders in the north such as the Bamum, the Chamba and, by the mid-nineteenth century, the Fulani of Adamawa. This pressure set in motion a series of leap-frogging migrations towards the south, into the Cameroun and Gabon forests. These migrations, in which each village moved a few miles at a time, in a manner similar to the contemporaneous Chokwe migrations in the south, eventually led to the colonization of a large section of the western equatorial forest by twenty or so culturally and linguistically related groups. The area they occupied seems previously to have been scantily populated. This may have been due to a reduction of population, caused perhaps by the slow drain of the slave trade, or by the introduction of such diseases as smallpox and sleeping sickness. Alternatively the dense forest may have not previously been attractive to agriculturalists and hunters, who preferred the forest margin when this was not threatened by savanna raiders. The advance parties of the Fang dispersion seem to have been capable hunters, and by the 1840s they were trading ivory for guns with the Gabon estuary. The acquisition of guns, and the new profitability of ivory-hunting, speeded the Fang advance towards the Gabon estuary and Ogowe river, thus severely restricting the Mpongwe sphere of influence.

The second major change in Gabon came in the 1860s and 1870s when three new developments occurred. Firstly, the credit system on which the old trade was based broke down. Secondly, Europeans, notably Paul du Chaillu, began to explore the interior of Gabon for themselves, and discovered direct access to the commercial hinterland.

Thirdly, ivory became exhausted and rubber became the major export. These three developments were closely related to one another. The Ogowe basin had several advantages as a source of rubber. Slaves, no longer in much demand for export, could be used to collect the rubber, which then reached the coast by the well-established river transport system. Canoe carriage made rubber and timber profitable export commodities, even though they were only worth about one-twentieth of the value of ivory. European firms therefore began setting up trading posts along the rivers and used the Mpongwe as hired agents. Trade was further increased by experiments in ground-nut and palm oil trading. The French, however, remained minor participants in the new commercial growth, and by the early 1870s were on the point of abandoning their settlements altogether. They never took such an active step, however, and within a decade Gabon was becoming a prized colony in France's Equatorial African empire.

One of the notable features of Gabon was the absence of any large political systems. None of the peoples, least of all the Fang, had administrative structures covering more than a single village or a group of adjacent villages. South of the Gabon the situation was different, and some of the people of the upper Ogowe and of the coastlands conducted trade with the Teke and Loango kingdoms north of the Zaïre river.[1]

The lower Zaïre area, athwart the southern boundary of the forest, was a much older area of external trade than Gabon. In the three centuries before 1790, slaving had gradually expanded from the Zaïre estuary, not only southward into Angola and eastward into the Kwango and Kasai basins, but also northward along the Loango coast. In the Loango kingdom which had come to dominate that coast in the seventeenth century, a growing dependence on the slave trade had had a number of effects. Firstly, it had led to the development of a large local population of slaves, who formed the basis of wealth in the kingdom. The more slaves a chief owned, the more land it was possible to cultivate and the higher his economic and social standing became. Secondly, the development of trade had meant that officers such as the Mafouk, who were responsible for trade negotiations, had become enormously powerful, usually at the expense of the monarchy. Thus the traditional structure of a great political and religious king supported by a large royal family was subverted. The power of the king was reduced,

---

[1] H. Deschamps, *Quinze ans de Gabon* (Paris, 1965). P. Alexandre, 'Proto-histoire Beti-Bulu-Fang', *Cahiers d'études africaines*, 1965, 5. H. Brunschwig, *Brazza explorateur* (Paris, 1966).

the pattern of succession was disrupted, and power shifted in fact, if not in theory, to the commercial officials and the slave-owning agricultural aristocrats. This pattern, with a weak nominal king and a range of powerful notables, apparently survived until the colonial period. From the 1860s the slave trade from the interior no longer supplied overseas markets but met the Loango demand for 'domestic' slaves.[1]

The south side of the Zaïre river, once the centre of the Kongo kingdom, had, by the nineteenth century, long since ceased to be a single empire. The royal dynasty still reigned in São Salvador, and was still revered in a spiritual way by many Kongo peoples. It held no political authority, however, beyond the confines of the village-capital, and the Kongo people were no longer even recognized as a single 'tribe', but were seen as three separate peoples, the Mussorongo in the north-west, the Mushikongo in the centre and the Zonbo in the east. Among these peoples a certain amount of European cultural influence survived; the 'kings' had to be crowned by a Christian missionary, and often went to considerable pains to obtain one from neighbouring Angola. Literacy and a knowledge of Portuguese were also significant among the various Kongo peoples, and in 1856 Alfredo de Sarmento was allowed to inspect the important royal archives, which were still being maintained. From the documents, he compiled a list of the twenty-eight kings who had reigned in the 200 years since the battle of Ambuila. These archives were unfortunately destroyed by fire towards the end of the century.

Although the Kongo region no longer represented a recognizable political entity, it remained an area of important trading activity. In the north, the Zaïre river was a favoured slaving area until the 1870s. The many creeks and islands made clandestine traffic easier than on the open coast, and the rapid current helped sailing vessels to get away quickly beyond the range of the coastal squadron. Boma was an important centre for receiving the slave caravans, which arrived loaded with cassava and beans to feed the waiting slaves in the barracoons. Monteiro, who studied the working of the slave trade in the 1860s, attributed its survival to three causes. The first was drought and famine, which caused subsistence communities to reduce the pressure of population by the short-term, but short-sighted, expedient of selling members of the community. The second factor was a judicial system which had come to make enslavement the punishment for even minor offences; this punishment was sometimes meted out not only to the

[1] Phyllis M. Martin, *The external trade of the Loango coast* (London, 1972).

offender but also to his family. A twisting of the judicial system to benefit chiefs in their capacity as judges, was a widespread effect of the slave trade. The third cause of the survival of extensive slavery was thought by Monteiro to be the widespread belief in witchcraft. Disease, death and other misfortunes were commonly thought to be caused by witches who had to be condemned. This belief may have been heightened by outbreaks of smallpox, and by the nineteenth-century spread of sleeping sickness from the Gabon coast.[1] These secondary factors, which facilitated slave trading, were of course all subordinate to the fact that the price of labour in the Atlantic basin remained higher than the price of any commodity which the lower Zaïre could produce. By the 1870s, however, the price of labour had fallen, and the operation of a free market had been broken by the European political decision to stop the slave trade. Both African and European traders had to seek new avenues.

The British and Dutch seem to have been most successful in diversifying their trade, and by the 1870s were sending half a million pounds' worth of European goods to the lower Zaïre each year for legitimate purchases. This trade was believed to be rapidly increasing, so that by the early 1880s British trade with the Zaïre was of comparable significance to that with the Niger. The main exports were palm oil and palm kernels, but a number of other trade items were encouraged. Ground-nuts were exported both from the river and from the coast. Coffee was grown in the Ndembu region north-east of Luanda and exported via the Zaïre coast to avoid Portuguese duty. Ivory was brought to the coast by Zombo traders from the Kwango regions, and some vine rubber was being produced by 1875. Red gum and white gum were produced and exported. Attempts were made to found mining companies to take over the Bembe copper mines, but both a Brazilian and a British company failed to compete successfully with traditional small-scale methods of extracting the malachite. The caravans reaching the coast were paid in local produce, notably salt and dried fish, as well as in imported cloth, manillas and other manufactures. Several thousand heavy flintlock muskets were imported each year and were very popular; although used with minimal skill, the noise of a large, overloaded musket was a major factor in deciding the outcome of village warfare. The Sorongo, who carried out a profitable piracy at the Zaïre mouth, were also able to mount small cannons on canoes to very good effect.

[1] J. J. Monteiro, *Angola and the river Congo*, 2 vols. (London, 1875).

Eastward from the lower Zaïre was the lower Kasai basin, a populous area of grass-covered hills and forested valleys, which much impressed the European explorers and colonizers of the 1870s and 1880s. The area was ethnically very fragmented, as shown in the previous chapter of this book. Some peoples, such as the Yaka and the Pende, had been brought under a form of unitary government by immigrant Lunda chiefs. Others, notably the Kuba, were governed by their own system of kingship. Others again were divided into independent chiefdoms and villages. These mainly lived at a self-sufficient subsistence level, with little regional or external trade. Typical, perhaps, were the Lulua at the heart of the Kasai basin.

The Lulua included substantial numbers of Luba immigrants among their number and some of their chiefs may have been of Lunda origin, although they did not recognize the supremacy of the *mwata yamvo*. These chiefs constantly disputed seniority among themselves. Their wealth was based on the tribute of their subjects who brought gifts of food, game-meat and craftsmanship in filial duty. In return they gave presents or held a feast with music and dancing. The rich agriculture was already based on the American crops, cassava and maize, supplemented with more nutritious crops such as ground-nuts and palm oil. The Lulua also grew and smoked tobacco and hemp. They were efficient artisans, ironworkers, weavers, potters and builders. Until about 1870 the Lulua peoples apparently produced nothing which was directly aimed at the export market. They were too far removed from the savanna markets to organize a transport system which could realize new economic potentials. A certain amount of indirect filtration of foreign goods may have reached them, as they reached their Kuba neighbours, from the trading areas of the lower Zaïre, or from Lunda, but only after about 1870 were they brought into the Central African caravan trading network. One opening was created by the arrival of Chokwe caravans, who established an important market at Kalamba.

The first item of trade to be exported from the Kasai was of course ivory. It was sold not only to the Chokwe, but also to Portuguese traders from Malanje. The Portuguese obtained contract porters from the Nzinga chiefs inside Angola. These carriers were bound to the expedition for its duration, which might be several years. Lopes de Carvalho and Saturnino de Souza Machado, for instance, travelled widely, storing goods in well-guarded camps, and only returned occasionally to Angola to sell their accumulated ivory. They carried with them salt, cloth and beads, which they traded for local valuables includ-

ing copper crosses and young women, until they had acquired a sufficiently attractive range of goods to buy ivory. In one transaction
Carvalho paid two children, five copper crosses, 5,000 cowries and 200
Venetian beads for a slightly damaged tusk. The Kasai ivory trade did
not flourish long, however, and within a few years the local supply was
exhausted. The Lulua began fetching it from their neighbours the
Songye, but very soon they ran up against the Swahili-Arab ivory-
hunting frontier. They thus became trapped in the same way that the
Luba had. The rapidly rising expectations of the people, and more
especially of the chiefs, had been met entirely by capitalizing on wasting
assets. When ivory was exhausted they were driven to seek desperate
alternatives. One of these was slaves.

At Kalamba, in the 1870s, a slave sold for sixteen metres of calico,
or six kilograms of gunpowder, or a musket. The majority of slaves
were women and children bought for resale within Africa. Many communities could afford to buy slave-women once the high-priced competition from the Atlantic coast had been removed. Only at this late
date did the trade introduce muskets on a large scale. This led to a
demand for powder, and a charge of gunpowder – measuring about
three thimbles – became a unit of currency. It could be used for the
purchase of food and household goods and for the valuation of export
commodities. The third export to develop from the Kasai was rubber,
sold in piles of 100 balls. The rubber was of good quality, and relatively
unadulterated, but inflation rapidly set in and the weight of the balls
shrank to only twenty-five grams in a few years. This rubber trade
eventually caused great hardship in the Zaïre basin. Just when the
supply was becoming scarce, and chiefs were desperate to extract
additional export revenue, a new political factor was introduced into
the situation: the Congo Independent State took over the government
of the Lulua. It used force on a wide and systematic scale to impose
compulsory rubber collecting by its subjects.[1]

Beyond the Kasai, in the far eastern part of the Zaïre forest, people
remained untouched by the growing turbulence of long distance trade
until very late in the pre-colonial period. When external influences did
penetrate, however, they had even more violent consequences than in
the west. Trade was introduced by Swahili-Arabs whose ivory supply
in the upper Lualaba basin had become exhausted. This, as has been
shown, led to severe disruption among the southern Luba, as traders
and chiefs resorted to slave trading and gun running to maintain their

[1] C. S. L. Bateman, *The first ascent of the Kasai* (London, 1889).

economic status. In the north, the Swahili-Arabs decided to move on to new ground and brave the dangers of the forest, in the hope that the rewards would more than compensate for their losses. They recruited local armies and began attacking forest communities, taking prisoners either for sale elsewhere or to be locally ransomed for ivory. On his great trans-African journey, Stanley hired Tippu Tip and his mercenaries to accompany him down the Lualaba towards the Zaïre river proper. Within five years Tippu's men had blazed a trail of destruction almost as far as Stanley Falls. When the Swahili-Arab progress down-river was stopped by the return of Stanley as Leopold's colonizing agent, they turned eastward and penetrated the forests of the Aruwimi basin, wreaking further havoc, but finding new riches of ivory.

To complete this survey one must look finally at the far north of Central Africa. During the nineteenth century, this area was affected by three different sets of external influences. The first, from the west, was the invasion of Fulani pastoralists from Nigeria, who set up the emirate of Adamawa in central Cameroun. The history of this great equestrian dynasty belongs more properly to the history of West Africa, but the consequences of its slave raids and conquests were felt deep into the south and east. Refugees fell back into the Cameroun forest, and victims were rounded up by raiding horsemen on the eastern plains of the Central African Republic. The second external influence in the northern woodland was the 'Arab' slave-raiding from the states on the southern side of the Sahara. By the end of the nineteenth century the raiders had reached the Ubangi river, and slaves from the Zaïre forest were being brought up by canoe to the departure points for the Sahara crossing. Finally the third external influence was the ivory trade from Khartoum. The Khartoumers employed a system of raids and ransoms which was not dissimilar to Tippu Tip's exploitation on the other side of the forest. Unlike him, however, they had not penetrated very far into the forest before the whole ivory-raiding system was brought to an end by the colonial partition. The southward advance of the Khartoumers was, moreover, delayed by the organized resistance of the Mangbetu kingdom on the Uele river.

The upper Uele basin, in the north-eastern corner of Central Africa, was rich agricultural farmland comparable to the banana groves of the East African lake region. The closely-settled Mangbetu practised agriculture of a quality not seen in the millet-growing plains of the northern savanna. Their plantains thrived with a minimal investment of labour, and were supplemented by crops of American origin, including excellent maize and cassava. They practised almost no animal husbandry, but received game-meat from client groups of Pygmies. Mangbetu smiths produced a sophisticated range of spears, swords, scimitars, adzes, knives and cutlasses, which they sold to their less skilled neighbours. They also manufactured jewelry out of copper brought in rough rings from Hofrat en Nahas in Darfur. The Mangbetu had a more extensive and centralized form of government than any of their neighbours either in the southern forest or in the northern Sudan belt. The king received regular tribute from his people, and held court in a royal complex occupied by his wives, courtiers and retainers, which reminded a European visitor of the great Lunda capital. In the late 1860s King Munza, after demonstrating his military power, was able to receive the first Khartoum ivory traders peacefully and on his own terms. This advent of foreign traders, however, rapidly turned sour on him, and the Mangbetu, like the Luba on the opposite side of the forest, were undermined by increasing numbers of gun-using traders. The garden-land of the upper Uele became a scene of violence and destruction, and the Mangbetu were unable to preserve their prosperity and independence.[1]

To the north and west of the Mangbetu and of their Central Sudanic neighbours, stretched a huge belt of eastern Niger–Congo peoples of rather different cultural origins. Among these were the Baya, Banda, Ngbandi and Azande. The bulk of these peoples lived in the open woodland, but some had colonized the forest margins, and a few had even migrated farther south and been absorbed into Bantu societies. In the late eighteenth century some of these eastern Niger–Congo peoples began to be conquered by Azande dynasties, of the Avungara clan, who spread eastward towards the headwaters of the north Zaïre basin and the Nile watershed. The conquerors sought new land, new rivers, new hunting grounds, and new subject peoples to be adopted and acculturated. The Avungara political system, although it grew rapidly during the nineteenth century, did not retain any cohesion, but fragmented into rival factions at each generation. By the 1870s there were numerous Azande kingdoms, each ruled by proud Avungara chiefs. These chiefs, however, were quite unable to resist the challenge of the Khartoum ivory traders, who rapidly spread into their territories. The traders developed an almost permanent state of war with the Azande, whom they greatly feared for their alleged cannibalism, and whom they consequently called the Niam-Niams.

[1] Georg Schweinfurth, *The heart of Africa*, 2 vols. (London, 1873).

In the region west of the Azande, another powerful clan, the Bandia, launched itself on an expansive career of conquest and state-building. The Bandia were of Ngbandi origin, and for some centuries had been spreading eastward up the Ubangi valley. Late in the eighteenth century they founded three or four kingdoms in areas they had colonized, and whose culture they had partially absorbed. The most powerful of these seems to have been the kingdom of Bangassou, founded among the riverain Nzakara whose old ruling clan was replaced by a new Bandia dynasty. Bangassou soon came into contact with the traders of the central Sudan. Whereas the fragmented, acephalous peoples of the Ubangi were unable to organize either resistance or co-operation, Bangassou was able to negotiate with slave dealers from a position of strength. The Bandia became prosperous middlemen, but only male slaves were sold to the trans-Saharan traders, since women and children could not survive the long overland journey to the north. Women captives were retained by the Bandia rulers, and played an important role in building the prosperity and population of their kingdoms. Sparseness of population was a major economic and political weakness among all Ubangi peoples, and the success of the Bandia, like that of the Chokwe in the south, was in large measure due to their absorption of additional people, and particularly of women who could enhance the demographic growth rate. Thus the Bangassou 'sultanate' flourished in the nineteenth century, while all around it the northern woodland was sparsely occupied by small, isolated, frightened villages of eastern Niger–Congo peoples, cowed under the shadow of the slave trade.[1]

CONCLUSIONS

The long-term significance of nineteenth-century development in Central Africa remains hard to judge. The real achievements in the economic and political management of small or medium societies were obscured, firstly by the destruction associated with the scramble for ivory and slaves, and secondly by the imposition of European rule. The destructiveness of the ivory trade, especially in its terminal stages, has been emphasized in the foregoing pages. The rising tide of violence, which began with the old Atlantic slave trade, increased rather than abated with the development of the ivory trade, and embroiled many more of the peoples of Central Africa, even into the heart of the forest. All peoples became accustomed to treating strangers as hostile. The

[1] Eric de Dampierre, *Un ancien royaume Bandia du Haut-Oubangui* (Paris, 1967).

violence was compounded by the gun trade as manufacturers and dealers sought outlets for their weapons in a period of rapidly advancing technology. The advent of colonial rule did not always bring an alleviation of the widespread suffering. The early colonial period in Central Africa was harsh and exploitative to a degree unmatched in the rest of Africa. It did, admittedly, see a suppression of the gun traffic. But French, Belgians and Portuguese all used extensive forced labour, and all surrendered part of their colonial sovereignty to concessionary companies, which were subject to few of the constraints imposed on democratically elected metropolitan governments. In the south-east corner of Central Africa, the peoples of modern Zambia, although also under chartered company rule, may have fared a little better and been subjected to less extreme forms of physical brutality and degradation. In all four regions, nevertheless, much individual hardship was suffered through labour-recruiting methods. The sparsity of population meant that labourers were taken to remote regions for long periods of time. To the victim, this contract labour often appeared very similar to the old nineteenth-century slavery. This was especially so in the case of labourers sent to the island plantations of São Tomé, whence they rarely returned.

The positive legacies of the nineteenth century became deeply hidden in the early decades of the colonial period. The economic achievements of Central Africans had represented real advances in the exploitation of their natural resources. Local economic networks throughout the southern savanna, and in the more accessible parts of the forest, were linked to the major commercial highways, so that produce from even remote parts of Africa began to reach world markets. Local economies were enhanced by increased consumption of traded commodities like salt, copper ornaments and textiles. In some areas, an expanding economic activity was matched by a growing political structure, which brought new forms of political integration to a formerly fragmented area. In the last quarter of the nineteenth century, however, these economic and political systems suddenly seemed inadequate to meet the challenge of outside economic enterprise and outside political ambition. The weaknesses which underlay the sudden loss of African initiative and the assumption of control by Europeans were many. Foremost, perhaps, was the inability of unaided African enterprise to evolve more efficient methods of bulk transport than caravan porterage. Railways and river steamers gave Europeans the economic means to compete profitably with traditional caravanning. Their military technology gave them the political means to compete with African kings and, more significantly perhaps, with the Arab and Swahili trade-princes whose power had been growing so rapidly in the last pre-colonial decades. As the Belgians advanced into Zaïre, as the Portuguese turned their trading posts into a colony, and as French and British companies staked out their claims, it seemed that the achievements of the past would count for nothing. All that went before was deemed irrelevant by the colonizers, and, all too often, by the colonized as well. But the legacy of business acumen and political ability was not totally submerged. Central Africans slowly found out that the small man could adapt, and could challenge the colonial monolith, the private lorry driver could compete with the international railway company, and the small retailer could thrive in conjunction with the foreign wholesaler. Although this African re-awakening was slower in Central Africa than in West Africa, or even East Africa, it did occur. Gradually the dismissal of the past was reversed and the old skills were adapted to the new circumstances in resistance, in co-operation and finally in re-emergence.

BIBLIOGRAPHICAL NOTE AND
FURTHER READING

An historian wishing to pursue his interest in Central Africa faces a series of hurdles. The first is linguistic. Central Africa is divided into one hundred or more cultural zones, each with a language of its own. Local historical experience is abundantly shared within each community, but neighbours are all too often excluded. The region has not one history but a hundred histories, each told in a different tongue. The modern historian who wants to bridge several societies and piece together a broad picture needs patience and skill. During the past hundred years a rising number of such specialists have published their interpretations, and it is on their work that this story has been based.

The most famous of the dedicated antiquarians to whom young scholars owe a debt was perhaps Dais de Carvalho. In 1890, after extensive travels and research, he published eight stout volumes on the Lunda people, their language, their culture, their economy, their history and their empire. Several works attempted to follow this path, Verhulpen on the Luba, van der Kerken on the Mongo, but none were on so comprehensive a scale.

The second source for Central African history is the rich range of writings by European travellers who explored its shores, its river lines, its trade paths, in the four hundred years after 1483. These sources present another linguistic problem. They are written in a dozen or more European languages. The famous seventeenth-century missionary history of Father Cavazzi is written in Italian. The forty-year war diaries of Antonio de Cadornega were scrawled in Portuguese. The great compendium of geographical reports edited by Olfert Dapper was written in Dutch. One of Central Africa's most determined explorers, Ladislaus Magyar, published his nineteenth-century diaries in German and Hungarian. Despite this proliferation of languages a few important works have been published in English. In the last twenty years of the sixteenth century Andrew Battell worked as a boatman for the Portuguese, and travelled widely with African armies as a prisoner-of-war, before retiring to Essex to dictate a most remarkable diary to his literate village vicar. Three centuries later J. J. Monteiro published his two travel volumes on Angola and the river Congo. The most famous work in English, however, is the missionary travelogue of David Livingstone who crossed Central Africa to reach the city of Luanda over land in 1854. His account of the early colonial communities in West Central Africa is as revealing as his reports on the African communities he visited.

The third source of ideas and evidence which historians can use and fruitfully reinterpret is the extensive scholarly literature published during the two generations in which Central Africa was ruled by colonial governments. This evidence also presents problems of language. Colonial Central Africa was partitioned four ways into French, Belgian Portuguese and British spheres. The historical, ethnographical and documentary materials of the period were usually published in the language of the colonial occupier. The works of the Angola missionary-anthropologists Gladwyn Childs and Carlos Estermann are exceptional in being available in English. Those who read French will profit greatly from the pioneering works of Louis Jadin on pre-colonial documentary history. Historians were not common in colonial Africa, though Ralph Delgado did publish a four-volume history of Angola. Despite the dearth of specialists the Belgians brought out a dictionary of colonial biography, and J. Bouchard wrote a history of Cameroun. Some history can be gleaned from the works of anthropologists like Max Gluckman in the British sphere and of geographers like Giles Sautter in the French sphere. One valuable part of the colonial tradition of scholarship was the translating and editing of historical texts. Two of the most meticulous examples are Ian Cunnisons' translation of the nineteenth-century travels of Gamitto to the Kazembe kingdom in Zambia, and Willy Bal's edition of Pigafetta's sixteenth-century description of the kingdom of Kongo in Angola.

The 1960s and the end of colonial rule brought an increase in historical writing. In *Kingdoms of the savanna* Jan Vansina surveyed the southern savanna. David Birmingham in *Trade and Conflict in Angola* explored the Portuguese archives for their African content. Englebert Mveng of Cameroun published the first Central African national history, *Histoire du Cameroun*. Eric de Dampierre finished his analysis of the Bangassou sultanate, *Un ancien royaume Bandia du Haut-Oubangui*, and Roger Anstey discussed nineteenth-century British trading enterprise in the region, *Britain and the Congo in the nineteenth century*.

The most original work on the history of Central Aftica has been the fruit of the new scholarship of the 1970s. This fertile decade brought striding advances both in historical method and in historical material, which are of much more than regional importance. The broadest recent survey of later prehistory is David Phillipson's book *The later prehistory of Eastern and Southern Africa*. Although mainly concerned with regions further east, it illuminates many questions of the Central Africa Iron Age. Pierre de Maret's thesis, *Chronologie de l'age du fer dans la depression de l'Upemba*, minutely explores the cultures of the upper Zaïre lakes. On to this interpretation of material evidence it is possible to graft several new works on oral tradition. Miller's pathbreaking study *Kings and kinsmen* has been followed by a set of essays on oral history, entitled *The African past speaks*. Andrew Roberts, *A history of the Bemba*, and Mutumba Mainga *Buloẓi under the Luyana kings*, are local histories of eastern and western Zambia, examining the rise of two important but very different states. Roberts has followed this up with the most comprehensive national history so far published for a Central African country, *A history of Zambia*. Two studies of coastal areas by David Patterson, *The northern Gabon coast to 1875*, and Phyllis Martin, *The external trade of the Loango coast 1576–1870*, have brought new sophistication to the analysis of economic interaction between Europe and Africa. Three very contrasted works have illuminated the role of the Portuguese in Angola. *Angola under the Portuguese: the myth and the reality* by Gerard Bender concentrates on the ideology of colonialism. In *Les Guerres grises* Réne Pélissier focusses on the patterns of African resistance. Gervase Clarence-Smith's work *Slaves, peasants and capitalists in Southern Angola 1840–1926* analyses the southern colonial economy. The latest works on the Zaïrean interior are the study of the great river traffic by Bob Harms, *The river of sorrows*, and Jan Vansina's history of the related Tio peoples, *The Tio kingdom of the middle Congo*. Vansina has also returned to the study of the Kuba of the southern forest and in *The children of Woot* magisterially revised his work of the 1950s. The great Luba empire has been re-examined by Thomas Q. Reefe, *The rainbow and the kings: a history of the Luba empire to 1891*. Finally, Birmingham and Martin are preparing a two-volume *History of Central Africa* in which seventeen authors have collaborated.

BIBLIOGRAPHY

Alexandre, P. 'Proto-histoire du groupe Beti-Bulu-Fang: essai de synthèse provisoire', *Cahiers d'études africaines*, 1965, 5, 4 (20), 503-60.

Almeida, F.J.M. de Lacerda e. *Travessia da Africa*. Lisbon, 1936.

Angola. *Catalogo dos Governadores do Reino de Angola*. Lisbon, 1825.

Anstey, R.T. *Britain and the Congo in the nineteenth century*. London, 1962.

Ardener, E.W. '. . . Trading polities between Rio del Rey and Cameroons 1500-1650', in Lewis, I.M., ed. *History and social anthropology*. London, 1968.

Arquivos de Angola. Review published occasionally since 1933 in Luanda.

Axelson, S. *Culture confrontation in the lower Congo*. Uppsala, 1970.

Bal, W. ed. *Description du royaume de Congo et des contrées environnantes par Filippo Pigafetta et Duarte Lopez* [1591]. Paris, 1963.

Bal, W. *Le royaume du Congo aux XVe et XVIe siècles*. Leopoldville, 1963.

Balandier, G. *La vie quotidienne au royaume du Congo du XVIe au XVIIIe siècle*. Paris, 1965. English tr. 1968.

Bastin, M.-L. *L'art décoratif Tschokwe*. Lisbon, 1961.

Bateman, C.S.L. *The first ascent of the Kasai*. London, 1889.

Battell, A. *see* Ravenstein, E.G. ed. *The strange adventures of Andrew Battell*. London, 1901.

Bender, G.J. *Angola under the Portuguese: the myth and the reality*. London, 1978.

Biebuyck, D. 'Fondements de l'organisation politique des Lunda du Mwaan-tayaav en territoire de Kapanga', *Zaïre*, 1957, 11, 8, 787-817.

Biographie coloniale Belge. Bruxelles, 1948-56. 5 vols.

Birmingham, D. *Trade and conflict in Angola: the Mbundu and their neighbours under the influence of the Portuguese, 1483-1790*. Oxford, 1966.

Birmingham, D. 'Early African trade in Angola and its hinterland', in *Pre-colonial African trade*, eds. Gray and Birmingham, London, 1970.

Birmingham, D. *A conquista portuguesa de Angola*. Lisbon, 1974.

Birmingham, D. and Martin, P.M. eds. *History of Central Africa*. 2 vols. Longman (in preparation).

Bohannan, P. and Dalton, G. eds. *Markets in Africa*. Evanston, 1962.

Bontinck, F. ed. *Brève relation de la fondation de la mission des Frères Mineurs capucins . . . au royaume de Congo*. Louvain, 1964.

Bontinck, F. ed. *Diaire Congolais de Fra Luca da Caltanisetta, 1690–1701.* Louvain, 1970.

Bontinck, F. ed. 'Histoire du Royaume de Congo (c. 1624)', *Études d'histoire africaine,* 1972, **4.**

Bouchaud, J. *La côte du Cameroun dans l'histoire et la cartographie des origines à l'annexion allemande* (1884). Douala, 1952.

Boxer, C.R. *Salvador de Sá and the struggle for Brazil and Angola 1602–1886.* London, 1952.

Boxer, C.R. *Race relations in the Portuguese colonial empire.* Oxford, 1963.

Boxer, C.R. *The Dutch seaborne empire 1600–1800.* London, 1965.

Boxer, C.R. *Portuguese society in the tropics.* Madison, 1965.

Boxer, C.R. *The Portuguese seaborne empire 1415–1825.* London, 1969.

Brásio. A. *Monumenta Missionária Africana: Africa Ocidental* (1st series). Lisbon, 1952 onwards.

Brásio, A. *Angola.* Pittsburgh and Louvain, 1966–71. 5 vols.

Brunschwig, H. *Brazza explorateur: l'Ogooué, 1875–1879.* Paris, 1966.

Burton, R.F. *The lands of Cazembe.* London, 1873.

Cadornega, A. de Oliveira de. *História geral das guerras Angolanas,* eds. M. Delgado and A. da Cunha. Lisbon, 1940–2. 3 vols.

Carvalho, H.A. Dias de. *Expedição ao muatiânvua: ethnographia e história tradicional dos povos da Lunda.* Lisbon, 1890.

Carvalho, H.A. Dias de. *O Jagado de Cassange na Provincia de Angola.* Lisbon, 1898.

Cavazzi, G.A. *Istorica descrizione de tre regni Congo, Matamba et Angola.* Bologna, 1687. Portuguese ed. Lisbon, 1965. 2 vols.

Childs, G.M. *Umbundu kinship and character.* London, 1949. Reprinted as *Kinship and character of the Ovimbundu.*

Childs, G.M. 'The kingdom of Wambu (Huambo): a tentative chronology', *Journal of African History,* 1964, **5,** 367–79.

Clarence-Smith, W.G. *Slaves, peasants and capitalists in Southern Angola 1840–1926.* Cambridge, 1979.

Cordeiro, L. *Questóes histórico-coloniais.* Lisbon, 1935–6. 3 vols.

Corrêa, E.A. da Silva. *História de Angola* (Collecção dos Classicos da Expansão Portuguesa no mundo, E). Lisbon, 1937.

Couto, C. *Os Capitães-Mores em Angola no século XVIII.* Luanda, 1972.

Cunnison, I. 'Kazembe and the Portuguese', *Journal of African History,* 1961, **2,** 1, 61–76.

Curtin, P. *The Atlantic slave trade.* Madison, 1969.

Cuvelier, J. *L'ancien royaume de Congo.* Brussels, 1946.

Cuvelier, J. *Documents sur une mission française au Kakongo, 1766–1776.* Brussels, 1953.

Cuvelier, J. and Jadin, L. *L'ancien Congo d'après les archives romaines, 1518–1640.* Brussels, 1954.

Dampierre, E. de. *Un ancien royaume Bandia du Haut-Oubangui.* Paris, 1967.

Davidson, B. *Black mother.* London, 1961.

Davies, K.G. *The Royal African Company 1672–1713.* London, 1957.

Degrandpré, L. *Voyage à la côte occidentale d'Afrique faits dans les années 1786 et 1787.* Paris, 1801. 2 vols.

Delgado, R. *A famosa e histórica Benguela*. Lisbon, 1940.

Delgado, R. *História de Angola*. Benguela and Lobito, 1948–55. 4 vols.

Delgado, R. 'O Governo de Souza Continho em Angola', *Studia*, 1960–2.

Deschamps, H. *Quinze ans de Gabon: les débuts de l'établissement français, 1839–1853*. Paris, 1965.

Dias, G.S. *Os Portugueses em Angola*. Lisbon, 1959.

Duysters, L. 'Histoire des Aluunda', *Problèmes de l'Afrique Centrale*, 1958, **12,** 75–81.

Estermann, C. *Etnografia do sudoeste de Angola*. Lisbon, 1956–61. 3 vols. (Later translated into English and French.)

Fagan, B.M. and others. *Iron Age cultures in Zambia*. London, 1967, 1969, 2 vols.

Faria, F.L. de. ed. *Uma relacão de Rui de Pinã sôbre o Congo escrita em 1492*. Lisbon, 1966.

Felner, A.A. *Angola*. Coimbra, 1933.

Felner, A.A. *Angola: apontamentos sôbre a colonização dos planaltos e litoral do Sul de Angola*. Lisbon, 1940. 3 vols.

Flint, E. 'Trade and politics in Barotseland during the Kololo period', *Journal of African History*, 1970, **11,** 1, 71–86.

Gamitto, A.C.P. *King Kazembe*, tr. I. Cunnison. Lisbon, 1960. 2 vols.

Garlake, P.S. 'Iron Age sites in the Urungwe district of Rhodesia', *South African Archaeological Bulletin*, 1971, **25,** 24–44.

Graça, J.R. 'Expedição ao Muatayanvua', *Boletim da Sociedade de Geografia de Lisboa*, 1890, **9.**

Gray, R. and Birmingham, D. eds. *Pre-colonial African trade*. London, 1970.

Guerreiro, F. *Relação annual das coisas que fizeram os padres da Companhia de Jesus* . . . 2nd ed. Coimbra, 1930–42. 3 vols.

Harms, R. *The river of sorrows*. New Haven, 1981.

Haveaux, G.L. *La tradition historique des Bapende orientaux*. Brussels, 1954.

Hiernaux, J., Longrée, E. de. and Buyst, J. de. *Fouilles archéologiques dans la vallée de Haut-Lualaba: I, Sanga (1958)*. Tervuren, 1971.

Hildebrand, P. *Le Martyr Georges de Geel et les débuts de la mission du Congo 1645–1652*. Anvers, 1940.

Ihle, A. *Das Alte Königreich Kongo*. Leipzig, 1929.

Jacobson, A. *Marriage and money*. Lund, 1967.

Jadin, L. 'Le Congo et la secte des Antoniens', *Bulletin de l'Institut Historique Belge de Rome*, 1961, **33,** 411–615.

Jadin, L. 'Aperçu de la situation du Congo et rites d'élection des rois en 1775', *BIHBR*, 1963, **35,** 246–419.

Jadin, L. 'Le clergé séculier et les Capucins du Congo et d'Angola . . . conflicts de jurisdictions 1700–1726', *BIHBR*, 1964, **36,** 185–483.

Jadin, L. 'Rivalités luso-néerlandaises au Sohio, Congo, 1600–1675', *BIHBR*, 1966, **37,** 137–359.

Jadin, L. 'Pero Tavares, missionaire jésuite et ses travaux apostoliques au Congo et en Angola 1629–1635', *BIHBR*, 1967, **38,** 271–402.

Jadin, L. 'Relations sur le Congo et l'Angola tirées des archives de la Compagnie de Jésus 1621–1631', *BIHBR*, 1968, **39,** 333–454.

Kalck, P. 'Pour une localisation du royaume de Gaoga', *Journal of African History*, 1972, **13**, 529–48.

Kalck, P. *Histoire de la république centrafricaine*. Paris, 1974.

Kerken, G. van der. *L'ethnie Mongo*. Brussels, 1944. 2 vols.

Laman, K. *The Kongo*. Uppsala, 1953–63. 3 vols.

Lima, J.J. Lopes de. *Ensaios sôbre a statistica das possessões portuguezas*, III. Lisbon, 1846.

Livingstone, D. *Missionary travels and researches in South Africa*. London, 1857.

Lucas, S.A. 'Baluba et Aruund: étude comparative des structures socio-politiques'. Ph.D. thesis, Paris, 1968.

Mainga, M. *Bulozi under the Luyana kings*. London, 1973.

Maret, P. de. *Chronologie de l'age du fer dans la depression de l'Upemba*. Doctoral Thesis, Brussels, 1978.

Martin, P.M. *The external trade of the Loango coast, 1576–1870*. Oxford, 1972.

Miller, J.C. 'Kasanje', in Heimer, F.W. *Social change in Angola*. Munich, 1973.

Miller, J.C. 'Requiem for the Jaga', *Cahiers d'études Africaines*, 1973, **49**, 121–49.

Miller, J.C. *Kings and kinsmen: early Mbundu states in Angola*. Oxford, 1976.

Miller, J.C. *The African past speaks: essays on oral tradition and history*. Folkestone, 1980.

Miller, J.C. 'Cokwe trade and conquest in the nineteenth century', in Gray and Birmingham, *Pre-colonial African trade*. London, 1970, 174–201.

Miracle, M. 'Plateau Tonga entrepreneurs in historical inter-regional trade', *Rhodes-Livingstone Journal*, 1959, **26**, 34–50.

Monteiro, J.J. *Angola and the River Congo*. London, 1875. 2 vols.

Mota, A. Teixeira da. *A Cartografia antiga da Africa central e a travessia entre Angola e Moçambique, 1500–1860*. Lourenço Marques, 1964.

Mveng, E. *Histoire du Cameroun*. Paris, 1961.

Nenquin, J. 'Notes on some early pottery cultures in northern Katanga', *Journal of African History*, 1963, **4**, 19–32.

Neves, A.R. *Memória da Expedião a Cassange*. Lisbon, 1854.

Oliveira, M.A. Fernandes de. *Angolana (documentação sôbre Angola), 1783–1883*. I. Luanda and Lisbon, 1968.

Pachai, B. ed. *The early history of Malawi*. London, 1972.

Paiva Manso, Viscount. *História do Congo*. Lisbon, 1877.

Patterson, K.D. *The northern Gabon coast to 1875*. Oxford, 1975.

Pélissier, R. *Les guerres grises*. Montamets, 1977.

Petermann, A. 'Ladislaus Magyar's Erforschung von Inner-Afrika', in *Petermann's Mittelungen*. Gotha, 1860.

Phillipson, D.W. 'Excavations at Twickenham Road, Lusaka', *Azania*, 1970, **5**, 77–118.

Phillipson, D.W. 'The prehistoric succession in eastern Zambia', *Azania*, 1973, **8**, 3–24.

Phillipson, D.W. 'Iron Age history and archaeology in Zambia', *Journal of African History*, 1974, **15**, 1–25.

Phillipson, D.W. *The later prehistory of Eastern and Southern Africa*. London, 1977.

Planquaert, M. *Les Yaka: essai d'histoire*. Tervuren, 1971.

Pogge, P. *Im Reiche des Muata Jamwo*. Berlin, 1880.

Pôrto, A.F. da Silva. *A travessia do continente africano*. Lisbon, 1938.

Pôrto, A.F. da Silva. *Viagens e apontamentos de um Portuense em Africa*. Lisbon, 1942.

Randles, W.G.L. *L'ancien royaume du Congo des origines à la fin du XIXe siècle*. Paris, 1968.

Ranger, T.O. 'Territorial cults in the history of Central Africa', *Journal of African History*, 1973, **14**, 581–97.

Ratelband, K. ed. *Reizen naar West-Afrika van Pieter van der Broecke 1605–1614*. The Hague, 1950.

Reefe, T.Q. *The rainbow and the kings: a history of the Luba empire to 1891*. California, 1981.

Rego, A. da Silva. *A dupla restauração de Angola (1641–1648)*. Lisbon, 1948.

Rego, A. da Silva, *Portuguese colonization in the sixteenth century*. Johannesburg, 1959.

Rego, A. da Silva. *O Ultramar Português no século XVIII (1700–1833)*. Lisbon, 1970.

Rinchon, P.D. *Les armements négriers au XVIIIe siècle*. Brussels, 1956.

Rinchon, P.D. *Pierre Ignace van Alstein*. Dakar, 1964.

Roberts, A.D. 'Tippu Tip, Livingstone and the chronology of Kazembe', *Azania*, 1967, **2**, 115–31.

Roberts, A.D. 'Pre-colonial trade in Zambia', *African social research*, 1970, **10**, 715–46.

Roberts, A.D. *A history of the Bemba: political growth and change in north-eastern Zambia before 1900*. London, 1973.

Roberts, A.D. *A history of Zambia*. New York, 1976.

Rodney, W. *A history of the Upper Guinea coast*. Oxford, 1970.

Rodrigues, J.H. *Brazil and Africa*. Berkeley, 1965. Portuguese ed. Rio de Janeiro, 1961.

Schweinfurth, G. *The heart of Africa*. London, 1873. 2 vols.

Scudder, T. *Gathering among African woodland savanna cultivators*. Lusaka, 1971.

Stanley, H.M. *Through the dark continent*. London, 1878.

Sutherland-Harris, N. 'Zambian trade with Zumbo in the eighteenth century', in Gray and Birmingham, *Pre-colonial African trade*. London, 1970, 231–42.

Sutton, J.E.G. 'New radiocarbon dates for eastern and southern Africa', *Journal of African History*, 1972, **13**, 1–24.

Tervuren Museum. *Miscellanea ethnographica*. Tervuren, 1963.

Theal, G.M., ed. *Records of south-eastern Africa*. Cape Town, 1899.

Turnbull, C.M. *The forest people*. New York, 1961.

Vansina, J. *Geschiedenis van de Kuba*. Tervuren, 1963.

Vansina, J. 'The foundation of the kingdom of Kasanje', *Journal of African History*, 1963, **4**, 355–74.

Vansina, J. *Introduction à l'éthnographie du Congo*. Brussels and Kinshasa, 1965.

Vansina, J. *Kingdoms of the savanna*. Madison, 1966.

Vansina, J. 'The bells of kings', *Journal of African History*, 1969, **10**, 187–97.

Vansina, J. *The Tio kingdom of the middle Congo*. London, 1973.

Vansina, J. *The children of Woot: a history of the Kuba peoples*. Madison, 1978.

Vellut, J.-L. 'Relations internationales du Moyen-Kwango et de l'Angola dans le deuxième moitié du XVIIIe siècle', *Études d'histoire africaine*, 1970, **I**.

Vellut, J.-L. 'Notes sur le Lunda et la frontière luso-africaine (1700–1900)', *Études d'histoire africaine*, 1972, **3**.

Verbeken, A. *Msiri, roi du Garenganze*. Brussels, 1956.

Verbeken, A. and Walraet, M. *La première traversée de Katanga en 1806*. Brussels, 1953.

Verhulpen, E. *Baluba et Balubïasés du Katanga*. Antwerp, 1936.

Walker, A.R. *Notes d'histoire du Gabon*. Montpellier, 1960.

Wilson, A. 'Long-distance trade and the Luba Lomami empire', *Journal of African History*, 1972, **13**, 4, 575–89.

Wing, J. van. *Études Bakongo*, 2nd ed. Brussels, 1959.

Wissman, H. von. *Second journey through Equatorial Africa*. London, 1891.

Wright, M. and Lary P. 'Swahili settlements in northern Zambia and Malawi', *African Historical Studies*, 1971, **4**, 3, 547–73.

INDEX

acculturation, Pygmy 52, 140–1
Adamawa 145, 151
Adamawa–Ubangian languages 2, 45, 46, 47, 51, 52
administration 97, 103, 113, 128, 132
adzes 106, 152
Afonso I, k. (Kongo) 33
Africanus, Leo (al-Hasan b. Muhammad) 47
agricultural settlements, white 36, 117; see also farmers, Portuguese
agriculture 41, 44, 79, 91, 97, 123, 141; see also farming
Alvaro I, k. (Kongo) 35, 58, 59; Alvaro II 35, 55, 56, 57, 59–60; Alvaro III 57, 60, 61, 79n.
Ambriz 67, 83, 126
Ambuila 63; battle 64, 66, 147
Ambun (=Bambun, Mbuun) people 89
American Civil War 117
American food crops 39, 44, 52, 89, 106, 149; see also maize, cassava, etc.
Ana de Souze (=Nzinga) 77
Anastacio, pombeiro 125
Angarussa, ch. 119
Angola – Portuguese Colony 35, 37, 53, 58, 74n., 80–1, 82, 107, 141; governor 58, 118; bishop, missions 37, 50; Kongo relations, wars 57–9, 60, 63, 64, 100; Luso-Africans 38, 67; Dutch 62, 63, 78
Angola (modern) 1n., 87, 108, 141; East 105, 118, 122; North 124–7; South 19, 115, 133; South-East 118–19; South-West 116–18
Angola, Early Iron Age 9; Later Iron Age 13; oral data 13, 15
Angola – slave trade, markets 68, 70, 71, 72, 124, 133, 146; trade, economy 67, 93, 126

Ansiku people (=Yansi) 43
Antonine movement 66
Antonio I, k. (Kongo) 64, 65
Arabs 46, 109, 115, 130n., 151, 155
archives, Kongo 147
Ardener, E. 45n., 51n.
arimos, private estates 82
aristocracy, Kongo 67; Loango 147
Arnot, Frederic 133
arrows, bow and arrow 24, 31, 47, 114, 132; arrowheads, iron 8, 18
artisans, craftsmen – local 91; see also smiths, potters, etc.; Portuguese, foreign 30, 32, 57
Aruwimi basin 151
Asante gold mines 49
Asian crops 4, 46, 51
Atlantic coast 23, 24, 35, 133, 141; – markets, trading complex 14, 24–39, 43, 44, 87, 116, 128; see also slave trade
Atlantic Islands 38
Atlantic plateaux 39, 83
Avungura clan 152
Azande people 49, 152

baboons 20
Babwa people 46, 47, 51
Bailundu kingdom 19, 86, 121
Bakole people 45
Bakongo peoples 147
balopwe chiefs 101
Balunda people 45
Bamba, Duke of 56
Bambuk mines 49
Bamilike people 50
Bamum people 50, 145
bananas 4, 5, 20, 25, 46, 51, 88, 91, 151
Banda people 152
Bandia people, clan 49, 153
Bandundu Province, Zaïre 78

Bangassou 'sultanate' 49, 153
Bangolo society 142
Bangui 108
Bantu-speaking peoples 2, 40, 41, 42, 43, 44, 45, 49, 51–2, 116, 152
Baptist Missionary Society 143
Baptista, pombeiro 125
bark-cloth 11
Barotseland see Bulozi
baskets 53, 105
Bastin, M.-L. 21n.
Bateman, C.S.L. 150n.
Battell, Andrew 24
battle-axes, iron 18
Baya people 152
bead currency 88, 91, 99
beads, local 49, 97; copper 6, 106; ostrich egg-shell 8
imported – Indian ocean 8, 9, 11, 12, 25, 105, 127, 131, 136–7; Atlantic 30, 39, 72, 106, 114, 142, 149, 150
beans 83, 88, 92, 147
Beatrix Kimpa Vita 66
beehives 122
Beecroft, J. 143
beer 8, 27
Belgium, Belgians 108, 109, 154, 155
bells, iron, royal 13, 22, 56, 79
belt, insignia 96
Bemba people, kingdom 9, 13, 104, 133–5
Bembe copper-mines 148
Bengo r. 58, 81, 126
Benguela coast, current 25, 121, 122; hinterland 116, 124; plateau 19, 74, 76, 81, 83, 84
Benguela trade 85, 101, 113, 116, 118, 124, 133
Benin kingdom 45, 49
Beti people 145
Biebuyck, Daniel 97.
Bight of Biafra 49, 141, 142
Bihe kingdom 19, 84–5, 86, 107, 116, 118, 121, 122, 133, 137; trade, trade routes 118, 122, 133, 137
Binza people 47
Bira people 46
Birmingham, David 24n., 38n., 74n., 76n., 86n., 100n.
Bisa people 9, 103, 104, 129, 136, 137
bishop, Kongo 35, 55
blacksmiths 29; see also iron-working
Bobangi people 43, 72, 87, 141
Bocarro, Gaspar 13n.
Boer trekkers 117
Bohannen, P. and G. Dalton (eds.) 90n., 92n.
Boma 67, 147
Boma–Sakata people 87

Bontinck, François (ed.) 65
Bornu 47
Botswana 119
bottles, glass 39
Bouchaud, J. 144n.
bourgeoisie 73
bowls, glazed 39
bowmen 36
Boxer, C. R. 81n.
bracelets, royal 22
Brásio, A. 64n., 76n., 79n.
brass pans 39
Brazil – economy, trade 26, 31, 33, 38, 71, 75, 81, 126; invasion from 62, 78; Brazilians, Luso-Brazilians 64, 71, 81 117; Brazilian mining company 148
bridewealth 12, 91, 106
British 71, 108, 143, 144, 148, 155; see also English
brokers, brokerage 73, 74, 81, 82; broker kingdoms 78, 80, 98, 107
bronze anklets 39
builders 149
'Bukkameale' ivory hunters 70
Bulozi (= Barotseland) 119
Bulu people 145
Bungu 28
Bunkeya 132, 133
bureaucracy, Lunda 96, 97, 112
burials, royal 95
Burton, R.F. 143
Bushmen (Kung) 20
Bushong (Kuba) 20, 92

Cabinda 67, 68, 73, 74, 83, 124
Caconda fort 86, 117, 121
Cadornega, A. de O. 79, 80 and n., 81
Cameron, Vernon 133
Cameroun 1n., 43, 45, 46, 49, 50, 142, 145
cannibalism 24, 34, 76, 152
canoes 25, 31, 91, 105, 119, 120, 146, 148; transport, trade 87–8, 141
Cape St. Catherine 72
Cape Town 81
capitals, royal 34, 36, 76, 95; see also Mbanza Kongo, musumba
captives, prisoners of war 12, 92, 98, 99
Capuchins, Italian 37, 62, 63, 64, 65, 66, 76, 78; Mukongo priest 65
caravans – absence 25, 49, 127; long-distance 73, 94, 97, 98, 109, 112, 118, 147; routes 61
caravans – Chokwe 149; Kasanje 123, 126; Kololo 120; Matamba 78; Ovimbundu (Bihe) 86, 121, 122, 123, 126; Swahili–Arab 130; Vili 41, 73, 81; Yao 103
Carvalho, Lopes de 149

cassava 39, 44, 52, 88, 92, 106, 147, 151; Lunda 96, 97, 103, 113, 128
cattle 9, 19, 36, 53, 84, 105, 106, 119, 134; – trade 117, 118, 136; – ranching 125, 126, 129; see also raiding, cattle
cattle figurines 8
Catumbela trading settlement 121, 122
cavalry empires 49
Cavazzi, G.A. 78 and n.
Cazengo 127
Central African Republic 151
central Sudan 45
Central Sudanic peoples 46, 51, 152
Chamba people 145
Chedzurgwe 11, 12
Chela escarpment 116
Chewa people 9, 13
Chibinda Ilunga 21 and n., 22, 23, 94
chieftainship 13, 15, 24, 48, 84, 88, 89
Chikangombe snake-god 14
child sacrifice 77
Childs, G.M. 84n., 86n., 124n.
Chileshye, chitimukulu 134
chisels 106
Chitapankwa, chitimululu 134
chitimukulu (king), Bemba 134
Chobe r. 119
Chokwe people, kingdoms 23, 92, 93, 122–4, 131, 134, 139, 140, 153; trade, caravans 122–3, 125–6, 128, 130, 149; mercenaries 115, 139
Chokwe–Lwena peoples 16, 93
Chondwe culture, site 4, 10
Christianity 30, 32, 33, 37, 56, 80, 133
Church, Kongo 35
churches, stone 30
'civilizing hero' 22
Clarence-Smith, W.G. 118.
class distinctions 48
clientship 3, 82, 140, 152
cloth, local 36, 49, 105, 119; weaving 29, 41, 66, 70, 91, 149; see also palm cloth, raffia cloth
cloth, imported 99, 114, 142
clothing 27, 30, 61
clubs, wooden 21
coffee 126, 129, 146
colocasia 88
colonial expansion, Lunda 96, 128
colonialism, colonial rule 109, 120, 127, 151, 154–5
colonization, white 117; see also settlement, white
commoners (Vili) 73
communications 94
concessions 154
Congo Independent State 139, 150
Congo river 26; see Zaïre

conquest, conquest state 28, 29, 89, 132
consuls, British 143
contract labour 154
conus shells 8
convicts, Portuguese 26, 38, 81, 114, 126; African 98, 114, 126
copper absence 4; tax, tribute 88, 113, 114, 133; trade 6, 9, 11, 41, 44, 88, 100, 103, 130, 131, 132; European trade 30, 68, 71, 73, 83, 129; import 131, 142; traders 69; royal wealth 36
copper bars, ingots 6, 11, 45, 91, 133; crosses (muambo) 6, 7, 95, 101, 113, 118, 132, 149
copper jewellery, ornaments 6, 8, 9, 31, 69, 105, 133, 152, 154; wire 6, 12, 69, 100, 113, 118, 133
copper mines 48, 68, 69–70; Bembe 148; Darfur, Hofrat en-Nahas 25, 47; Katanga 118, 131, 138; Kongo 59, 63, 64; Lualaba, Tenke 6, 100, 102, 103, 119; Lunda 113; Lusaka 9; Mindouli 44, 68; Mpande 138; Samba 10, 102, 137; Teke 41; Urungwe 11
copper production – smelting 6, 69, 133; working 22, 29, 135
Copperbelt, Zambia 4, 10
Corrêa, E.A. da Silva 127n.
Correia, Bras 57
Correia de Sá, Salvador 78
Correia de Souza, João 59
cotton 30, 82, 117, 126; woven 11
councils, royal 97
court culture 30, 33; Mangbetu 152
Courts of Equity 143
Coutinho, F. de Souza (governor) 82
cowries 8, 9, 88, 91, 150
crafts, craft specialization 12, 27, 29, 52, 109
credit 143, 144–5
crop yields 106; crop changes 141; see also American crops, etc.
cross-shaped ingots see copper crosses
cultivation, intensive 40
cults 13
Cunnison, Ian 129n.
currency 29, 69, 88, 89, 91, 'bar' 143; beads 88, 91, 99; copper bars, manillas 88, 91, 143, 148; copper crosses 6, 7, 95, 101, 113, 118, 132, 149; copper wire, bracelets 100; cowries 68, 91; 'crew' 143; elephant hair bangles 113; gunpowder charge 150; nzimbu shells 28–9, 56, 63, 64, 68, 88; palm, raffia cloth 68, 91, 135; salt 38
Curtin, P.D. 75n., 124n.
cutlasses 152

Dahomey kingdom 49
dam-building 105
Damaraland 117
Dambwa culture 4, 7
Dampierre, E. de 49n., 153n.
Dande river, valley 58, 63, 81, 126
Darb al-Arba 'īn route 47
Darfur 25, 47, 152
Delgado, Ralph 64n., 82n.
depopulation see population decline
Deschamps, H. 146.
Dias de Carvalho, Henrique 95n.
Dias de Novais, Paulo 36; Dias, Bartholemeu 36
diet 106
digging sticks 8
Diogo I, k. (Kongo) 33
diplomatic envoys 125; recognition 77
dogs 8
Dondo fair 121
Douglas, Mary 90n.
drainage channels 105
drought 76, 106, 147
drums 22, 56
du Chaillu, Paul 145
Duala 45, 49, 50, 108, 142, 143, 144
Dutch occupation of Angola 62, 63, 78;
ships 49, 50, 60, 141; slave trade 62, 71, 75;
traders 35, 38, 60, 61, 64, 69, 71, 83, 148
duties, import 63
Duysters, Léon 97n., 139n.
dyewoods 25, 30, 60, 71; see also redwood
dynasty, Kongo 26; Ndongo 78, 82

Early Iron Age 1, 8, 21, 40; farmers,
societies 3, 4, 7, 14, 20, 24, 141
earthworks, Lunda 95
East Africa 3, 9, 24, 87, 129, 151, 155
economic development 26, 91
economy, Lunda 96; Luba 136
education, European type 62; see also
teachers; in Europe 32
Efik people 45
Egypt 47
elephants, elephant-hunting 47, 70, 134,
136; elephant numbers 70, 104, 122,
133, 138
elephant hair bangles 113; elephant-tails 69
embroidery 91
English 60, 67, 83, 86, 126, 141
Enkoje fort 83
epidemics 66
escrivão, clerk 80
Estermann, Carlos 118n.
Ethiopia 46
ethnography 1, 27n., 51n., 52
European goods 30, 38, 60, 70, 76, 148;
see also cloth, metals; ships 125

European landed estates, plantations 36,
75, 81, 82; dress 117; visitors 1, 13, 26,
42; settlements 64; titles 61 67;
influence 26, 29, 53
Evora 36

factions, feuds 34, 35, 93, 114, 115, 137,
139
factor/inspector 79
Fagan, B.M. et al. 8n.
fairs 38, 60, 82, 121
famine 66, 76, 106
Fang people 43, 45, 145
farmers, agriculturalists 40, 84, 96, 101,
103, 113, 134; forest, forest margins 1,
4, 20, 40, 52, 140, 141; mixed farmers
19, 127; cash-crop 126; Portuguese 26,
81, 127
farming – Stone Age 46; Early Iron Age
1, 21, 40
feira staple market 125
Felner, A. de Albuquerque 118n.
Fernando Po 143
figurines 8, 17
fire, fire ceremonies 13, 15, 42, 101
fish 5, 6, 7, 105; dried 27, 31, 53, 97, 135;
traps, lines 31
fishing 20, 29, 41, 91, 92; coastal 17,
25, 45, 117; fishing port 117
fishing peoples 43, 44, 52, 88, 107, 140,
141; fishing/trading people 87; fishing
economy, industry 2, 7, 19, 102, 103
128, 134, 137; fishing rights 21
Flint, E. 120n.
food 114, 126, 128
food producing economy, peoples 2, 40
43, 44
food production, Portuguese 81
forced labour 154
forest, equatorial 1, 26, 40, 46, 51, 140,
145; forest margins 4, 20, 51, 152
forest peoples, cultures 1, 44, 46
forts 82, 83, 85, 86, 130
fragmentation, political, ethnic 87, 93
Freetown 143
French 67, 71, 83, 108, 144; ships 60, 86,
141
French Equatorial Africa 1n., 146, 159
Fulani 49, 145, 151
Fuller, Jackson 143
Furtado de Mendonça, João 58

Gabon 41, 43, 68, 144
game, game meat 5, 8, 9, 27, 97, 105,
106, 152
Gamitto, A.C.P. 130n.
'Gaoga' 47

Garcia II k. (Kongo) 62, 63, 64 and n., 65
Garenganze 132, 133, 139
gathering, gathering peoples 8, 20, 52, 101, 105, 109; *see also* hunter-gatherers
Geel, Georges de 62
gens d'eau, 'water people' 44
Germany 69, 108
Gipsies 81
goats 20, 51, 56
gold 25, 26, 30, 129; mines, supposed 59, 64; ornaments 11, 61
Golungu Alto 127
government agents 126
Graça 97n., 98, 114 and n., 115n.
grain, granaries 91, 105, 109, 128
grassland resources 26
graves, grave goods 6, 15
Gray, J.R. and Birmingham, D. (eds.) 38n., 124n., 130n.
Greenberg, J.H. 51n.
Grenfell, George 143
grindstones 9
ground-nuts 88, 146, 148, 149
Guinea 107; *see also* West Africa
gum 117, 148
gunpowder 37, 72, 115, 130, 142
guns 107, 130, 131, 132, 134, 138, 152; absence 136; field guns, cannon 82, 86, 148; use in war 36, 72, 115, 131; trade 72, 83, 115, 122, 138, 142, 145, 148, 150, 154; gunsmiths 122

hammocks 79
harbours 26
Hausa 50
Haveaux, G.L. 93n.
head-loading 70
hemp-smoking 149
hens, poultry 8, 56
Herero people 19, 116
hides 27, 105
Hiernaux, J. de Longrée and K. de Buyst 7n.
hoes 8, 106, 114, 121, 127, 131, 135, 136
Hofrat en-Nahas 47, 152
Holo people 80, 100
honey 105, 119
horses, horsemen 47, 79, 151
houses 9, 91
house servants 73
Huambo kingdom 19, 84, 86, 121
Huila kingdom 87, 116, 117
Humbe 117
Hungu refugees 100
hunter hero 21, 22, 94
hunting charms 22
hut poles 105
Hutchinson, consul 143

Ila–Tonga peoples 10
Ilunga Kalala, k. (Luba) 137
Ilunga Sunga, k. (Luba) 137
Imbangala 23, 24 and n., 34, 75, 77, 79, 84, 98, 129
immigrants 38, 52
imports, exotic 128
India, Indian goods 33, 60
Indian Ocean 115, 127
indirect rule (Portuguese) 77–8
industries, local 3, 91
inflation 63, 68
Ingombe Ilede 10, 11
initiation 19, 20, 24, 41
innovation, economic 48
interlacustrine region 1, 108, 151
intermarriage 81
interpreters 73
invaders 115
investment 82, 123, 126
iron 30, 69, 88, 105, 106, 114, 121, 131, 137; use 4, 8, 9, 22, 48
iron goods 51, 72, 127, 142; tools, knives 6, 8, 9, 30, 69, 106; weapons 8, 18, 21, 69; ornaments 6, 8, 9, 13; bells 6; needles 6, 8, 9
iron imports, bars 45, 69
iron symbols (*ngola*) 18
iron-working 4, 29, 36, 40, 121, 126, 149; Portuguese 82; ore, mines 19, 69, 105, 127
irrigation, natural 105
Isamu Pati mound 8
Ituna 134
Ituri forest 141
ivory hunters, hunting 49, 70, 104, 120, 122, 123, 145
ivory trade, coastal 25, 30, 41, 49, 71, 116, 117, 142, 144, 145; western hinterland 30, 60, 69, 83, 118, 121, 141, 153; Centre 79, 104, 120, 122–3, 136, 137, 139, 144, 149, 150; eastern 11, 14, 102, 104, 129, 130, 131, 132, 133, 138; northern 47, 70, 71, 73, 140, 150, 151
ivory working, ornaments 9, 11, 31, 69; royal wealth 36

Jacobson, A. 43n.
Jadin, L. 66n.
Jagas 34, 59, 84, 90; 'our Jaga' 79
Jesuits 36, 37, 57, 62, 76
jewellery 12, 152
Jews 58, 81
João II, k. (Portugal) 32
justice, judges 38, 115, 147, 148

Kafue r. 10
Kakongo kingdom 68, 72, 73

Kalahari Sands 8
Kalamba 149, 150
Kalck, P. 47n.
Kalombo Falls 4, 5, 10
Kalomo culture 4, 7, 8, 10
kalonga Maravi ruler 13
Kalukembe 85
Kalundu culture 4, 7
Kalundwe people 101, 102, 137
Kamnama culture 4
kanapumba, Lunda officer 97
Kandanda 3
Kaniok, Kanioka 102, 114
Kanongesha 100
Kansanshi mine 6
Kapwirimbwe culture 4, 9
Kasai Province, Zaïre 87
Kasai river, people 16, 43, 92, 122, 125,
    141, 146; lower 20, 87–93, 94, 149;
    middle 39, 98, 102; upper 39, 87, 93,
    94, 110, 122, 123; trade network 43
Kasanje depression 17
kasanje title 23, 79
Kasanje kingdom 72, 79–80, 107, 116,
    119, 122, 125, 136; king 79, 95; slave
    raiders 84, 87; trade, traders 79, 86, 98,
    115, 122, 125, 126; town 100
Kasongo (Luba) 101, 102, 104, 114
Kasongo Lunda 100
Katanga 9, 13, 118, 119, 131, 132, 133;
    Katanga, chief 131, 138
Katoto, Katanga 13
kazembe title 102, 128 and n., 129, 130
    139; *see also mwata kazembe*
Kazembe kingdom 104, 128 and n., 130,
    131, 133, 134, 136
Kete people 114
Khartoum traders 49, 151, 152
Khoisan people 2, 3
kidnapping 81
Kikonja kingdom 102, 135
kilolo chiefs 97, 101
kilombo war camps 23
Kilwa 25
Kimbanga, Mt 65
KiMbundu language 15 and n., 74n.; *see*
    Mbundu peoples
kimpaku 'sorcerer' 62
Kimpanzu clan 65
Kimulaza clan 65
King Akwa 142
King Bell (= Mbele) 142
King Denis 144
King Glass 144
king-list, Kongo 147
Kingolo kingdom 84
kingship 13, 14, 15, 23, 52, 89, 94; sacral
    28, 42, 101; prestige 30, 31

kinguri lineage, title 21, 22, 23
Kinsembo 126
Kinshasa 32, 56, 67, 108
kinyama title 22
Kinyama, k. (Lovale) 120
Kisale, lake 5
Kisama 19, 37, 76
knives 30, 69, 106, 152
kola nuts 36, 88
Kololo people 119, 120, 127
Kongo peoples, influences 16, 17, 26, 80,
    87, 89, 92, 93; kingdom 26–36, 38, 53,
    55–67, 80, 100, 107, 147; east, north-east
    north 67, 100; south 67, 76, 100; king
    27, 31, 33, 35, 55, 56, 105; slave trade
    31–4, 43, 72–3, 83
Kuba (Bushong) people 20, 52, 87, 88, 90
    and n., 91, 92, 106, 122, 149; region 39
Kulembe kingdom 19
Kumu peoples 46
Kumwimba, k. (Luba) 137
Kunene r. 1n.
Kung (Bushmen) 20
Kuvale people 116
Kwango river, area 15, 38, 52, 67, 74, 79,
    82, 89, 98, 146, 148; peoples, states 30,
    83, 92, 93, 100; Kwango-Kasai area 90,
    125
Kwanyama people 117
Kwanza river, valley 17, 19, 37, 74, 76,
    78, 81, 83, 121, 126; upper 23, 119;
    lower 15, 23
Kwisi people 116

labour 25, 31, 33, 120, 154; regiments
    (Lozi) 105
Lacerda e Almeida, Francisco 129, 130
    and n.
Lala people 3, 9
Lamba people 102, 131, 132
lances 132
land 21, 31, 48
language 44, 140–1; Adamawa–Ubangian
    2, 51; Ambun 89; Bantu 2, 40, 41, 46,
    47, 51, 109, 141, 145; Central Sudanic
    2, 41, 51, 109, 141; Dutch (South
    Africa) 50, 108; English (South Africa)
    108; Herero 116; Khoisan 2; Kikongo
    92; Kimbundu 38, 80; Ngbandi 51;
    Niger–Congo family 2, 46; – eastern
    109; Portuguese 80, 108, 147; Spanish
    108
Late Stone Age 3, 14
Later Iron Age 1, 4, 8, 9, 10, 14, 22, 24,
    40, 48
Latin America 75
lawyers, Portuguese 30
lead 39

Leite de Faria, Francisco 28
Lele people 87, 88, 90
Lemba 65
Lengola people 46
Lenje people 128
Leopold II, k. (Belgium) 139, 151
Lewanika, k. (Lozi) 120
Lewis, I.M. (ed.) 51n.
Liboko people, kingdom 17, 18, 19, 76
Libreville 144
Lima, J.J. Lopes de 127n.
lineages 17, 18, 21, 22, 23
linguistic evidence 1, 4
Lisbon 36, 56; *see also* Portugal
literacy 147
livestock 40, 97, 106
Livingstone, David 120 and n., 125, 130
Loango 42, 44, 53, 68–74, 81, 86, 107, 124, 146; king 42, 76
Loango Bay 68; coast 41, 68, 78; salt 41, 68
Lomami r. 102, 104
lorry drivers 155
Lovale 118, 119, 120, 133, 137; *see also* Luena-Lovale peoples
Lozi 7, 104, 105, 119, 120, 128, 134
Lualaba valley, peoples 6, 92, 101, 118, 137, 141; upper 5, 102, 119, 132, 150; lakes 135, 137; copper 6, 22, 95, 100, 102, 113, 119
Luanda Island 28, 58, 63; coast 36; plateau, hinterland 17, 19, 37, 74, 77, 79, 116
Luanda town 56, 57, 62–3, 64, 79n., 80, 81, 85, 108
Luanda trade, traders 60, 63, 67, 72, 77, 83, 86, 95, 113, 122, 124–7
Luangwa pottery 9, 10; basin 128, 133
Luapula r. 102, 103, 104, 106, 113, 128, 130, 132, 133
Luba Kalundwe 98, 104; Luba Kaniok 98, 137; Luba Kasongo 104; Luba Lomani 136–9
Luba peoples 22, 101, 114, 122, 123, 132, 149–50, 152; empire 104, 133, 135–9
Lucas, Steven A. 101n.
Luchaze territory 122
lueji lineage 21
Luena people 22, 93; Luena–Lovale peoples 18; Luena r. 118
Lukala iron mines 19
lukano bracelet 94, 101
lukonkeshia 'mother of the king' 94, 97, 112, 125
Lulua people 92, 102, 123, 149
Lunda–Chokwe culture 23
Lunda economy 96, 115, 125, 130, 131, 137; copper 118, 119; ivory 123

Lunda Province, Angola 87
Lunda state, empire 85, 93–101, 102, 107, 124, 127, 132, 136; origins 21, 22, 94; decline 130, 131, 132, 139; chiefs, kings 13, 94, 95, 105, 123, 149, 152; peoples 9, 20, 39, 87, 92, 128; emblems, symbols 22, 90, 93
Lundaized ruling group 100, 103
Lundu kingdom 15
Lusaka district 4, 10
Luso-Africans 38, 44, 67, 115, 116 and n., 125; 'kingdom', economy 86, 98
Luso-Brazilians 71
luxuries, luxury goods 30, 31, 72, 105, 106

Machado, Saturnino de Souza 149
Madeira 81
mafouk trading official 73, 146
Magyar, L. 113, 114n.
maize 39, 44, 52, 88, 92, 96, 106, 149, 152
makoko (Teke king) 69, 89
Makwe 10
malacaite 6, 148
Malanje 125, 149
Malawi (=Maravi) 4, 10, 13, 14, 18, 104, 136
Malawi, lake 13, 103
Malemba 68, 73
maloango (Loango king) 72, 73
malungu cult, figurines 14, 18
'Mambari' caravans 86, 120
Mamvu people 51
Manda 25
Manganja people 14, 15
Mangbetu people 46, 51, 151, 152
mani kabunga shrine guardian 28
manillas 88, 91, 143, 148
Manuel I, k. (Portugal) 32
Manuel ne Vunda, Antonio 56
Manyema 137
market gardens 117
market place, market cycle 29, 77, 79, 80, 88, 89, 91, 100, 107; absence 3, 49, 140
market production, sector 41, 68, 69, 126, 128
marriage 3, 12, 13, 21, 45; between titles 21
Martin P.M. 42, 70n., 147
masons, request for 57
Massangano 78, 81
Matadi rapids 28
Matamba 34, 77, 78, 79, 80, 90, 100, 116
matrilineal peoples, clans 42, 94
Mayombe forest, area 41, 43, 52
Mbala people 87, 93
Mbanza Kongo 26, 28, 35
Mbara people 11
Mbele (= King Bell) 142

Mbochi people 44
Mbunda 118, 119, 120
Mbundu 15, 16, 19, 23, 36-8, 74-80;
    captives, refugees 32, 84, 90
Mbwela 119, 120
medicine 38
Mediterranean world, manufactures 24, 30
messianic movement 66
mestizo population 81
metal working 5, 6, 53, 135
mfumu court councillors 101
middle class, Kongo 35
'Middle' Iron Age 4
middlemen 105
migrations 28, 45, 123, 126, 141
Mikuka secret society 142
military force, power 74, 80, 85, 114, 132,
    140; leadership 13, 77; training 24, 75,
    77, 82, 97
Miller J.C. 15n., 24n., 34n., 75n., 94n.,
    124n.
millet 5, 44, 52, 88, 96; eleusine millet 8
Mina (Gold Coast) 33
Mindouli copper mines 44, 68, 69-70
mineral resources 25, 26, 36, 37, 38;
    prospecting 59
mines see copper, silver, gold
mining companies 148
mining engineers requested 59
minorities (Portuguese) 26
Miracle, Marvin 128n.
mirrors 30
missanga currency beads 99
missionaries 26, 33, 35, 37, 57, 80, 118,
    147; Dominican 56, 57; Jesuit 57, 62;
    Capuchin (Italian) 62, 63, 64, 65
'Mobara, people of' (=Mbara) 11
Moçâmedes 74n., 117; Baron of 116
modernization policy 33
'Molua' (=Lunda) 100
Mona Kimbundu market 139
Mongo peoples 45, 52, 87, 90, 92, 141
monogamy 62-3
monopoly, trade Kongo 30, 55, 61, 67;
    Loango 72; Luba 136; Lunda 97, 99,
    104, 115; Mpongwe 145; Portuguese
    61, 70, 76, 85, 120, 122; Yeke 133
Monteiro, J.J. 118n., 127n., 147, 148n.,
    Montiero, J.J. and A.P.C. Gamitto 129
moradores residents 81
Mossul people 67, 126
Mozambique 10, 118
Mpande, chief 132, 138
Mpinda 61
Mpongwe people 144, 145, 146
Mpumbu (=Pombo) 32, 43
Msiri, Yeke chief 132, 138
muambo copper crosses 113

'Mubires' (=Vili) 68, 72
Mulambwa, k. (Lozi) 120
mulattoes 35, 126; see also mestizo
Munza, k. (Mangbetu) 152
Murdock, G.P. 46, 51n.
Mushikongo people 147
musical instruments, ivory 69
muskets see guns; musketeers 64, 72, 79,
    115
musumba royal compound 95, 96, 98, 99,
    103, 105, 112
Mutapa confederacy 11
Muteba ya Chikombe k. (Lunda) 112
Mutumba Mainga 105n.
Muzura, chief 13n.
mwamba title (Bemba) 134
mwant yav see mwata yamvo
Mwashya saltsprings 133
mwata kazembe 103, 104
mwata yamvo title (Lunda) 23, 94, 97, 98,
    115; empire 96, 109, 112, 113, 125,
    129, 131, 139, 149; tribute 97, 100, 113,
    114; trade 39, 114, 128; capital, musumba
    95, 113, 132
mwine ntanda land chiefs (Luba) 101

Nachikufu 3
Nakapapula 3
Namibia 119
Naweji I mwata yamvo 98
Naweji ya Ditende k. (Lunda) 112
Ndebele people 127
Ndembu people, region 76, 100, 148
Ndola 108
Ndombe pastoralists 84, 85, 116
Ndongo kingdom 17-18, 24, 75-7, 79, 82,
    86, 93; kings 36, 76, 77, 82; salt trade
    37-8
Ndulu kingdom 84, 121
Negro peoples 40, 45
Nenquin, J. 7n.
nets, game, fishing 31, 91, 106
Ngalangi kingdom 84
Ngambwe people 117
Ngangela people 19, 79
Ngangulu people 44
Ngbandi people, language 46, 47, 51,
    152, 153
Ngiri r. 44, 141
ngola title, symbol 18, 74n., 78; kingship
    19, 36
ngola a kiluanje shrine 19, 75; kingdom 19,
    75
Ngola Ari Kiluanji (Ndongo) 78, 81, 82,
    84; Ngola Ari II 82
Ngoni people 134
Ngoyo kingdom 68, 72, 73
'Niam-Niam' (=Azande) 152

Niari valley 69
Niger delta 108; trade 148
Niger–Congo peoples 152, 153; see also
    under language
Nigeria 50
Nile, upper 46
Nilotes 46
Njau kingdom 116
Nkisi r. 28
Nkumbe people 116, 117, 118
North-Central Africa 13–48, 49n., 51,
    140–53
Novo Redondo 83, 96
Nsundi 52
Nyamwezi 87, 115, 131, 133, 136; see also
    Yeke
Nyaneka–Nkumbi people 19
Nyangwe kingdom 139
Nzakara people 153
nzimbu shell currency 28–9, 56, 63, 64, 88
Nzinga princess 77, 78, 79; Nzinga
    chiefs 149

Ogowe people 42; river, basin 70, 146
oil palms 5, 88, 102, 135
Okango 'kingdom' 56
Okavango peoples, region 19, 118
oral evidence, traditions 3, 18, 21, 41, 88,
    93, 102; chronicles 26, 138; sources 1,
    13, 24, 109
orchilla (dyestuff) 117
ornaments 91, 114, 128
ostrich feathers 118
Ovambu people, region 19, 117, 118
Ovimbundu people, states 15n., 16, 17,
    19, 74 and n., 79, 83–7, 117, 121–2;
    trade, traders 81, 100, 115, 116, 118,
    125, 126, 133, 137

Pachai, B. (ed.) 14n.
padroado 55
palm cloth 25, 27, 41, 68, 70, 137
palm trees 5, 24, 58, 102, 135; see also oil
    palms; palm oil 114, 126, 137, 149;
    palm wine 20, 21, 24, 36
paraphernalia, religious 28
pastoralists 83, 85, 101, 109, 116, 119,
    120, 127; pastoral produce 105
patrilineal succession 94, 102
patronage, royal 27
Paul V, Pope 56, 79n.
Pedro III, k. (Kongo) 60; Pedro IV 65, 66
Pende people 17, 18, 78, 87, 90, 93, 99,
    149
Petermann, A. 115n.
Phillipson, D.W. 4n., 9n., 10n.
Phiri clan 13, 14, 15
plague 64

Plancquaert, M. 34n.
plantains 151; see also bananas
plantations 81, 82, 113, 154
planting economy 2, 19
Pogge, P. 95n., 115 and n.
political power 12, 15, 30, 73, 130, 132;
    expansion 15, 18, 23, 39, 96, 107, 134,
    154; stability 22, 35, 135; fragmentation
    35–6
political system 13, 15, 29, 48, 53, 68,
    88–90, 91–2, 146, 154
polygamy 65, 91
pombeiros trading agents 32, 35, 60, 67, 78,
    79, 81, 125, 129
Pombo (= Mpumba) 32
Pope, papacy 26, 35, 56, 58, 60, 62
population – sparse 1, 3, 39, 44, 90, 108,
    116, 122, 141, 144–5, 153; denser 1, 88
population growth 4, 29, 48, 50, 52, 84,
    91, 92, 153; decline, loss 37, 44, 75, 79,
    140, 145; movement 88, 90, 96;
    pressure 147
porridge 8
Port Clarence 143
porters, porterage 63, 64, 82, 126, 132,
    149, 154
Pôrto, A.F. da Silva 119, 120n., 122, 133
Portugal 26, 57, 80, 82, 108, 114; policy
    32, 33, 34, 37, 126, 129
Portuguese 25, 36, 117; citizenship 81;
    colonies, settlements 33, 74, 116; see
    also São Tomé, Angola, Benguela;
    community, Kongo 57, 58; customs
    duties 67; governors 38, 58, 77, 82, 85,
    96; priests 28, 55
Portuguese invasion, penetration 34, 35,
    63, 74, 75, 76, 82, 86, 117; military
    strength 64, 77, 82, 86
Portuguese trading contact 30, 55, 80,
    116, 128; trading posts 52, 121, 155;
    ships 25, 28, 55; reports 11, 13, 27n.,
    45, 75
'Portuguese' traders, agents 60, 61;
    troops 64
Portuguese West Africa 74n.; colonial
    rule 154, 155
pottery 3, 53, 88, 114, 121; pot-making
    10, 20, 28, 29; potters 8, 10, 149;
    pottery clay 8, 121
pottery, imported – glazed china 30
pottery styles, traditions 1, 4, 5, 7;
    Chondwe 10; Early Iron Age 10;
    Ingombe Ilede 11; Kalomo 10;
    Kisalian 7; Later Iron Age 10, 11;
    Luangwa 9, 10, 11; Lungwebungu 8;
    Mulongo 7; 'red slip' 7; Tonga 11
prazos (Mozambique) 82
prestige goods 94, 106

prices 63, 76, 78
priests, Catholic 28, 30, 32, 33, 35, 55, 56, 57; traditional 14, 24, 42
Príncipe Island 60
prophets, black 66
Proprietary Colony 36
protection money 70, 117
provincial rulers, governors 29, 33, 61, 65, 72, 132, 226
Pungu a Ndongo 82, 84
Pygmies 2, 40, 41, 44, 45, 47, 51, 70, 140–1, 152; clientage 46, 52

queen-mother 42
Quilengues 116

radio-carbon dating 3, 4n., 7
raffia cloth 13, 20, 30, 88, 91, 114, 135; see also palm cloth
raiding 10, 28, 59, 63, 124; cattle 87, 104, 107, 116, 117, 119, 120, 121, 127, 134; salt 134; slaves – Angola 37; Arab 151; Bemba 134; Chokwe 124; Fulani 49; Lunda 96, 98; Kasanje 79, 84, 87, 107; Kongo 32, 34; Nyamwezi 139; Ovimbundu 117; Swahili–Arab 139
railways 154, 155
rainbow symbol 101
rainfall 36, 41, 109, 113
rainmaking 14, 15, 17, 42, 78
Ranger, T.O. 15n.
ransoms 151
Ratelband, K. (ed.) 61n.
Ravenstein, E.G. (ed.) 42n.
refugees 23, 39, 52, 76, 84, 89, 90, 94, 100, 151; Brazilian 117
religion 14, 16, 38, 48, 62, 80, 109, 135; syncretism 66; sanctions 114
reliquary basket 101
revenue Angola 114; Lunda 103, 114; Kongo 35
Rhodesia see Zimbabwe
rift valley lakes 1n.
road and dyke work 82
Roberts, A.D. 130n., 134n., 135 and n.
rock shelters 3, 4
Rodney, W. 71n.
Rome see Pope
royalties 70
rubber 121, 123, 146, 148, 150
rum, Brazilian 71, 106, 114; local 117

Sá, Salvador de 63
Saker, Alfred 143
salt coastal 27, 41, 63, 68, 70, 83; seaborne, imported 25, 142, 149; bars, rock salt 38, 95; Lualaba, Luapula 100,

102, 103; trade 37, 48, 106, 127, 131, 135, 137, 154; to Lunda 98, 113, 128; to Pygmies 41, 70
salt production 17, 29, 41, 68, 126, 135; mines, springs 19, 133; Portuguese salt pans 82, 85
Samba people 18, 137; copper working 137
Sanaga region 145
Sanga 4, 5, 6, 102, 132; pottery 5
Sankuru r. 88
São Salvador 55, 58, 61, 62, 63, 65, 66, 147
São Tomé 25–6, 33, 36, 53, 55, 57–8, 60, 154
Sarmento, Alfredo de 147
satellite colonies, chiefdoms 96
savanna – northern, north-western 26, 47, 49–51; southern 1, 3, 12, 15, 22, 48, 52, 109, 113, 127; savanna cultures 1, 46
Schecter, R. 101n.
Schoffeleers, J.M. 14n., 15n.
Schweinfurth, G. 152n.
scimitars 152
Scudder, T. 8
Sebanzi hill 10, 11
secret societies 142
Sekeletu, k. (Kololo) 120
Sela kingdom 86
serfs, farm 96, 105, 113, 114
sertanejo backwoodsmen 85, 96
settlement mounds 7, 105
settlement, white, foreign 115, 118
shea butter 105
shells 12, 24, 31, 39, 63; collecting 17; see also under currencies
Shinje people 79, 90, 100
Shire r. 14, 15
Shona people 15
shrines 15, 17, 18, 62, 65, 86; shrine guardians 18, 28
Shyaam, k. (Kuba) 92
silk 30, 79
silver mines, mythical 37, 38
skins 114
slave trade, internal – Angola 63, 64, 75, 124–5; Bemba 135; Benguela/Ovimbundu 83, 85, 116, 121, 125, 137; Cameroun/Gabon 142–4, 151; Kazembe 104, 128, 129; Mbundu, Matamba, Ndongo 74–9; Kongo, lower Congo 31 32, 53, 146, 147; Loango, Teke, Cabinda 43, 70, 71, 72, 73, 125; Luba 138–9; Lunda/Lulua 98, 99, 101, 113, 128, 139, 152; Swahili–Arab 130, 139; Yeke 133, 139
slave trade, overseas 24, 26, 33, 37, 50, 59, 153; Saharan 47, 151, 153
slave-trading society, economy 32, 34, 63

slave-trading society, economy (*cont.*)
74, 99; markets 35, 43, 68; slave-getting 37, 47; *see also* raiding, slave
slavery 48, 64, 120
slaves – domestic 73, 96, 105, 117, 126, 128, 147, 150; labour 25, 26, 117, 128; plantation labour, serfs 37, 81, 82, 96, 105; prisoners of war 113, 133; wives 26; slave class 32
slaves as wealth 146; as payment of tolls, fines, tribute 114, 119, 133
sleeping sickness 145, 148
small stock 8, 52
smallpox 145, 148
smiths 57, 152; smith-kings 18; copper-smiths 69; *see also under* copper, iron
smoke signals 79
snake-god 14, 15; snake symbol 101
soap factory 82
social organization, culture 26, 109
societies, localized 109
Sofala 25
Sohio 28, 60, 61, 62, 63, 64, 65, 67
Songo people 79; princess 85
Songye people 135, 150
sorcery 65
sorghum 5, 8, 88
Sorongo people 67, 147, 148
Sotho people 119
South Africa 107
South-central Africa 49, 108, 127–35
southern Africa 108
Spain 37, 57, 60; war with Portugal 62
Spanish-speaking South Africans 144
spears 21, 31, 114, 152
specialization 3, 91, 127
spindle-whorls 11
spirits, alcohol 31, 44, 72, 78, 95, 106, 142, 143
Stanley, H.M. 151
Stanley Falls 151
states, state-building 1, 20, 48, 84, 107
steamers, rivers 126, 154
stockades 130
stone technology 3; tools 3; bored stones 8
subsistence communities 48, 105, 127, 149; agriculture 49
succession, royal 63, 73, 79, 137, 146
Sudan, E 46, 47
sugar 25–6, 81, 88, 117, 125, 127; Brazil 71
Suku people 78, 93, 100
Sumbwa Nyamwezi (=Yeke) 131, 132
surfboat men 73
Sutherland-Harris, Nicola 129n.
Sutton, J.E.G. 4n.
Swahili 109, 116, 130n.; Swahili–Arab 130 and n., 131, 134, 138, 139, 140, 150, 151, 155
swana mulope title (Lunda) 97
swana mulunda mother of the people 94
swords 47, 152
symbols of office 96; *see also ngola*

Tanganyika, Lake 101, 134, 137
Tanzania 4, 10, 103, 131
taxes 27, 61, 63, 72, 98, 112, 114, 132, 136; tax collectors, tax farming 37, 38, 65
teachers, Portuguese 30, 32, 55
technology 48, 55, 57, 91, 126, 154
Teke people (=Tyo, Ansiku) 34, 43, 44, 87, 88, 89, 92, 141, 146; plateau, mines 41, 68, 70, 72, 88
Tenke 6
Tete 14, 103, 129
Tetela people 45, 52
textiles 25, 31, 79, 106, 129, 154; Asian 95, 103; Mediterranean 30, 47; industry 53; *see also* cloth
Thandwe 10
Theal G.M. 131n.
Tikar kingdom 50
timber 73, 126, 142, 144, 146
Tippu Tip 130n., 134, 151
tithes 82
titles, Lunda 21, 22, 23, 94, 97, 98
tobacco 39, 81, 88, 92, 149; Brazilian 39, 44, 71; pipes 39
tolls 98, 119, 121
tomatoes 39
Tomistas *see* São Tomé
Tonga people 11, 13, 104, 105, 127; *see also* Ila–Tonga
tooth-filing 9
trade, exchange 3, 26, 91, 92, 106, 132; cabotage 30; contacts 89; legitimate 143, 144, 148; market-orientated 19; monopoly 30, 39; Pygmy 41
trade, exchange – arrow poisons 137; beads 8, 25, 30, 49, 105, 127, 136, 137, 142, 149; beads, copper 106; beads, glass, imported 9, 11, 72, 131, 142, 149, 150; beer 6, 106; building materials 105, 127; cattle, livestock 106, 117, 118, 136; cloth 29, 49, 73, 78, 127, 131, 143, 149; bark cloth 135; palm, raffia cloth 27, 30, 41, 69, 79, 95, 98, 137; foreign cloth 30, 36, 63, 72, 131, 135, 137, 142, 144, 148; cotton cloth 106, 136; clothing 106; coffee 148; copper, early trade 6, 9, 11; copper, coastal hinterland 30, 41, 44, 69, 71, 73, 83; interior trade, copper 88, 98, 129, 130, 131, 137; copper ornaments 105, 154; cowries 8,

trade, exchange (*cont.*)
9, 150; drums 137; dyewoods, dyestuffs 30, 71, 117, 144; elephant tails, elephant-hair bangles 69, 73, 113; European trade-goods 118, 128, 148; fish 6, 83, 105, 127, 137, 140, 148; food 30, 43, 83, 127, 131, 141; gold 30; grain 3, 6, 49, 127, 140; groundnuts 146, 148; gum 117, 148; guns *see under* guns; hides, skins 3, 85, 136, 137; honey 105; horses 47; iron 30, 51, 69, 88, 131, 137; iron goods 72, 127, 142; iron ore 105; ivory *see under* ivory; luxuries 106; manufactures, local 43, 48, 136, 137; meat 3, 49, 51, 83, 127; metal goods 31, 72, 95, 128, 143, 144; ochre 127; ornaments 128, 136; ostrich feathers 118; palm oil, kernels 6, 70, 137, 142, 143, 146, 148; pepper 30; pottery 30, 31, 88, 106, 114, 121, 128, 142; raw materials 43, 48, 106; rubber 121, 123, 133, 139, 146, 148, 150; salt *see under* salt; shea butter 105; shells 12, 25, 106, 127, 128; slaves *see under* slave trade; spirits, alcohol 31, 71, 72, 78, 95, 106, 142, 143; textiles *see under* textiles, cloth; timber 73, 142, 146; tobacco 31, 71, 72, 78, 95, 98, 106; tools 3, 106, 121, 127, 131, 135, 136; wax 117, 121, 122, 126, 133, 139, 142; weapons 47, 105, 135; wine 79
trade, long-distance 2, 25, 42, 47, 95, 98, 125, 135, 136; external 113, 115, 120, 149; trans-Saharan 30, 47, 49, 153; local 121, 127, 133, 135
trade-routes central 119, 123, 125, 126; eastern 11, 67, 85, 91, 107, 133; northern 55, 73, 89, 120, 140; western, southern 38, 39, 77, 61, 68, 81–2, 115, 121
traders, African 7, 11, 34, 94; coastal hinterland 68, 69, 73, 80, 86, 120; interior 120, 123–4, 136; Swahili–Arab 130 and n., 133, 134, 138–9, 150–1; Yao 103, 104; Yeke 131–3, 134, 138, 139
traders, European – Dutch 35, 70, 71; Portuguese, maritime 26, 30, 45, 53, 70, 71; Portuguese, interior 32, 35, 55, 58, 85, 118, 129, 133, 149
trading centres 11, 121, 130, 142, 146; communities, families 35, 68, 118, 130; expeditions 35; officials 73; relations, contacts 93, 116, 128
trading systems, networks 24, 43, 60, 77, 109, 115, 117, 122, 125, 138, 149, 154
transport 82, 122, 154; *see also* porters, etc.

tribute 28, 29, 70, 100, 103, 135, 136; political 27, 96–7, 105, 112–13, 119, 128, 152; to Portuguese 37, 64
tribute/reward – baskets 105; beads 97; beer 27; canoes 119; cloth, clothing 27, 103; copper, copper goods 29, 103, 113; crafts 149; fish 27, 29, 97, 105, 119; food 114, 149; fruit 119; game meat 27, 97, 105, 119, 149, 152; grain, cassava 97, 105, 119; hides, skins 27, 105, 114; honey 105, 119; iron, iron tools 29, 97, 105, 114, 119; livestock, pastoral produce 97, 105; pottery 29, 114; salt 27, 29, 113, 119, 128; slaves 96, 105, 114; weapons 114, 119; woodwork 105
'trust' *see* credit
tsetse fly 7, 17
tubers, forest 46, 108
tubungu elders (Lunda) 20, 97
tukwata messengers (Lunda) 97, 98, 112
Tumbuka 14
Twa *see* Pygmy
Twickenham Road, Lusaka 9, 10
Tyo (= Teke) people 43

Ubangi r. 43, 44, 46, 47, 141, 151, 153; Ubangi–Chari watershed 1n.
Uele region 46, 151, 152
Ujiji 137, 138
undi king (Maravi) 14
Unyamwezi 133; *see also* Nyamwezi
Upper Guinea Coast 71
urban growth 108
Urungwe 9, 11
utensils 91

va-shambadzi agents 103
Van Wing, J. 28
Vansina, J. 52n., 88n., 90n., 92n., 97n., 137, 139n.
Vasconcellos, L. M. de 76
Vatican archives 64
Vellut, J.-L. 80n., 93n., 98n., 116n.
Verbeken, A. 133n., Verbeken, A. and Walraet, M. 129n.
Vili people, caravans (= Mubires) 41–3, 44, 68, 69, 72, 73, 80, 81
villages 1, 2, 4, 12, 17, 29, 48, 107
violence 107, 152, 153

Wadai–Darfur area 47
wage-payments 29
war 59, 64, 76, 77, 97, 102, 115, 125; war camps 23; war leaders, chiefs 23, 24, 132
water-carriers 73
wax 117, 121, 122, 123, 126, 133, 139, 142

weapons, iron 8, 18, 21, 69
weaving, weavers 29, 41, 69, 70, 149
West Africa 1, 3, 24, 30, 80, 141, 155
west-central Africa 49n.
West Indies 71
whaling 117
Wilson, Ann (Hilton) 104n., 139n.
wine, Spanish 50; wine-tapping 91;
　wine-cups 24
witchcraft 65, 148
wives as tribute 96
women, slave 153; as investment 123
woodland, woodland savanna 3, 40, 46,
　105, 108, 151, 152; margin 1, 5, 108
woodwork 105
wool, woolens 30, 121
Wright, Marcia and Peter Lary 135n.

xylophones 25, 79

Yaka people 78, 93, 100, 149; Yaka-Suku
　peoples 87
yala mwaku lineage (Lunda) 21
yams 88
Yanzi Ambun people 87
Yao 103, 104

Yavo ya Mbanyi, k. (Lunda) 112
Yeke (= Sumbwa Nyamwezi) 131–3, 134,
　138, 139

Zaïre 9, 10, 13, 22, 93, 105, 108, 109, 155;
　east, north-east, south east 7, 46, 51,
　115, 130; south, south-west 4, 22, 118;
　central 87
Zaïre river 26, 43, 53, 88; bend 44, 72,
　87; lower 25, 28, 41, 43, 52, 64, 67,
　108, 141, 146 and passim.
Zaïre–Zambezi watershed 39
Zambezi r. 11, 14, 105, 118, 129; lower
　115, 128; middle 1n., 10, 22, 119, 128;
　upper 7, 8, 16, 86, 100, 101, 104, 115,
　118, 128
Zambia 1, 4, 13, 93, 154; east 4, 10, 104;
　north 3, 4, 22, 103, 130; north-west,
　west 3, 22, 103, 130; south 4, 7, 10,
　11, 104, 127
Zande see Azande
Zanzibar coast 129, 133
Zimbabwe 4, 9, 119
Zumbo, Zombo people (traders) 67, 100,
　147, 148
Zumbo (Zambezi) 103, 128

Printed in the United States
65222LVS00005B/54

9 780521 284448